Dubai

DIRECTIONS

WRITTEN AND RESEARCHED BY

Gavin Thomas

ROUGH
GUIDES

NEW YORK • LONDON • DELHI
www.roughguides.com

Contents

Introduction   4

Ideas   9

The big six sights 10
Old Dubai 12
Souks 14
Futuristic Dubai 16
Sharjah 18
Al Ain 20
Luxury hotels................................... 22
Restaurants: Middle Eastern 24
Restaurants: international 26
Cafés and cheap eats 28
Drinking... 30
Shopping malls................................. 32
Things to buy................................... 34
Sporting Dubai.................................. 36
Dubai on (and in) water 38
Desert Dubai.................................... 40
Future Dubai.................................... 42

Places   45

Bur Dubai 47
Deira 62
The Inner suburbs............................ 78
Sheikh Zayed Road.......................... 92
Jumeirah 106

The Burj Al Arab and around 114
Dubai Marina.................................. 127
Sharjah.. 138
Al Ain.. 147
Abu Dhabi....................................... 155
The east coast................................ 162

Accommodation   167

Essentials   181

Arrival.. 183
Information....................................... 183
City transport................................... 184
Tours, cruises and desert safaris 186
Kids' Dubai 189
Festivals 190
Major sporting events 191
Directory.. 191

Chronology   195

Language   199

Index   205

Introduction to

Dubai

Dubai is like nowhere else on the planet. Often claimed to be the world's fastest-growing city, in the past four decades Dubai has metamorphosed from a small Gulf trading centre to become one of the world's most glamorous, spectacular and futuristic urban destinations, fuelled by a heady cocktail of petrodollars, visionary commercial acumen and naked ambition.

◄ Coffee pots, Ibn Battuta Mall

In many ways, modern Dubai is a panegyric to consumerist luxury – a self-indulgent haven of magical hotels, superlative bars and restaurants and extravagantly themed shopping malls. If it were less opulent and prodigal it might be merely tawdry, but the sheer pizazz with which Dubai has carried through its plans to woo the tourist and business dollar lifts it to a hitherto undreamt-of level of contemporary chic, embodied by stunning developments such as the futuristic Sheikh Zayed Road, the extraordinary mock-Arabian

▲ Tilework, Iranian Mosque, Bur Dubai

When to visit

The best time to visit Dubai is in the cooler winter months from December through to February, when the city enjoys a pleasantly Mediterranean climate, with average daily temperature in the mid-20°Cs – although, not surprisingly, room rates (and demand) are at their peak during these months. Temperatures rise significantly from March through to April, and in October and November, when the thermometer begins to nudge up into the 30s on a regular basis, though the heat is still relatively bearable, and shouldn't stop you getting out and about.

During the summer months from May to September the city boils – especially in the suffocating months of July and August – with average temperatures in the mid-30s to low 40s (and sometimes higher). Although the heat is intense, even after dark, room rates at most of the top hotels plummet by as much as seventy-five percent, making this an excellent time to enjoy some authentic Dubaian luxury at relatively affordable prices, so long as you don't mind spending most of your time hopping between air-conditioned hotels, shopping malls, restaurants and clubs.

Madinat Jumeirah and the unforgettably beautiful Burj Al Arab – not to mention the ongoing mega-developments at Dubai Marina and elsewhere – testament to the ruling sheikhs' determination to make Dubai one of the world's essential destinations in the twenty-first-century.

Perhaps not suprisingly, Dubai is often stereotyped as a vacuous consumerist fleshpot, appealing only to those with more cash than culture, though this one-eyed cliché does absolutely no justice to the city's beguiling contrasts and rich cultural make-up. There's far more to Dubai than designer boutiques and five-star hotels, a fact amply demonstrated by the old city centre, with its string of vibrant commercial districts centred on a higgledy-piggledy labyrinth of old-style souks, interspersed with fine old traditional Arabian houses lined up along the banks of the breezy Creek, whose serene waters provide Dubai with many of its most unforgettable views, as well as a living link with its maritime past. It's here, too, that you'll get the best sense of Dubai's remarkable ethnic diversity – a cosmopolitan cultural hothouse of races and languages which makes Dubai one of the world's most genuinely multicultural cities, with streets full of Indian and Pakistani traders, West African gold dealers, Filipina maids, Russian bargain-hunters, robed Emiratis and tanned expat Europeans.

In the last analysis, it's this marvellous eclecticism that is the heart of Dubai's appeal. Of course, for many visitors the entire city is simply an excuse to go shopping or lie on the beach and

▼ Al Sabkha Abra Station, Deira

▲ Sheikh Zayed Rd

be pampered senseless. But scratch the surface and Dubai reveals a world of fascinating contrasts, from traditional Arabian shisha cafés to chic contemporary cocktail bars; or from down-at-heel Indian

▶ Camels on beach, Dubai Marina

tea stalls with Bollywood tunes warbling from the radio to cool clubs with leading international DJs manning the decks. It's this cosmopolitan cultural fabric, just as much as the city's increasingly spectacular tourist attractions, that remains the essence of Dubai's appeal, and which is likely to provide a benchmark for the city's future development as it continues with its plans to become the world's top tourist destination.

▼ Jumeirah Beach Park

Dubai
AT A GLANCE

BUR DUBAI

On the south side of the Creek, Bur Dubai is the oldest part of the city and home to many of its most interesting traditional Arabian heritage houses, as well as the atmospheric Textile Souk.

SHEIKH ZAYED ROAD

Sheikh Zayed Road's dizzying array of skyscrapers – bounded to the north by the glittering Emirates Towers and to the south by the soon-to-be-completed Burj Dubai, the world's tallest building – represent Dubai at its most futuristic.

▲ Abra on Creek, with Textile Souk in background

▲ Sheikh Zayed Road

DEIRA

North of the Creek, the bustling district of Deira is where you'll find most of Dubai's traditional commercial activity, much of it still conducted in the area's vibrant array of old-fashioned souks.

► Belly-dancing costumes, Gold Souk, Deira

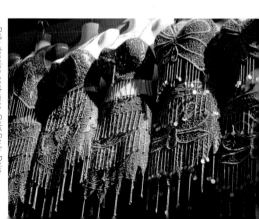

◄ Mercato

JUMEIRAH

Home to dozens of shopping malls and a smattering of low-key sights, the sprawling beachside suburb of Jumeirah is the traditional address-of-choice for Dubai's European expats.

Dubai sights, including the wave-shaped *Jumeirah Beach Hotel*, the extraordinary mock-Arabian Madinat Jumeirah complex, and the unforgettable Burj Al Arab.

DUBAI MARINA

The epicentre of modern Dubai, the vast new Dubai Marina development is the city's next Big Thing, home to a string of luxurious beachside resorts and an extraordinary number of cranes.

▲ Burj Al Arab and Jumeirah Beach Hotel

BURJ AL ARAB AND AROUND

The sleepy suburb of Umm Suqeim is home to a trio of iconic

▲ Beach, Dubai Marina

Ideas

The big six sights

Modern Dubai has plenty of wow factor, and the city's top contemporary sights, such as the soaring Emirates Towers and the magnificent Burj Al Arab, are guaranteed to make even the stiffest jaw drop. There are also numerous captivating attractions in the old city centre, ranging from the traditional souks of Deira and the wind-towered houses of Bastakia to the beautiful Creek itself.

▲ Bastakia

Dubai's most perfectly preserved traditional district, with a fascinating little labyrinth of old-fashioned Arabian houses topped by innumerable wind towers.

P.52 ▸ BUR DUBAI

▼ Deira souks

At the heart of old Dubai, the city-centre district of Deira comprises a long, labyrinthine tangle of absorbing bazaars, ranging from the famous Gold Souk's glittering array of shops to the aromatic alleyways of the Spice Souk.

P.62–67 ▸ DEIRA

▶ Madinat Jumeirah

An astounding mock-Arabian city, home to a string of lavish hotels and leisure facilities – the quintessential Dubaian example of opulent kitsch on an epic scale.

P.118 ▶ THE BURJ AL ARAB AND AROUND

◀ Emirates Towers

A dazzling pair of triangular-topped modernist marvels, soaring high above the futuristic Sheikh Zayed Road.

P.93 ▶ SHEIKH ZAYED ROAD

▼ Burj Al Arab

One of the world's most instantly recognizable contemporary buildings, this superb, sail-shaped hotel towers gracefully above the coast of southern Dubai, providing the city with its most iconic landmark.

P.114 ▶ THE BURJ AL ARAB AND AROUND

▼ The Creek

Running through the heart of old Dubai, the tranquil waters of the Creek provide some of the city's most memorable views, and a welcome, breezy respite from the crowded city-centre streets.

P.49 ▶ BUR DUBAI

Old Dubai

Despite contemporary Dubai's headlong rush into modernity, determined conservation efforts have succeeded in saving significant parts of the city's old architectural heritage from the developers, offering visitors an absorbing insight into local life in the days before five-star hotels and shopping malls. Most of the city's heritage buildings are found on or near the Creek in the city-centre districts of Bur Dubai and Deira, while the flotillas of traditional Arabian dhows and abras that still ply the Creek add a further splash of old-fashioned colour.

▲ Jumeirah Mosque

The most impressive of Dubai's innumerable mosques, rising imposingly above the drab suburbs of northern Jumeirah – and also open to visitors during informative thrice-weekly tours.

P.106 ▶ JUMEIRAH

▲ Al Ahmadiya School and Heritage House, Deira

An interesting pair of museums tucked away next to one another behind the Gold Souk, with illuminating displays on both domestic and scholastic life in early twentieth-century Dubai.

P.68–69 ▶ DEIRA

▲ Dhow Wharfage

Home to hundreds of superb old Arabian dhows moored up along the Deira Creekside – one of central Dubai's most incongruous but magical sights.

P.67 ▸ DEIRA

▶ Majlis Ghorfat Um Al Sheef

Hidden away in the prosaic suburbs of the southern city, this attractive little traditional *majlis* (meeting house) offers a touching reminder of life in pre-oil-boom Dubai.

P.110 ▸ JUMEIRAH

▼ Sheikh Saeed Al Maktoum House

The finest traditional house in Dubai, and former home of the ruling Maktoum family, now housing an absorbing collection of atmospheric old city photographs.

P.55 ▸ BUR DUBAI

Souks

The cultural essence of traditional Dubai can be found in its quaintly old-fashioned souks, living proof of the city's long history as one of the principal trading centres of the southern Gulf, and still an important element in its economic life. Most are located in the vibrant district of Deira, where the city's gold, spice, perfume and food souks jostle for elbow room near the tip of the peninsula.

▲ Textile Souk

The traditional heart of Bur Dubai, the rambling Textile Souk has bags of old-world character and reams of cheap fabrics and clothing.

P.47 ▸ BUR DUBAI

▲ Spice Souk

The most atmospheric and old-fashioned of Deira's myriad souks, with narrow alleyways stuffed full of fragrant merchandise, from frankincense to rose-petal tea.

P.65 ▸ DEIRA

◀ Deira Fish, Meat and Vegetable Market

Entertainingly everyday souk – more carrots than carats – with huge piles of fruit, veg and household utensils, plus gory hunks of meat and a vast spread of Gulf-fresh seafood, from sardines to sharks, laid out on display.

P.70 ▸ DEIRA

▼ Souk Madinat Jumeirah

Superb modern souk in traditional Arabian style at the heart of the Madinat Jumeirah complex.

P.121 ▸ THE BURJ AL ARAB AND AROUND

▼ Gold Souk

It all glitters – and it *is* gold. This famous Deira souk remains one of the cheapest places in the world to stock up on gold jewellery, from ornate traditional Arabian pieces to sleek contemporary designs.

P.62 ▸ DEIRA

Futuristic Dubai

Kitsch, quirky, over-the-top, and frequently stunning – modern Dubai has plenty of contemporary architectural landmarks which show the city at its most futuristic, though many also hark back to the city's maritime past, with a clutch of sail-shaped constructions including the Dubai Creek Golf Club, National Bank of Dubai and, of course, the inimitable Burj Al Arab.

▲ Burj Al Arab

The ultimate Dubaian modernist icon, and the last word in the city's myriad sail-inspired architectural creations.

P.114 ▶ THE BURJ AL ARAB AND AROUND

▼ National Bank of Dubai

Rising high above the Creek, the National Bank of Dubai's sail-shaped glass facade offers central Dubai's most striking tribute to the city's maritime traditions; it's particularly memorable towards dusk, when the setting sun turns the entire facade into a huge wall of brilliantly reflected light.

P.70 ▶ DEIRA

▲ Jumeirah Beach Hotel

Towering high over the beach in southern Dubai, this startlingly original wave-shaped hotel remains one of the city's most famous landmarks.

P.117 ▸ THE BURJ AL ARAB AND AROUND

▼ Dubai Creek Golf Club

Dubai's answer to the Sydney Opera House, the engagingly quirky Dubai Creek Golf Club's sail-shaped outline remains one of the city's quaintest and most instantly recognizable sights.

P.78 ▸ THE INNER SUBURBS

▲ Sheikh Zayed Road

Dubai at its most futuristic, the neck-cricking skyscrapers of Sheikh Zayed Road provide a compendium of contemporary architectural design, ranging from the unquestionably wonderful to the irrefutably weird.

P.92 ▸ SHEIKH ZAYED ROAD

Sharjah

Just 10km down the coast from central Dubai, conservative Sharjah presents a startling contast to its glamorous and emancipated neighbour. The emirate's puritanical laws are unlikely to warm many tourist hearts, but the city compensates with a cluster of excellent museums covering pretty much every aspect of traditional Islamic art and culture. There are further attractions at the city's excellent art museum and quaint Al Hisn Fort, while carpet-baggers will be in seventh heaven at the immense Blue Souk, home to one of the country's finest, and cheapest, selections of fine hand-made rugs and kilims.

▼ Souk Al Arsah

The prettiest souk in Sharjah, if not the entire country, with an atmospheric little labyrinth of alleyways lined with an appealing selection of handicraft and carpet shops.

P.143 ▶ SHARJAH

▼ Al Hisn Fort

A quaint traditional fort at the heart of contemporary Sharjah, now home to an interesting selection of exhibits devoted to local life in the emirate.

P.139 ▶ SHARJAH

▲ Blue Souq

A huge, eye-catching modern souk in quasi-Arabian style housing a wide array of shops, including plenty of carpet shops offering rugs at some of the cheapest prices in the UAE.

P.145 ▶ THE CITY

▼ Sharjah Islamic Museum

One of the finest museums in the UAE, boasting a superb selection of artefacts from around the Islamic world.

P.141 ▶ SHARJAH

▲ Bait Al Naboodah

An atmospheric traditional house with exhibits recreating life in the emirate in the early years of the twentieth century.

P.142 ▶ SHARJAH

Al Ain

Inland UAE's only major city, sedate Al Ain is the perfect place to head for if you want to have a look at how the rest of the country lives, and offers a peaceful respite from the crowds and nonstop action of Dubai. Built around an idyllic little oasis, the city boasts a good selection of diverse attractions, from down-to-earth local food and livestock markets to a string of fine old forts and other archeological remains, as well as the chance to hop over the border into the neighbouring Omani town of Buraimi.

▼ Al Ain Museum

A rewarding museum devoted to life in Al Ain and Abu Dhabi emirate in days gone by, including an outstanding selection of archeological displays.

P.149 ▸ AL AIN

▼ Al Ain Oasis

An idyllic retreat from the heat and dust of contemporary Al Ain, with peaceful little pedestrianized roads running through shady plantations of luxuriant date palms.

P.151 ▸ AL AIN

▶ Al Ain Souk

An engaging market attracting a cosmopolitan crowd ranging from Indian stall holders to local Bedouin women.

P.151 ▸ AL AIN

▲ Al Kandaq Fort

A superbly restored Omani fort in Buraimi, with elaborate bastions and delicately carved towers and battlements.

P.152 ▸ AL AIN

◀ Livestock market

A rustic livestock market, with crowds of locals bartering over anything from chickens to cows.

P.150 ▸ AL AIN

◀ Sultan Bin Zayed Fort

This quaint little mud-brick fort, attached to the Al Ain Museum and famous as the birthplace of the much-loved Sheikh Zayed, now houses an interesting collection of old photographs of Abu Dhabi emirate.

P.150 ▸ AL AIN

Luxury hotels

Dubai has some of the most stunning hotels on the planet, from the futuristic *Burj Al Arab* – the world's first "seven-star" hotel – to traditional Arabian-themed palaces such as *Al Qasr* and the *One&Only Royal Mirage*. When it comes to creature comforts, all the city's top hotels do outrageous luxury as standard, with sumptuous suites, indulgent spa treatments, spectacular bars and gorgeous private beaches, and the size and style of the very best places makes them virtually tourist attractions in their own right – self-contained islands of indulgence in which it's possible to spend day after day without ever feeling the need to leave.

GROSVENOR HOUSE

▲ One&Only Royal Mirage

The most atmospheric and intimate of Dubai's Arabian-themed hotels, with superb Moorish decor and a magnificent array of facilities, from traditional shisha courtyards to one of the city's most beautiful nightclubs.

P.179 ▸ DUBAI MARINA

▶ Burj Al Arab

A stay in Dubai's ultimate architectural icon – and self-professed "seven-star" hotel – doesn't come cheap, but does offer the last word in contemporary luxury, from personal butlers to private helicopters.

P.114 & 177 ▶ THE BURJ AL ARAB AND AROUND

◀ Al Qasr

A marvellously opulent and seriously over-the-top Arabian-themed palace at the heart of the stunning Madinat Jumeirah development.

P.178 ▶ THE BURJ AL ARAB AND AROUND

▲ Grosvenor House

A super-stylish high-rise hotel, brimful of contemporary urban chic, and with some of southern Dubai's most delectable bars and restaurants.

P.178 ▶ DUBAI MARINA

▶ Park Hyatt

This serene hotel in quasi-Moroccan style occupies a picture-perfect Creekside setting amid the verdant grounds of the Dubai Creek Golf Club.

P.174 ▶ THE INNER SUBURBS

Restaurants: Middle Eastern

Not surprisingly, Middle Eastern (aka "Lebanese") food takes pride of place in Dubai's burgeoning eating scene. Restaurants all over the city – from streetside shwarma stalls to fancy hotel establishments complete with live bands and belly dancers – offer varying takes on the classic dishes of the region, usually featuring a big range of tasty mezze through to delicately grilled kebabs, often with a good selection of shisha on the side. Iranian food is also popular, while the cooking of North Africa is represented by a small but excellent selection of Moroccan places serving up sumptuous tagines and helpings of traditional pigeon pie.

▲ Shahrzad

The best Iranian food in the city, served up in a gorgeously romantic setting brimful of 1001 Nights-style atmosphere.

P.75 ▸ DEIRA

▲ Tagine

Dubai's prettiest Moroccan restaurant, and with food to match, from pigeon pie to fruity tagines.

P.136 ▶ DUBAI MARINA

▲ Kan Zaman

In a breezy Creekside setting, this unpretentious place remains enduringly popular with local and expat Arabs for its cheap but excellent Middle Eastern food and shisha.

P.60 ▶ BUR DUBAI

▼ Al Nafoorah

Formal Emirates Towers restaurant serving up possibly the best Middle Eastern cooking in the city.

P.101 ▶ SHEIKH ZAYED ROAD

▼ Bastakiah Nights

Stylish Middle Eastern fare in an incomparably romantic setting in an old Bastakia heritage building.

P.61 ▶ BUR DUBAI

Restaurants: international

Dubai has a superb spread of international restaurants, and its top eating establishments offer a veritable feast for the senses, with gourmet food served up in some of the city's most magical locations, whether atop the soaring skyscrapers of Sheikh Zayed Road, alongside the tranquil waters of the Creek, or amid the idyllic palm-studded grounds of the southern city's beachside hotels. Italian, Thai, Japanese, Chinese and Indian cooking are particularly popular, and there's also an outstanding clutch of European fine-dining establishments, epitomized by the superlative *Verre*, which provides single-handed proof of the city's growing culinary credentials.

▲ Thai Kitchen

An idyllic Creekside restaurant serving up a good spread of traditional Thai food in mezze-style portions.

P.90 ▸ THE INNER SUBURBS

▼ Verre

The best restaurant in Dubai, this Gordon Ramsey-managed temple to fine dining remains the undisputed king of Dubai's eating scene.

P.75 ▸ DEIRA

▲ Nina's

Wonderfully fresh, light and inventive contemporary takes on the classic dishes and flavours of India.

P.135 ▸ DUBAI MARINA

▼ Eauzone

Probably the most romantic restaurant in Dubai, set in tented pavilions amidst the floodlit pools and palmy gardens of the magical *One&Only Royal Mirage* hotel.

P.134 ▸ DUBAI MARINA

◀ Zheng He

Top-notch traditional and contemporary Chinese cuisine in a superb setting opposite the *Burj Al Arab*.

P.123 ▸ THE BURJ AL ARAB AND AROUND

Cafés and cheap eats

Food in Dubai isn't all about five-star hotel restaurants and Michelin-starred chefs – indeed some of the city's most memorable eating experiences are yours for a few dollars, or less. Indian and Pakistani curry houses are scattered all over the city centre, often with surprisingly good food, while there are also plenty of Middle Eastern eateries, from streetside shwarma stands to lively local restaurants serving up excellent mezze and kebabs. And if these don't appeal, there is no end of other unpretentious cafés and restaurants all over the city, from European coffee houses to no-frills noodle joints, where you can eat well without emptying your wallet.

▲ The Noodle House

A brisk, breezy and no-nonsense modern restaurant serving up excellent, moderately priced Southeast Asian food at long communal tables.

P.101 ▸ SHEIKH ZAYED ROAD

▼ Lime Tree Café

The archetypal Jumeirah Road hangout, attracting a loyal clientele of expat wives passing the time over excellent sandwiches and coffee – plus healthy lashings of local gossip.

P.112 ▸ JUMEIRAH

▶ Yakitori

A wonderfully quirky little restaurant – like a slice of downtown Tokyo magically transported to innermost Dubai – offering excellent Japanese food at bargain prices.

P.61 ▶ BUR DUBAI

◀ XVA

Cheap and tasty Arabian-influenced café fare in the courtyard of a marvellous old traditional Bastakia house.

P.60 ▶ BUR DUBAI

▼ India House

The classic Bur Dubai curry house, with a tasty selection of vegetarian food at cut-throat prices.

P.59 ▶ BUR DUBAI

▼ Beirut

A classic Al Diyafah Road shwarma café. Get a seat at the roadside terrace, tuck into a kebab and watch the night-time streetlife rush past.

P.86 ▶ THE INNER SUBURBS

Drinking

You won't go thirsty in Dubai, and the huge number of drinking holes tucked away all over the city attests to the extraordinary degree to which this Muslim city has gone in accommodating infidel tastes. Dubai's best bars encapsulate the city at its most beguiling, opulent and theatrical, whether your taste is for lounging on cushions in alfresco Arabian-themed venues or supping champagne in cool contemporary cocktail bars – and there are usually superlative views thrown in for good measure too.

▲ Bar 44

On the 44th floor of the superb *Grosvenor House* hotel, this smooth contemporary cocktail bar offers a chic perch from which to enjoy peerless views over the ever-expanding Dubai Marina development.

P.137 ▸ DUBAI MARINA

▼ Vu's Bar

A chic contemporary bar – the highest in Dubai – perched up on the stratospheric heights of the 51st floor of the Emirates Towers, with breathtaking views over the city below.

P.105 ▸ SHEIKH ZAYED ROAD

▶ Rooftop

Tucked away on the rooftop of the beautiful *One&Only Royal Mirage* hotel, this is one of Dubai's ultimate romantic bars, with superb Arabian-themed decor and smooth sounds from the resident DJ.

P.137 ▸ DUBAI MARINA

▼ Buddha Bar

Modelled after its famous Parisian name-sake, this superb bar-restaurant has bags of pseudo-Oriental cool, complete with excellent pan-Asian food and crisp cocktails.

P.134 ▸ DUBAI MARINA

▲ Koubba

Stylish and indulgent Arabian-themed terrace bar, with unforgettable views of the *Madinat Jumeirah* and *Burj Al Arab*.

P.124 ▸ THE BURJ AL ARAB AND AROUND

▼ 360º

Seductive contemporary chill-out venue, perched at the end of a breakwater overlooking the Burj Al Arab and Jumeirah Beach Hotel, with a dressy young crowd fashionably slumped over cocktails and shisha while the resident DJ spins his stuff.

P.123 ▸ THE BURJ AL ARAB AND AROUND

Shopping malls

Shopping malls are big in Dubai. The modern equivalent of the traditional Arabian café and souk, the city's malls act as a magnet to local Emiratis, who cruise the shops and chew the fat with friends over coffee just as they have for centuries, even if it's now *Starbucks* rather than shisha that's king. The seriousness with which Dubai takes its shopping is also evident in the lavishness of many of its malls, some of which are tourist attractions in their own right. And of course there's plenty of retail therapy on offer too, with a staggering array of shops ranging from cheap supermarkets to the most exclusive of designer outlets.

▲ Mall of the Emirates

The biggest mall in Dubai, for the time being at least, with a huge array of classy retail outlets in a slightly surreal setting next to the huge indoor Ski Dubai snowdrome.

P.121 ▶ THE BURJ AL ARAB AND AROUND

▲ Wafi City Mall

Quirky Egyptian-themed mall and leisure complex complete with obelisks, copious hieroglyphs and huge pharaonic statues – plus a good selection of upmarket shops and eating and drinking venues.

P.85 ▶ THE INNER SUBURBS

▲ BurJuman

Central Dubai's premier shopping
destination, this huge modern mall houses
a vast selection of shops ranging from the
low-brow bag-fillers to the most chic of
contemporary designer outlets.

P.57 ▸ BUR DUBAI

▼ Mercato Mall

Surreal Italian-themed mall, with a range
of upmarket shopping outlets housed
in an engagingly kitsch fake Florentine-
cum-Venetian miniature city.

P.108 ▸ JUMEIRAH

▲ Ibn Battuta Mall

Dubai's king of retail kitsch, this
kilometre-long mall takes its inspiration
from the journeys of the famous Moroccan
traveller Ibn Battuta, with seven eye-popping
sections styled after regions ranging from
Andalucia to India.

P.133 ▸ DUBAI MARINA

Things to buy

International brands – from Marks & Spencer to Armani – may have taken a firm hold of much of the city's retail trade, but there are plenty of authentically Arabian souvenirs to look out for during a visit to Dubai. Carpets are a particularly good deal, with a vast array of rugs to choose from and cut-price deals if you shop around, while there's also a plentiful supply of other local specialities, from authentic antique Omani silverware to the kitschest of kitsch souvenirs – not to mention the huge quantity of fake designer clothing, watches, bags and other accessories for which the city remains famous.

▲ Carpets and kilims

Dubai is one of the best places in the world to go shopping for carpets and kilims, with innumerable shops offering rugs from all over Asia – anything from museum-quality Persian heirlooms to inexpensive prayer mats and kilims (such as those pictured, from Al Orooba oriental carpetes).

P.58 ▸ BUR DUBAI

▼ Designer fakes

If you want the fashion statement without the bank statement, Dubai is the perfect place to pick up near-perfect copies of designer watches, bags and other gear at far-from designer prices, as well as plenty of imitation clothing.

P.63 ▸ DEIRA

▶ Gold and precious stones

Dubai is heaven for gold lovers, with the precious metal selling at far far lower prices than most other places in the world. There's also a thriving trade in precious stones, with plenty of cut-price diamonds, in particular.

P.63 ▶ DEIRA

▼ Kitsch souvenirs

Cuddly toy camels, Burj Al Arab-shaped glass paperweights or miniature china Arabs with attitude – if you want it, someone in Dubai probably makes it. Check out the shops in Karama for a particularly good selection of quirky collectibles.

P.84 ▶ THE INNER SUBURBS

▲ Arabian antiques

There are plenty of excellent-quality antiques lurking amongst the clutter of kitsch, if you hunt a little, including fine antique silver jewellery and khanjars (ceremonial daggers) from Oman (such as those pictured, from the Souk Al Arsah in Sharjah).

P.143 ▶ SHARJAH

Sporting Dubai

Sport and Dubai might seem unlikely bedfellows given the emirate's climate, culture and location, but creating a series of high-profile sporting events has been a long-term part of Dubai's ongoing plans to capture the world's tourist market. The city's prestigious tennis and golf tournaments attract top international names, including Roger Federer (who has used the city as a winter training camp), Tiger Woods (who's designing a golf course here), and David Beckham (who brings his wife shopping here), while the immensely popular rugby sevens tournament and the world's richest horse race add further ballast to the city's burgeoning sporting credentials.

▲ **Dubai Rugby Sevens**

This wildly popular international sevens tournament attracts some of the world's leading teams – and provides an excuse for one of Dubai's most raucous spates of partying.

P.191 ▶ ESSENTIALS

▲ **Dubai World Cup**

The world's richest horse race, with a cool US$6 million in prize money.

P.191 ▶ ESSENTIALS

▲ Dubai Desert Classic

A prestigious and lucrative European PGA tournament, held at the Emirates Golf Club near Dubai Marina.

P.191 ▸ ESSENTIALS

▷ Dubai Duty Free Tennis Open

The world's leading male and female singles players slog it out in Garhoud.

P.191 ▸ ESSENTIALS

▼ Dubai Desert Challenge

Top rally drivers and bikers descend on Dubai to race one another across the desert.

P.191 ▸ ESSENTIALS

Dubai on (and in) water

It's not all desert in Dubai – indeed the city has traditionally looked outwards towards the sea, rather than inland towards its sandy hinterlands. For a genuine taste of Dubai's centuries-old maritime traditions, a trip across the Creek on one of the city's abras or an evening cruise aboard an old-style dhow can't be bettered. And if you want to get in the water rather than on it, there are plenty of chances to swim, snorkel and dive on both coasts of the UAE.

▲ Abra rides

Forget five-star luxury and designer frills, the 50-fils ride across the Creek in one of the city's rickety old abras remains Dubai's most definitive experience, offering superb views of the Creekside and a genuine taste of the Dubai of yesteryear.

P.51 ▶ BUR DUBAI

▼ Wild Wadi Waterpark

Splash around on inflatable tubes, shoot along waterslides atop high-powered flumes of spray or tackle the stomach-churning Jumeirah Sceirah at the spectacular Wild Wadi Waterpark.

P.117 ▶ THE BURJ AL ARAB AND AROUND

▲ Creek cruises

Sail along the Creek and enjoy the night-time city illuminations on a dinner cruise aboard one of Dubai's beautiful old dhows.

P.188 ▸ ESSENTIALS

▼ Diving and snorkelling

Explore the Gulf's spectacular underwater environment, at its finest along the east coast emirate of Fujairah.

P.191 ▸ ESSENTIALS

Desert Dubai

Getting out into the desert is likely to be high on your agenda during a visit to Dubai, and there is no shortage of opportunities to fill your boots with sand and get a taste for the city's starkly beautiful desert surroundings. Most visitors' encounters with the desert are limited to the enduringly popular half-day desert safaris offered by myriad tour operators in Dubai, though there are plenty of other ways of getting out into the wilderness, whether you fancy a spot of wadi-bashing or mountain hiking, or a less challenging stay at one of the emirate's two luxury desert camps.

▲ Desert safaris

Go dune-bashing, try your hand at sand-skiing or quad-biking, then settle down over a shisha for a spot of traditional belly dancing.

P.186 ▸ ESSENTIALS

◀ Camel racing

Visit the Nad Al Sheba race-track for one of Dubai's most evocative sights, as dozens of camels gallop across the sands to the enthusiastic cheers of local dromedary fanciers.

P.95 ▸ SHEIKH ZAYED ROAD

▶ Dune-bashing

Dubai's ultimate desert thrill. Get on board a 4WD and hold on tight as you're bounced at high velocity up and down the dunes – or hire a 4WD and have a go yourself.

P.186 ▸ ESSENTIALS

▼ Bab Al Shams and Al Maha desert resorts

Two stylish desert resorts, combining five-star luxury with an authentic taste of life amongst the sands.

P.180 ▸ ACCOMMODATION

◀ Desert adventure activities

Have a crack at sand-skiing, dune-buggy riding, camel riding or traditional falconry. Just don't forget your sun-cream.

P.188 ▸ ESSENTIALS

Future Dubai

If you thought Dubai already had it all, think again. Over the next decade a spectacular series of developments will transform the place beyond all recognition and, it's intended, establish it as one of the planet's ultimate tourist destinations. The world's tallest building – the Burj Dubai – and first luxury underwater hotel are already nearing completion, while a sequence of massive artificial islands, complete with innumerable hotels and leisure facilities, plus a state-of-the-art metro system are also in the pipeline. And, just for good measure, there's the world's largest theme park, too. Watch this space.

▲ Dubailand

The ultimate Dubai development, this vast new theme park – covering an area the size of Singapore – will be the jewel in the city's 21st-century crown, with attractions ranging from state-of-the-art sporting stadia to animatronic dinosaurs and full-size reproductions of the ancient wonders of the world.

P.97 ▸ SHEIKH ZAYED ROAD

▲ Burj Dubai

The world's tallest building – already over a hundred storeys high at the time of writing (though its ultimate height remains a closely guarded secret). It's intended to house the world's first Armani hotel and form the centrepiece of a massive new residential and retail development at the southern end of Sheikh Zayed Road.

P.96 ▸ SHEIKH ZAYED ROAD

▶ The World

Nearing completion, this new offshore complex of artificial islands built in the shape of a map of the world could only have been dreamt up in Dubai. If you don't believe it, look out of the window of your plane.

P.128 ▸ DUBAI MARINA

▲ The Palm, Jebel Ali and The Palm, Deira

Two huge new palm-shaped artificial islands to complement the recently opened Palm Jumeirah, likely to host a vast array of luxurious hotel and leisure facilities.

P.128 ▸ DUBAI MARINA

▼ Hydropolis

The world's first luxury underwater hotel, offering the chance to sleep with the fishes, though only for those with very deep wallets.

P.131 ▸ DUBAI MARINA

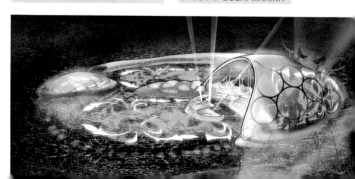

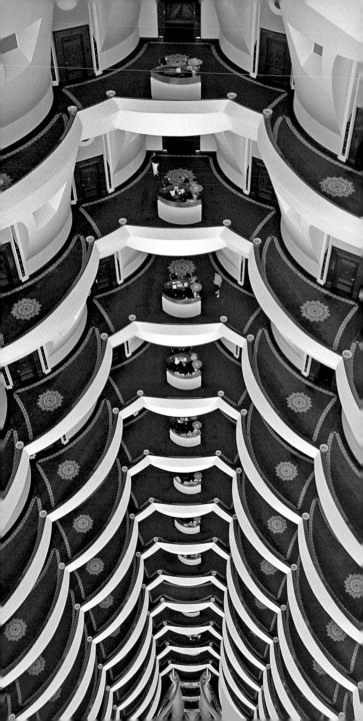

Places

Bur Dubai

Strung out along the southern side of the Creek, the district of Bur Dubai is the oldest in the city and encapsulates all the various strands that have gone into the making of Dubai's cosmopolitan cultural fabric, from traditional Arabian mosques and Emirati houses through to neon-lit modern shopping strips stacked high with electronics, computers and designer watches, while innumerable down-at-heel curry houses, catering to the district's predominantly Indian and Pakistani population, add a further splash of ethnic colour. At the heart of the area, the old-fashioned Textile Souk provides Bur Dubai with its major point of reference, bounded to the north by the more modern shopping areas centred around Al Fahidi Street and Khalid Bin Al Waleed Road. Tucked away amidst the endless shops are a sequence of absorbing traditional attractions, including the excellent Dubai Museum, the historic old quarter of Bastakia and a smattering of other traditional buildings – most notably the Sheikh Saeed Heritage House and Heritage Village, two of a series of reconstructed old Emirati buildings that straggle along the Creek at the western edge of the district in Shindagha quarter.

The Textile Souk

Most shops open 10am–10pm, although many close during the afternoon around 1–4pm. At the heart of Bur Dubai, the Textile Souk (also known as the Old Souk) occupies an immaculately restored Emirati-style traditional bazaar, its long line of attractive sand-coloured stone buildings

▼ THE CREEK, BUR DUBAI SIDE

Bur Dubai **PLACES**

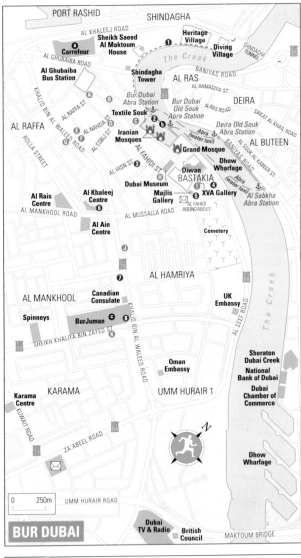

BUR DUBAI

ACCOMMODATION		Time Palace	C	India House	3	SHOPS	
Admiral Plaza	E	XVA	I	Kan Zaman	1	Bateel Dates	c
Ambassador	B			Sherlock Holmes	H	BurJuman	c
Arabian Courtyard	H	**EATING & DRINKING**		Viceroy Bar	J	Carrefour	a
Astoria	D	Antique Bazaar	J	XVA Café	I	Damas	c
Dallas Hotel	F	Automatic	6, 7	Yakitori	G	International	
Four Points Sheraton	J	Basta Arts Café	5			Aladdin Shoes	b
New Penninsula	A	Bastakiah Nights	4			Al Orooba	
Regent Palace	K	Bayt Al Wakeel	2			Oriental Carpets	c
Royal Ascot	G	Dôme	8			Virgin Megastore	c

▲ TEXTILE SOUK

shaded by a fine wooden roof, keeping things pleasantly cool even in the heat of the day. Look up and you can still see interesting decorative carvings and latticed windows here and there, as well as a few old bits of unplastered coral wall, while at the far end of the souk, next to the Saleh Abdullah Mohd Tea Stall (a good place for a reviving cup of masala tea, incidentally) there's a particularly impressive little alleyway flanked by no fewer than eight wind towers. Despite its decidedly Arabian appearance, virtually every shop in the souk is now occupied by Indian traders flogging reams of garishly coloured low-grade sari cloth (along with assorted tourist tat) – a classic example of contemporary Dubai's endless cultural miscegenations – and though the shopping opportunities (for more on which, see the box on p.58) may be limited, it remains an attractive, pleasantly traffic-free spot for an idle stroll at any time of the day or night.

The Creek

Cutting a broad, salty swathe through the middle of the city centre, the Creek (Al Khor in Arabic) lies both physically and cuturally at the very heart of Dubai. All that now remains of a river which historical sources say once flowed inland all the way to Al Ain (and was even known to the ancient Greeks, who named it the River Zara), the Creek was the location of the earliest settlements in the area – first on the Bur Dubai side of the water, and subsequently in Deira – and also played a crucial role in the history of the recent city. One of the first acts of the visionary Sheikh Rashid, the so-called father of modern Dubai, on coming to power in 1939 was to have the Creek dredged and made navigable to larger shipping, thus diverting trade from the then far wealthier neighbouring emirate of Sharjah (whose own harbour was allowed to silt up, with irreversible consequences). It was Rashid's opening up of the Creek to international trade, and the resulting establishment of Dubai as a major regional commercial centre, just as much as the later discovery of oil, that paved the way for the city's latter-day prosperity.

Although the Creek's economic importance has dwindled in recent decades following the opening of the enormous new coastal docks at Port Rashid (another creation of the canny Sheikh Rashid) and Jebel Ali, the Creek continues to see plenty of small-scale commerce, almost all of it transported on the innumerable old-fashioned wooden dhows which continue to ply between Dubai and neighbouring countries, and which moor up along the Deira side of the water at the Dhow Wharfage (see p.67) – adding an improbably picturesque and old-fashioned footnote to the contemporary city centre. Commerce apart, the Creek remains the centrepiece of Dubai and its finest natural feature, a broad, serene stretch of water, which is as essential a part of the fabric and texture of the city as the Thames is to London, providing cooling breezes and a welcome stretch of open space, as well as many of the city's finest views and a continuing link with the city's maritime past.

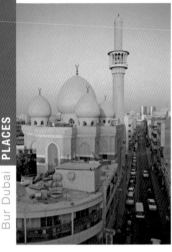

▲ IRANIAN MOSQUE

of predominantly blue tiling decorated with geometrical floral motifs. The second (about 50m west towards the *Time Palace Hotel*) is a contrastingly plain, sand-coloured building, its rooftop enlivened by four tightly packed little egg-shaped domes.

Shri Nathje Jayate Temple

Textile Souk. Daily 6am–noon & 5–10pm. Hidden away at the far end of the Textile Souk, the tiny hybridized Hindu-cum-Sikh Shri Nathje Jayate temple is one of Dubai's most curious and appealing little sights. Amazingly, given the number of Indians in Dubai, this is the city's only Hindu temple, and its diminutive size and obscure location give it a charmingly secretive, almost clandestine air, like the meeting house of an early Christian sect in Imperial Rome. Visitors are welcome (leave your shoes outside), though you can't take photos. The temple's main room is decorated with assorted images of the Hindu gods Shiva, Hanuman and Ganesh, along with the revered South Indian guru Sai Baba and a few swastikas. One flight of

It's also worth exploring the lanes that run inland, parallel to the main drag, boasting further examples of traditional (albeit heavily restored) Emirati architecture, as well as a fine pair of **Iranian Shia mosques**, which stand close to one another at the western end of the souk on 11C St, close to the *Time Palace Hotel*. The first sports a superb facade and dome covered in a lustrous mosaic

▼ BUR DUBAI BY NIGHT

Crossing the Creek by abra

Despite contemporary Dubai's obsession with all the marvels of modern technology, getting from one side of the Creek to the other in the city centre is still a charmingly old-fashioned experience, involving a trip across the waters in one of the hundreds of rickety little boats – or abras – which ferry passengers between Deira and Bur Dubai. There are two routes: one from the Deira Old Souk Abra Station (next to the Spice Souk entrance) to the Bur Dubai Abra Station (at the north end of the Textile Souk), and another from Al Sabkha Abra Station (at the southern end of the Dhow Wharfage in Deira) to the Bur Dubai Old Souk Abra Station (in the middle of the Textile Souk). Boats run on both routes around the clock and cost 50 fils per crossing. Whichever route you take, it's a wonderful little journey, offering superb views of the fascinating muddle of Creekside buildings with their tangles of souks, wind towers, mosques and minarets, and is certainly the most fun you can have in Dubai for 50 fils. Boats leave as soon as full (meaning, in practice, every couple of minutes) and the crossing takes a few minutes. Note that small bumps and minor collisions between boats are common when docking and departing, so take care or you might find yourself not so much up the Creek as in it.

Abra cruises

A more leisurely alternative to the standard Creek crossing is to charter your own abra, which gives you the freedom of the waters and the chance to sail the Creek for as far as your fancy (or wallet) suggests. Starting from somewhere in the city centre, you should be able to do the return journey to Al Maktoum Bridge in thirty minutes, while in an hour you can probably get down to the Dubai Creek Golf Club and back (although obviously this will depend on exactly where you start from – see below). Chartering an abra can be a bit tricky, however. Part of the problem is that there's no single recognized place to hire a boat. You'll often be approached by people around the four abra stations offering trips, or at various other points along the river (try at the abra stations themselves; behind the *Sheraton Dubai Creek Hotel* in Deira; on the Creekside edge of Bastakia; or west of the Bur Dubai abra station near the Shindagha Tower), although in the eternal traditions of Sod's Law, when you actually want to charter a boat, you probably won't be able to find one. The second problem is agreeing a fare. You'll be quoted anything from 60dh up to 120dh for an hour's charter (or 40–80dh for 30 minutes). Aim for 60dh per hour, bargain hard if necessary and remember that the price should be the same irrespective of how many people are going to be using the boat.

stairs leads from here up to the Sikh Gurdarbar, adorned with pictures of the ten Sikh gurus. A second flight of stairs opposite (cover your head with a piece of cloth from the box at the top) leads to the Gurmandir, a large room which is used for both Hindu and Sikh religious ceremonies, with the Sikh mantra "Satnam Waheguru" ("Oh God your name is true") painted on the walls.

To reach the temple, go to the far end of the Textile Souk, turn right by T. Singh Trading and then left by Mohammadi Textiles down the alleyway by the temple – home to a cluster of picturesque little Indian shops selling a quaint array of bangles, coconuts, flowers, bells, bindis, almanacs and other religious paraphernalia. Flights of stairs lead up to the temple from the alleyway; leave your shoes at the lockers just past Gate no. 2, and enter via Gate no. 1.

The Grand Mosque and Diwan

Immediately south of the Shri Nathje Jayate temple lies the altogether more visible and imposing Grand Mosque, the biggest in Dubai: a large, sand-coloured building topped by eighteen tiny domes and the city's tallest minaret, rising elegantly above Bur Dubai's skyline. The original Grand Mosque was built around 1900 but demolished in the 1960s; the current edifice dates only from the 1990s, although it manages to look quite a lot older than that.

On the other side of the Grand Mosque (go back across the end of the Textile Souk, then turn right along the side of the Creek), protected by ostentatiously high black railings, the **Diwan**, or Ruler's Court, is home to the offices of senior government figures including the ruling sheikh himself (hence its alternative name). The building itself is large but uninspiring – a big white box topped by a few oversized reproduction wind towers. Rather more eye-catching is the attached **mosque**, topped by an unusually flattened onion dome and a slender white minaret which rivals that of the nearby Grand Mosque in height. There are also fine views from here back across the Creek to the Dhow Wharfage at Deira, with the wind towers of the Spice Souk in the background.

Bastakia

Immediately east of the Diwan, the recently restored Bastakia (or Bastakiya) quarter is the most impressive fruit of Dubai's recent efforts to salvage something of the city's old architectural and cultural heritage before it was completely lost to the bulldozers and developers. This entire little district of wind-towered houses and narrow lanes (originally built by merchants from Bastak – hence the name – in southern Iran in the 1920s), was threatened by wholesale demolition in the late 1980s, but has now been rescued from near dereliction and restored to its original condition – indeed, probably to something quite a lot neater than its original condition. The quarter now offers a fascinating snapshot of old Dubai, with a disorienting rabbit-warren of tiny alleyways, built deliberately narrow in order to provide pedestrians with welcome shade, and twisting between the high, bare, dun-coloured walls of dozens of fine old traditional houses capped with beautiful wind

▼ GRAND MOSQUE

towers, each one carved in its own unique pattern. For the moment, however, Bastakia remains a work in progress. Restoration work continues in various places, while the entire quarter remains rather empty and under-used, despite the presence of a couple of good cafés and two of the city's best galleries, although hopefully this will change in future. Bastakia can either be reached via the waterfront, on the far side of the Diwan, or from Al Fahidi Street, where a small lane leads into the quarter next to the Basta Arts Café and Majlis Gallery.

Much of the charm of Bastakia lies in just wandering around and getting lost, but there are also a couple of interesting local galleries (as well as a couple of good places to eat – see below). The first is the **Majlis Gallery** (daily except Fri 9.30am–8pm; ☎04-353 6233, ⊛www.majlisgallery.com), on Al Fahidi Roundabout, next to the main entrance into Bastakia. Founded in 1976 by English interior designer Alison Collins (who still co-owns it), the gallery hosts monthly exhibitions showcasing the work of international artists who are invited to come and stay in Dubai and paint Emirati scenes – often with memorable results. The second is the **XVA**

Wind towers

Often described as the world's oldest form of air-conditioning, the distinctive rectangular-shaped wind towers (*barjeel*) that top many old Dubai buildings (as well as numerous modern buildings constructed in faux-Arabian style) formerly offered an ingeniously simple way of countering the Gulf's searing temperatures in a preelectrical age – as well as solving the problem of ventilating houses in a country where windows (where they existed) were almost always kept closed to protect the occupants' privacy. Traditionally the largest and most highly decorated wind tower was placed over the bedroom, with smaller ones over other rooms. They're built up to about 6m high, are open on all four sides and channel any available breezes down into the building via four triangular flues. Of course, wind towers don't produce the arctic blast of icy air conditioning that nowadays seems to be considered *de rigueur* in Dubai's smarter establishments, but stand next to one and you'll notice a slight but significant drop in temperature – particularly welcome in summer, and doubtless a life-saver back in the city's pre-air-con days.

Although the wind tower has become one of the iconic architectural symbols of Dubai and the UAE, they were actually introduced to the city by Iranian merchants who came to settle in the city in the early twentieth century. Many built houses in Bastakia, whose collection of wind towers is the largest and finest in the city (at least, excepting the forest of fake wind towers at the recently constructed Souk Madinat Jumeirah), with subtle variations in design from tower to tower, meaning that no two are ever exactly alike.

▲ DUBAI MUSEUM

Gallery (Sat–Thurs 9am–9pm; ☏04-353 5383, Ⓦwww .xvagallery.com), hidden away at the back of Bastakia next to the F.A.E. boutique. The main focus here is on Middle Eastern artists, though the traditional old house itself is a work of art in its own right, and well worth a look over a long cool drink in the gallery's courtyard café.

Dubai Museum

Al Fahidi St. Mon–Thurs, Sat & Sun 8.30am–8.30pm, Fri 3–9pm. 3dh.
The excellent Dubai Museum occupies the old Al Fahidi Fort, a rough-and-ready little structure whose engagingly lopsided corner turrets and unadorned coral-and-gypsum walls – it looks like a giant sandcastle – offer a welcome contrast to the city's other "old" buildings, most of which have been restored to a state of pristine perfection. Dating from around 1800, the fort is the oldest building in Dubai, having originally been built to defend the town from the very real threat of pirates and other roving mercenaries; it also served as the residence and office of the ruling sheikh. The large courtyard is flanked by a few rooms containing exhibits

of folklore and weaponry, while in the courtyard itself stands a traditional *barasti* house, topped by a basic wind tower, made out of neatly cut palm branches and thatch – the constituent branches are spaced so that breezes are able to blow through the interior, which remains surprisingly cool even in the heat of the day.

The museum's real attraction, however, is its sprawling underground section, a buried wonderland which offers as comprehensive an overview of the traditional life, crafts and culture of Dubai as you'll find anywhere. A sequence of rooms (full of the sound effects and life-size mannequins without which no Dubai museum would be complete) cover every significant aspect of traditional Dubaian life – Islam, local architecture and wind towers, traditional dress and games, camels, falconry, uses of the palm leaf and water in the desert, pearl diving, desert wildlife (with stuffed animals) and dhow building (a lifesize boat under construction) – in stimulating detail, while many rooms also feature interesting short films on various subjects, including brief but fascinating historic footage of pearl divers at work. There's also a line of shops featuring various traditional trades and crafts – carpenters, blacksmiths, potters, tailors, spice merchants and so on – kitsch but undeniably engaging, although the holographic images of artisans add a rather spooky touch.

Al Fahidi Street

Al Fahidi Street is Bur Dubai's de facto high street, bisecting the area from east to west, and also marking the transition point between the textile-focused Creekside area to the north, and that to the south, which is devoted to phones, computers, cameras, watches and all things electronic. Al Fahidi Street itself has a mix of both, with clothing, shoe and jewellery emporia squeezed in between shops packed with Sony camcorders, Nokia phones and Titan watches (some of them may even be genuine, although the constant offers of fake watches, bags and other counterfeit goods as you make your way down the strip might make you think otherwise), while the alleyways to either side are dotted with innumerable downmarket curry houses catering to the area's predominantly Indian and Pakistani community.

Khalid Bin Al Waleed Road

The dual-carriageway Khalid Bin Al Waleed Road (popularly known as "Computer Street") marks the edge of Bur Dubai proper, and a distinct change of pace from the narrow streets and souks of the old city centre to the more modern districts beyond, epitomized by the huge BurJuman mall (see p.57) which nestles on a corner near the road's eastern end. The strip is best known, however, for its dense array of computer and electronics shops, concentrated around the junction with Mankhool Road, a good place to pick up cheap digital stuff or simply to enjoy the after-dark atmosphere, when the strip lights up in a long blaze of neon, and local shoppers come out to haggle over the latest technological temptations.

Sheikh Saeed Al Maktoum House

Shindagha. Sat–Thurs 8am–8.30pm, Fri 3–9.30pm. 2dh. On the northwest side of Bur Dubai, the Creekside Shindagha area is home to a clutch of lovingly restored traditional Emirati homes which line the edge of the Creek as it curves round opposite the tip of the Deira peninsula before reaching the sea. The finest of these is the Sheikh Saeed Al Maktoum House, the principal residence of Dubai's ruling family from

▼ SHEIKH SAEED AL MAKTOUM HOUSE

1896 to 1958. Work on the house was begun in 1896 – making it one of the oldest buildings in Dubai – by Sheikh Maktoum bin Hasher Al Maktoum, and three further wings were added by subsequent members of the Maktoum family, including Sheikh Saeed bin Maktoum Al Maktoum, former ruler of Dubai (and grandfather of the current ruler), who lived here until his death in 1958.

The house is now home to the **Museum of Historical Photographs and Documents of Dubai Emirate**, a very dry name for a surprisingly absorbing collection of old photographs of Dubai through the decades, with beautifully photographed images of the city from the 1940s onwards showing its amazing transformation from a small Gulf town to global megalopolis. The old shots of Bur Dubai are particularly striking: the time-warped records of a quintessential Arabian city, packed with wind-towered houses and big blank walls and appearing almost Biblical (there's even a shot of a swarm of locusts). Other exhibits include models of different types of dhow, along with more striking old photographic images of boats and fishermen and a room full of photos of various craggy-featured Al Maktoum sheikhs – the startling family resemblence makes it surprisingly difficult to tell them apart.

The museum also has extensive exhibits of local coins (featuring a large selection of the East India Company and Indian colonial coins which were used as common currency in Dubai from the late eighteenth century right through until 1966, when Dubai and Qatar introduced a joint currency to replace them). There's also a colourful selection of colonial-era stamps, while upstairs a couple of further rooms are filled with lovely old maps of Dubai and the Arabian peninsula, plus some mildly interesting documents detailing assorted administrative and commercial dealings between the British and Emiratis during the later colonial period.

Heritage and Diving villages

Shindagha. Mon–Thurs, Sat & Sun 8am–10pm, Fri 8–11am & 4–10pm. Free. Beyond the Sheikh Saeed Al Maktoum House, a further

▼ BATEEL DATES

Khidri with
Marzipan
Pistachio
Dhs. 98.00 /kg

cluster of fine old traditional houses line the edge of the Creek. Several of these buildings have now been converted into restaurants (including *Kan Zaman*; see p.60), while one of the largest is given over to the so-called **Heritage Village**. The "village" comprises a large sandy courtyard lined with small shops; most open only during the Dubai Shopping festival, though a few at the rear of the courtyard stay open year round selling the usual kitsch souvenirs along with some more interesting antiques. The atmosphere is pretty moribund during the hotter months, but livens up somewhat from October to April, when there are occasional displays of traditional dancing, cooking and other Emirati pursuits. The adjacent **Diving Village** offers more of the same, with another, notably less imposing, string of traditional buildings around a sandy courtyard dotted with a couple of wooden boats and a few *barasti* huts, plus two boat-shaped phone booths.

Shops

Bateel Dates

BurJuman. Sat–Thurs 10am–10pm, Fri 2–10pm. This smart deli is devoted to all things date-related (30–100dh per kilo), both plain, stuffed with ingredients such as almonds and slices of lemon or orange, and covered in chocolate. Other offerings include date biscuits, date juice and date jam, plus a few other local specialities like acacia honey and fig rolls, and a small selection of fine chocolates. There's another branch at Deira City Centre.

BurJuman

Corner of Khalid Bin Al Waleed and Sheikh Zayed roads. Sat–Thurs 10am–10pm, Fri 2pm–10pm. ✆www .burjuman.com. The flagship city centre mall, BurJuman remains enduringly popular with tourists and locals alike thanks to its vast array of shops (over 300 – pick up a map at the entrance) and convenient location. The sheer size of the place means that it easily swallows up the thousands of visitors, and remains pleasantly calm even at busy times. The older and fairly run-of-the-mill section of the mall hosts branches of pretty much every local and international retailer that does business in the city, ranging from BHS, Mothercare and Virgin to shops selling Emirati-style robes, jewellery, dates and carpets. At the south end of the mall, a swanky new extension combines stylish architecture with a chain of upmarket shops including Cartier, Dior, D&G, Hermès, Burberry, Hugo Boss and Saks Fifth Avenue.

Carrefour

Al Ghubaiba Rd. Daily 8am–midnight (Fri from 9am). The Bur Dubai branch of this vast French hypermarket chain might not be the most atmospheric place to shop in the city, but is one of the best places to pick up just about any kind of Middle Eastern foodstuff you fancy, including dates, sweets like halva and baklava, teas, tropical fruits, nuts, spices, Arabian honey, turkish coffee, saffron, caviar, feta cheeses, labneh and olives – and pretty much every international brand you can think of. Other branches are at Deira City Centre and the Mall of the Emirates.

▲ INTERNATIONAL ALADDIN SHOES

of the Textile Souk stocks a gorgeous selection of colourful embroidered ladies slippers (25–35dh) – pretty little souvenirs, although they can be a bit tight unless you've got skinny feet – along with lovely embroidered belts.

Khalid Bin Al Waleed Street

The massed computer and electronics shops lining Khalid Bin Al Waleed Street around the junction with Mankhool Road are heaven for technophiles in search of a deal, with everything from cut-price PCs to mobile phone accessories at bargain prices – at least if you know what you want and are prepared to shop around. It's also worth checking out the Al Ain Centre on nearby Mankhool Road, which is stuffed with all sorts of digital gadgets.

Damas

BurJuman. Sat–Thurs 10am–10pm, Fri 2–10pm. Dubai's leading chain of jewellery shops, the ubiquitous Damas has branches in virtually every mall in the city. Gold and diamond jewellery predominate, and designs range from classic Italian to chintzy Arabian.

International Aladdin Shoes

Next to Bur Dubai Old Souk Abra Station. Sat–Thurs 10am–10pm, Fri 4–10pm. In a prime position right next to the Bur Dubai Old Souk Abra Station, this eye-catching little stall (no sign) in the midst

Al Orooba Oriental Carpets

First floor, BurJuman. Sat–Thurs 10am–10pm, Fri 2–10pm. This lovely shop is mainly given over to carpets from all the main Asian rug-producing centres (from 600dh up to 50,000dh), but also stocks a fine range of other decorative items and collectables including tablecloths, pashmina and organza shawls, Islamic

Tailoring in Bur Dubai

Although not as well known for its tailoring industry as places like Hong Kong, Bangkok or India, Bur Dubai is a decent place to get tailor-made clothes run up at fairly modest prices, either in the Textile Souk itself or at any of the other cloth shops to the south (try the large Rivoli shop on Al Fahidi Street). All the shops in this area should be able to put you onto a tailor, who can either copy any existing garments you bring along, or run up new ones from scratch.

silverware, Omani khanjars (daggers), walking sticks, coffee pots, frankincense burners and a fine array of prayer beads in lapis lazuli, amber, turquoise and other stones.

Virgin Megastore

BurJuman. Sat–Thurs 10am–10pm, Fri 2–10pm. Along with the usual international CDs and DVDs, Virgin also stocks a superb collection of Arabic pop and other music from Morocco to Iraq – anything from traditional oud music or Um Kalthoum through to May Hariri and the REG Project, as well as recordings by many Gulf and Emirati musicians. Listening posts allow you to browse before you buy. Other branches at Deira City Centre and Mall of the Emirates.

Cafés

Basta Arts Café

Bastakia. Daily 8am–10pm. Set in the idyllic garden of a traditional old Bastakia house (it's on Al Fahidi Street, right next to the main entrance to Bastakia), this lovely little café offers a serene retreat from the modern city outside. The menu features a reasonable selection of salads and sandwiches with an Arabian twist - from grilled halloumi sandwiches to "souk salad" (chicken and couscous) – plus a big selection of herbal teas and unusual juices (but not alcohol).

Bayt Al Wakeel

Textile Souk, near the main entrance. The small menu of rather pedestrian Arabian fare here won't win any awards, but the super-convenient location near the entrance to Textile Souk and the attractive setting on a terrace

sticking out into the Creek behind a traditional old Emirati house compensate. Mezze from around 15dh. Unlicensed.

Dôme

BurJuman. Daily 7.30am till late. This brisk and attractive European-style café makes a convenient lunch stop at the BurJuman, with a superb range of gourmet sandwiches (from 22dh) and excellent coffees, plus an eclectic selection of international mains (from 24dh) running from fish and chips via pizzas and seafood to nasi goreng. Unlicensed. Other branches at Madinat Jumeirah and Jumaira Plaza.

India House

Al Hisn St. Daily 7am–12.30am (closed Fri 11.30am–1.30pm). This long-established vegetarian restaurant is the biggest and perhaps the best of the innumerable no-frills Indian eateries that dot Bur

▼ BASTA ARTS CAFÉ

▲ ANTIQUE BAZAAR

Dubai. There's a baffling range of choices, with every type of vegetable in every conceivable kind of curry, dosa or thali, while further specials are plastered up on the walls. Even with all the trimmings you'll struggle to spend more than 20dh. Unlicensed.

Kan Zaman

Heritage Village, Shindagha. Daily 5.30pm–2.30am. Occupying a beautiful Creekside location in the Shindagha heritage area around Sheikh Saeed Al Maktoum House, this large Middle Eastern restaurant is popular with local familes, who come here to chew the fat, nibble some mezze and puff on a sisha, while old-style Arabic music wails in the background. The menu is strangely confusing, but basically boils down to the usual range of traditional Middle Eastern mezze and meat dishes, all cheap, tasty and dished up in generous portions. Mezze from 10dh, mains from 22dh. Unlicensed.

XVA Café

Bastakia. Daily except Fri 9am–9pm. Buried deep in the labyrinthine alleyways of Bastakia, but well worth the search (it's towards the back of the quarter, near the F.A.E. boutique), the courtyard café of this lovely gallery-cum-guesthouse (see p.53) serves up good Middle Eastern-style vegetarian fare (around 20–25dh), including flavoursome salads (tuna, burgul, bean, fattoush), tasty sandwiches and other light meals and snacks. Unlicensed.

Restaurants

Antique Bazaar

Four Points Sheraton, Khalid Bin Al Waleed Rd ☎04-397 7444. Sat–Thurs 12.30–2.30pm & 7pm–2am, Fri 7pm–2am only (music and dancers from 9pm daily). This pretty little Indian restaurant looks like a forgotten corner of a Rajput palace, littered with carved wooden pillars, antique tables and assorted Indian artefacts. The menu covers all the basic North Indian favourites – tandooris, birianis, chicken and veg curries – with reasonable aplomb, and there's the added incentive of a very passable resident band churning out Bollywood tunes, plus a couple of female dancers twirling around in gauzy costumes. Not the place for a quiet romantic dinner, but good fun otherwise. Mains from around 30dh.

Automatic

Khalid Bin Al Waleed Rd (on corner of 18 St) and Al Khaleej Centre, Mankhool Rd. Daily noon–midnight. Popular with expat Arabs, this citywide chain offers dependable Middle Eastern fare in its string of comfortable and fuss-free restaurants. None is particularly atmospheric, but prices are cheap and food is reliably good, with the full array of mezze and grills, plus a decent seafood selection – or try the grilled pigeon and chips. Mains from around 20dh. There are other branches on Al Rigga Street in Deira; in the Beach Centre, Jumeirah; at the Ibn Battuta Mall; and in Jumeira Tower on Sheikh Zayed Road.

Bastakiah Nights

Bastakia ☎04-353 7772. Daily 4pm–midnight. This Middle Eastern restaurant is one of the most beautiful places to eat in central Dubai, occupying a superbly restored old house in Bastakia – the perfect place to indulge in a few orientalist fantasies whilst sitting in the courtyard puffing on a shisha. The menu runs through the usual gamut of Middle Eastern favourites, plus a few more unusual offerings such as stuffed grape leaves and traditional veg and lamb stews. Dishes are well prepared and reasonably priced, although portions are a bit stingy. Mezze from 18dh, mains from 35dh.

Yakitori

Royal Ascot Hotel, Khalid Bin Al Waleed Rd ☎04-352 0900. Daily 12.30–3pm & 6.30-11.30pm. Hidden away on the fifth floor of the *Royal Ascot Hotel*, this lively and informal little Japanese restaurant is one of Dubai's weirdest and most wonderful ethnic enclaves – and probably as close as you'll get to Tokyo without actually going there. The largely Japanese clientele, Japanese-language menu (with English translation, fortunately), Japanese TV programmes and Japanese sushi and teppanyaki chefs all conspire to give you the sensation of having fallen suddenly through a hole in space into deepest Ginza, an impression strengthened by the cheap, fuss-free and delicious food, with all the usual noodles, sushi, sashimi, yakitori, kushi katsu and tempura, plus excellent set menus (35–45dh).

Pubs

Sherlock Holmes

Arabian Courtyard, Al Fahidi St. Daily noon–2am. One of the nicer English pubs in Bur Dubai, with a relaxed atmosphere, flock wallpaper, leatherette chairs and glass cases full of vaguely Sherlock Holmes-related memorabilia. It does decent pub food, and regular beer promotions keep things busy; drink enough beer and you might even enjoy the live Filipina karaoke singer.

Viceroy Bar

Four Points Sheraton, Khalid Bin Al Waleed Rd. Daily 11–2am. This traditional English-style pub is the nicest in Bur Dubai, complete with fake oak-beamed ceiling, authentic wooden bar and oodles of comfy leather armchairs – although it's so dark you can hardly see what you're drinking. There's a decent range of draught beers and other bevvies, plus assorted sports on the overhead TVs, and it's also a conveniently short stagger to the excellent *Antique Bazaar* Indian restaurant (see opposite).

Deira

North of the Creek lies Deira, the second of the city centre's two principal districts, founded in 1841, when settlers from Bur Dubai crossed the Creek to establish a new village here. Deira rapidly overtook its older neighbour and remains notably more built-up and more cosmopolitan than Bur Dubai, with a heady ethnic mix of Emiratis, Arabs, Indians, Pakistanis, Somalis, African traders, Russian bargain-hunters and Western tourists thronging its packed streets. For the visitor, Deira's main attraction is its myriad souks – most obviously the famous Gold Souk and the atmospheric Spice Souk – although in many ways the entire district is one enormous bazaar through which it's possible to wander for mile after mile without ever surfacing. The district is also home to a pair of interesting traditional buildings – the Heritage House and Al Ahmadiya School – while along the banks of the Creek itself you'll find the atmospheric Dhow Wharfage, an authentic taste of Dubai past, along with a clutch of striking modernist buildings centred on the landmark National Bank of Dubai – an icon of Dubai's dazzling present.

Gold Souk

Sikkat Al Khail Rd. Deira's famous Gold Souk is usually the first stop for visitors to the district, and attracts a cosmopolitan range of customers, from

For information on crossing the Creek by abra and abra cruises, see p.51.

▼ THE CREEK, DEIRA SIDE

Shopping in the Gold Souk

The gold industry in Dubai is carefully regulated, so there's no danger of being ripped off with substandard or fake goods, but there are still a few useful basic things to know if you're planning on buying gold here. First of all, gold jewellery is **sold by weight** (the quality and detail of the decoration and workmanship, however elaborate, isn't usually factored into the price). Secondly, the **price of gold is fixed** in all shops citywide (and is often posted up inside) – although the exact figure fluctuates daily depending on the international price of gold. Therefore, if you ask how much a piece of jewellery is, it will first be popped on the scales and weighed, and the cost then calculated according to the day's gold price. Once you've established this basic price, it's time to start **bargaining**. A request for "best price" or "small discount" (virtually all the Gold Souk shops are run by Indians, who are well versed in the intricacies of barter – not to mention high-pressure salesmanship) should yield an immediate discount of around 20–25 percent over the basic price; you may be able to lower the price still further depending on how canny you are and how desperate they are for a sale. As ever, it pays to shop around and compare prices (and tell the shop you're in that you've found a better deal elsewhere, if necessary). If you're buying more than one item in a shop, you should press for further discounts. If you can't find what you want in the Gold Souk itself, there are several sizeable malls – Goldland, The Gold Centre, Gold City and Gold House – all exclusively devoted to gold, lined up along the Corniche opposite the Gold Souk Bus Station, a short distance to the north, as well as numerous other shops dotted around the city.

Shopping for **precious stones** is more complicated, and it pays to do some research before leaving home. **Diamonds** are a particularly good buy in Dubai, often selling at half (or even less) the price they would retail for in the West. As well as the Gold Souk, it's also worth visiting the excellent Gold and Diamond Park in southern Jumeirah (see p.121).

If authenticity isn't a worry when buying gold and precious stones, the same cannot be said of the thriving local trade in **counterfeit goods**, still going strong despite modest attempts in recent times by the Dubai authorities to crack down on this illicit trade. Spend any amount of time in the Gold Souk and you'll be repeatedly importuned with offers of "cheap copy watches", "copy bags" and the like. If you decide to investigate further you'll be led to an obscure lock-up shop somewhere in the surrounding alleyways stuffed with counterfeit designer goods – watches, bags, sunglasses and other designer accessories. Prices aren't especially cheap ($50 and up for watches and bags), but still a fraction of the cost of the real thing, and quality is excellent (indeed it's often suggested that some counterfeits are actually manufactured in the same factories which produce the genuine items). Not surprisingly, for many visitors the acquisition of a top-notch fake Chanel bag or Gucci watch at a fraction of the price of the original may be the shopping highlight of a visit to the city, although the designers of the originals aren't going to thank you for saying so, or for supporting this under-the-counter trade. Be prepared to bargain like crazy, and don't be afraid to walk away if you can't get the price you want – you'll have plenty of other offers.

▼ GOLD CITY

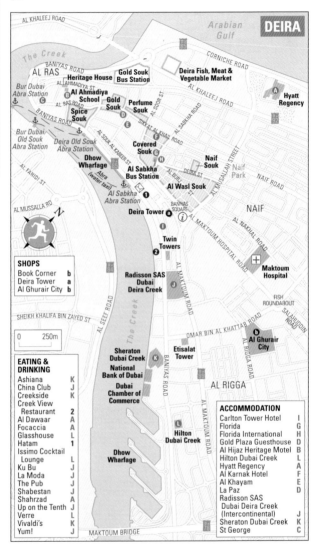

DEIRA

Arabian Gulf

The Creek

AL KHALEEJ ROAD

BANIYAS ROAD

CORNICHE ROAD

AL RAS

Heritage House

Gold Souk
Bus Station

Deira Fish, Meat &
Vegetable Market

AL AHMADIYA ST

Bur Dubai
Abra Station

Al Ahmadiya
School

AL KHALEEJ ROAD

Hyatt
Regency

AL RAS ROAD

Gold
Souk

Perfume
Souk

Spice
Souk

AL SABKHA ROAD

AL SABKHA ROAD

BANIYAS ROAD

AL SOUK AL KABEER ST

SIKKAT AL KHAIL ROAD

Bur Dubai
Old Souk
Abra Station

Deira Old Souk
Abra Station

Covered
Souk

Naif
Souk

AL MUSSALLAH STREET

Naif
Park

Dhow
Wharfage

Al Sabkha
Bus Station

AL BUR

DEIRA ST

AL FAHIDI ST

Abra
(water taxi)

Al Wasl Souk

NAIF ROAD

Al Sabkha
Abra Station

NAIF

AL MUSSALLA RD

BANIYAS
SQUARE

Deira Tower

AL MAKTOUM HOSPITAL ROAD

AL NAKHAL ROAD

N

Twin
Towers

Maktoum
Hospital

SHOPS

Book Corner	b
Deira Tower	a
Al Ghurair City	b

Radisson SAS
Dubai
Deira Creek

AL MAKTOUM ROAD

FISH
ROUNDABOUT

SALAHUDDIN ROAD

SHEIKH KHALIFA BIN ZAYED ST

The Creek

OMAR BIN AL KHATTAR ROAD

0   250m

AL SEEF ROAD

AL RIGGA ROAD

Al Ghurair
City

Sheraton
Dubai Creek

Etisalat
Tower

**EATING &
DRINKING**

Ashiana	K
China Club	J
Creekside	K
Creek View	
Restaurant	2
Al Dawaar	A
Focaccia	A
Glasshouse	L
Hatam	1
Issimo Cocktail	
Lounge	L
Ku Bu	J
La Moda	J
The Pub	J
Shabestan	J
Shahrzad	A
Up on the Tenth	J
Verre	L
Vivaldi's	K
Yum!	J

National
Bank of Dubai

AL RIGGA

Dubai
Chamber of
Commerce

BANIYAS ROAD

AL MAKTOUM ROAD

Hilton
Dubai Creek

ACCOMMODATION

Carlton Tower Hotel	I
Florida	G
Florida International	H
Gold Plaza Guesthouse	D
Al Hijaz Heritage Motel	B
Hilton Dubai Creek	L
Hyatt Regency	A
Al Karnak Hotel	F
Al Khayam	E
La Paz	D
Radisson SAS	
Dubai Deira Creek	
(Intercontinental)	J
Sheraton Dubai Creek	K
St George	C

Dhow
Wharfage

MAKTOUM BRIDGE

Western tourists to African and Asian traders buying up pieces for re sale at home. The souk itself – centred around a pedestrianized street of small shops sheltered beneath a wooden roof – isn't particularly exotic, but the sheer quantity of gold jewellery lined up in the shop windows is staggering, and it offers a pleasantly cool and laid-back respite from the city outside, even if the constant offers of "cheap copy watch" from roving rogue traders can become wearisome.

▲ GOLD SOUK

The souk's main attraction, of course, is price: gold in Dubai is among the cheapest in the world, and massive competition keeps prices keen. The jewellery on offer ranges from fabulously ornate Arabian creations to elegantly restrained pieces oriented towards European tastes. Particularly appealing are the traditional Emirati bracelets, fashioned from solid gold (and often exquisitely embellished with white-gold decoration) and hung in long lines in shop windows – they were traditionally used for dowries, as were the heavier and more ornate necklaces also on display. As well as gold, there are plenty of places selling jewellery mounted with precious stones, most obviously diamonds, as well as a range of other gems from emeralds to tanzanite.

Spice Souk

Opposite Deira Old Souk Abra station. Dubai's Spice Souk (also known as the Deira Old Souk) is perhaps the most interesting and atmospheric – and certainly the most fragrant – of the city's myriad bazaars. Large sections of the main covered walkway through the souk have been taken over by cheap shops selling toys and household goods, and most of the spice merchants can now be found tucked away in the narrow alleyways immediately to the north. Run almost exclusively by Iranian traders, the shops here stock a wide variety of culinary, medicinal and cosmetic products, with tubs

Souk opening hours

There are no set hours for the myriad shops in Deira's various souks. In practice, most shops open at 10am and close at 10pm or later; many also close during the afternoon from around 1 to 4pm.

▲ SPICE SOUK

of merchandise set out in front of a sequence of tiny shops. All the usual spices can be found – cinnamon, cardamom, cumin, coriander – along with more unusual offerings such as saffron (Dubai is one of the cheapest places in the world to buy this delicate and highly prized spice), dried cucumbers and lemons (a common ingredient in Middle Eastern cuisine), incense, and heaps of hibiscus and rose petals, used to make a delicately scented tea. The souk is also famous for its frankincense, which is sold in several different forms – the most common type looks like a kind of reddish, crumbling crystalline rock; frankincense burners can be bought in the souk for a few dirhams. Most stalls also sell natural cosmetic products such as pumice (it looks rather like coal) and *alum*, a clear rock crystal used to soothe the skin after shaving. Male visitors in search of a pick-me-up will also find plentiful supplies of so-called "natural viagra".

It's also worth exploring the back of the Spice Souk area, stretching north from here towards the Gold Souk. The shops themselves are uninteresting (toys and cheap homeware are, once again, the order of the day), but the souk itself is unusually pretty, with a couple of tiny squares linked by rambling alleys lined with green lamps topped with Islamic crescent moons.

Perfume Souk
Sikkat Al Khail St and Al Soor St.
The area immediately east of the Gold Souk is traditionally known as the Perfume Souk, and although the area's scent shops are now probably outnumbered by places selling women's clothing (everything from traditional black robes and shalwar kameez through to belly-dancing costumes), there are still a decent number of small-scale perfumeries dotted around the streets here. These sell a range of international brands (not all genuine) along

▲ PERFUME SOUK

colourful, low-grade cloth for women's clothes, along with large quantities of mass-produced junk including piles of plastic toys and cheap household goods. It's all rather down-at-heel and a bit shabby compared to the Gold and Spice souks, but makes for an interesting stroll even so, especially in the area at the back of the Al Sabkha Bus Station, the busiest and densest part of the bazaar – expect to get lost at least once. The souk then continues, more or less unabated, on the far side of Al Sabkha Road, where it's known variously as the Naif Souk and Al Wasl Souk, before reaching Al Musallah Street.

with rather more flowery – some might say overpowering – local scents. The latter usually come presented in chintzy little glass bottles, which are virtually collectables in their own right.

Covered Souk

South of Naif Rd between 67C St and Al Sabkha Rd. The sprawling Covered Souk (a misnomer, since it isn't) comprises a rather indeterminate area of small shops stuffed into the narrow streets and alleyways which run from south of Naif Road down virtually to the Creek. Most of the shops here are Indian-run, selling vast quantities of

Dhow Wharfage

Baniyas Rd, between the Deira Old Souk and Al Sabkha abra stations. The Dhow Wharfage offers a fascinating glimpse into the maritime traditions of old Dubai which have survived miraculously intact at the heart of the twenty-first-century city. At any one time, the wharfage is home to hundreds of beautiful wooden dhows (some as much as a hundred

▼ DHOW WHARFAGE

PLACES

Deira

▲ AL AHMADIYA SCHOOL

years old), which berth here to load and unload cargo; hence the great tarpaulin-covered mounds of merchandise – anything from boxes of dates to massive air-conditioning units – that lie stacked up along the waterfront. The dhows themselves range in size from the fairly modest vessels employed for short hops up and down the coast to the large ocean-going craft that are used to transport goods around the Gulf, over to Iran, and sometimes further afield to India, East Africa and Southeast Asia. Virtually all of them fly the UAE flag, although they're generally manned by foreign crews who live on board, their lines of washing strung out across the decks and piles of cooking pots giving the boats a quaintly domestic air in the middle of downtown Dubai's hustle and bustle. Hang around long enough and you might be invited to hop on board for a chat (assuming you can find a shared language) and a cup of tea.

Al Ahmadiya School

Just off Al Ahmadiya Street. Mon–Thurs, Sat & Sun 8am–7.30pm, Fri 2.30–7.30pm. Free. Hidden away in the backstreets north of the Gold Souk, the Al Ahmadiya School is one of the most beautiful surviving examples of traditional Arabian architecture in the city, now converted into an interesting little museum devoted to the educational history of the emirate. Founded in 1912 under the charitable auspices of the pearl merchant Sheikh Mohammed bin Ahmed bin Dalmouk, Al Ahmadiya was the first public school in UAE, and many of the city's leaders studied here, including Sheikh Rashid, although the school was also notably egalitarian – only the sons of wealthy families were expected to pay, and education for poorer pupils was free. The curriculum initially focused exclusively on the traditional Islamic disciplines of Koranic study, Arabic calligraphy and mathematics, though the syllabus was later expanded to cover practical subjects such as diving and the pearl trade, as well as more modern disciplines including English, sociology and science. By 1962, over eight hundred students had been enrolled in the increasingly over crowded school, which was soon afterwards relocated to new and larger premises nearby, while the original building was allowed to fall into ruin. In 1995 the building was meticulously restored by the city authorities in their belated attempt to rescue surviving examples of traditional architecture and culture amidst the swiftly modernizing city.

The school occupies a simple but attractive two-storey sand-coloured building, topped by a pair of wind towers, its plain outlines embellished by Koranic inscriptions on the ground floor and latticed windows upstairs, plus finely carved arches. Interesting touchscreens and displays cover the history of the school, while exhibits include pictures of former sheikhs, clay water pots, government letters, old photos and a life-sized model showing three tiny pupils being instructed

by a rather irritable-looking teacher brandishing a wooden cane. There's also an interesting ten-minute film containing interviews with former students, plus some intriguing old footage of the school in its heydey showing neatly robed pupils lined up in the courtyard chanting Koranic verses.

Heritage House

Al Ahmadiya St. Mon–Thurs, Sat & Sun 8am–7.30pm, Fri 2.30–7.30pm. Free. The sprucely restored Heritage House offers visitors a glimpse into the former lifestyle and traditions of pre-modern Dubai. The house was originally built in 1890 and subsequently enlarged and embellished at various times over the next fifty years, most notably in 1910 by the pearl merchant Sheikh Mohammed bin Ahmed bin Dalmouk, who was also responsible for establishing the adjacent Al Ahmadiya School. The building gives a good idea of a traditional Emirati house, with its imposing but windowless street facade opening onto a large sandy courtyard, a characteristic

▼ HERITAGE HOUSE

feature of inward-looking Arabian houses, providing daylight and ventilation to the rooms arranged around it, and with a cattle pen on one side and a couple of trees in the middle – a miniature desert at the heart of an urban mansion.

Each of the rooms is enlivened with exhibits and mannequins evoking aspects of traditional Emirati life, while piped background noises of conversation and daily activity (complete with an intermittently screaming baby in the main room) add a slightly surreal touch. In the entrance *majlis* (the room in which male guests were traditionally received, business conducted and news exchanged), mannequins loll around on cushions drinking coffee, while in the nearby ladies' *majlis* a child has her hands painted with henna, while others spin thread, work on their embroidery or grind spices. Finely carved wooden doors with stylized palm and floral motifs lead into the main room, where further mannequins in rich traditional dress and jewellery share a space with incongruous Western luxury imports, including an old gramophone, a wireless and a Seth Thomas clock.

Deira Fish, Meat and Vegetable Market

Al Khaleej Rd. Daily 7.30am–11pm.

The extensive Deira Fish, Meat and Vegetable Market offers a welcome respite and change of scenery from central Deira's crowded streets and souks. The best time to visit is early in the morning, when the fish and meat markets are in full swing, though the market remains busy throughout the day. The fruit and veg section features a photogenic array of stalls piled high with all the usual fruit alongside more exotic offerings such as rambutans, mangosteens, coconuts, vast watermelons, yams and big bundles of fresh herbs, as well as a bewildering array of dates in huge, sticky piles. The less colourful and far more malodorous fish section is stocked with long lines of sharks, ocean-fresh tuna and all sorts of other fish right down to little sardines – if you're lucky someone will offer you a prawn. There's also a small and rather gory meat section tucked away at the back, the perfect place for vegetarians to reaffirm their principles.

The National Bank of Dubai and around

Deira's contemporary face is embodied by the arresting sequence of buildings that line the Creekside along Baniyas Road, a kilometre or so east of the old city centre. The most striking and one of the city's most famous sights is the **National Bank of Dubai** building, opened

▼ DEIRA FISH, MEAT AND VEGETABLE MARKET

▲ NATIONAL BANK

in 1998, its Creek-facing side covered by an enormous, curved facade of sheet glass, modelled on the sail of a traditional dhow, which seems positively to catch fire with reflected light towards sunset (it's best seen from the Bur Dubai side of the water). It was designed by Carlos Ott, who was also responsible for the striking interior of the nearby *Hilton Dubai Creek* (see p.172).

Next to the National Bank building sits the shorter and squatter **Dubai Chamber of Commerce**, an austerely minimalist glass-clad structure of 1995 which seems to have been designed using nothing but triangles – a design subliminally echoed in the adjacent **Sheraton Dubai Creek**, whose wedge-shaped facade pokes out above the Creekside like the prow of some enormous concrete ship. Opposite the Sheraton stands the **Etisalat Tower** (1986), designed by Canadian architect Arthur Erikson and instantly recognizable thanks to the enormous golf ball on its roof (a feature which can also be seen on Etisalat's new building on Sheikh Zayed Road, and on its Abu Dhabi headquarters).

There's also another large **dhow wharfage** just east of the Chamber of Commerce, much less visited than that in central Deira but just as eye-catching, with the old-fashioned boats superbly framed against the sparkling glass facades of the surrounding modernist high-rises.

Shops

As well as the shops described below, there are of course endless shopping possibilities in Deira's myriad souks, especially the Gold Souk (for more on shopping in which, see p.62), Spice Souk (p.65) and Perfume Souk (p.66).

Al Ghurair City

Al Rigga Rd. Sat–Thurs 10am–11pm, Fri 2–11pm. The oldest mall in Dubai, Al Ghurair seems small and rather plain compared to more recent complexes, but still pulls in a good crowd thanks to its decent selection of mainstream high-street shops such as BHS, Timberland,

▼ SOUTHERN DHOW WHARFAGE

PLACES Deira

French Connection and Mexx. Locals head upstairs, where you'll find a number of outlets specializing in Arabian perfumes and *abbeya* (the black robes worn by Gulf women), and others with windows full of mannequins modelling extremely flouncy frocks made out of the colourful piles of fabrics sold within. A couple of shops also sell men's robes and headscarves.

Book Corner
First floor, Al Ghurair City, Al Rigga Rd. Sat–Thurs 10am–11pm, Fri 2–11pm. The second-biggest bookshop in the city (recently eclipsed by the newly opened Borders at the Mall of the Emirates). This vast but rather uninspiring emporium's best feature is its good range of local-interest titles on all aspects of Emirati and Arabian life and culture, although the stock of travel guides is woefully out of date.

Deira Tower
Baniyas Square. Home to the biggest collection of rug shops in the city, the so-called "Carpet Souk" here comprises thirty-odd shops spread over the ground and first floors of this large office block. There's a massive amount of stuff on sale, ranging from huge, museum-quality Persian heirlooms to ghastly framed carpet pictures and other tat, but it's mostly good quality.

Restaurants

Ashiana
Sheraton Dubai Creek, Baniyas Rd ☎04-228 1111. Sat–Thurs 12.30–3.30pm & 7.30pm–1am, Fri 7.30pm–1am. An elegant and pleasantly old-fashioned Indian restaurant with Rajput-style decor and a well-chosen selection of nourishing North Indian favourites, including all sorts of kebabs and a decent choice of vegetarian and fish/seafood curries, plus a few well-prepared desserts (try the apricot and fig kulfi). There's also a live singer and band nightly from 8.30pm, performing anything from ghazals to Bollywood hits. Mains from 50dh.

China Club
Radisson SAS Hotel Dubai Deira Creek, Baniyas Rd ☎04-222 7171. Daily 12.30–3pm (Fri from 11.30am) & 7.30–11pm. The best Chinese restaurant in

▼ ASHIANA

▲ CREEKSIDE

Creek View Restaurant

Baniyas Rd. Daily noon–2am.

This convivial little open-air Creekside restaurant draws in a good local crowd most nights during the cooler parts of the year thanks to its appealing combination of cheap and tasty Middle Eastern food (all the usual mezze and grills, with pretty much everything under 20dh), a decent shisha list, and views of the neon-fringed waters of the Creek. It's also open for lunch, but is usually rather moribund until after dark.

Al Dawaar

Hyatt Regency, Deira Corniche ☎04-317 2222. Daily 12.30–3.30pm & 7–11.30pm. Dubai's only revolving restaurant, balanced atop the gargantuan *Hyatt Regency* and offering superlative city views – each revolution takes 1hr 45min, so you should get to see the whole 360-degree panorama if you don't eat too fast. Food is buffet only (140dh at lunch, 175dh at dinner, excluding drinks), featuring a

central Dubai, with tastefully simple modern decor and some seating in cosily intimate, high-backed booths. The smallish menu mixes well-prepared Chinese standards – dim sum, live seafood, Peking duck, stir fries and noodles – along with a few more unusual offerings like duck soup with egg white and pine nuts, all delivered on huge white plates by well-drilled staff. Mains from around 45dh.

Creekside

Sheraton Dubai Creek, Baniyas Rd ☎04-207 1750. Sat–Thurs 12.30–3pm & 6.30pm–midnight, Fri 6.30pm–midnight. A pleasant Japanese restaurant with Creek views and a good spread of authentic fare – anything from sushi and sashimi to temaki, donburi and tempura, as well as noodle dishes, soups, grills and nice bento boxes for that authentic packed-lunch-in-Tokyo experience. It also has regular sushi-, teppanyaki- and seafood-themed food nights, with set menus from around 100dh. Mains from 40dh.

PLACES Deira

▼ CREEK VIEW RESTAURANT

mix of Mediterranean, Arabian, Asian and Japanese dishes plus US steaks – not the city's greatest (or best-value) culinary experience, but a decent accompaniment to the head-turning vistas outside.

Focaccia

Hyatt Regency, Deira Corniche ☎04-317 2222. Daily except Sun 12.30–3pm & 7pm–midnight. This rambling modern Italian restaurant has the feel of a rather smart country club, with a casual ambience, soothing Gulf views and a menu of revivifying pasta, fish and meat dishes such as beetroot risotto, lobster taglione, veal tortellini and pork chop ragout. Mains from 45dh.

Glasshouse

Hilton Dubai Creek, Baniyas Rd ☎04-212 7550. Open 24hr. Colourful and casual brasserie with funky

▼ GLASSHOUSE

decor and a tempting range of Mediterranean-style dishes – salads, pasta, steaks and fish – with fresh flavours and some inventive combinations like pan-fried hammour with chorizo potato salad or shrimp and avocado salad. Mains 70–80dh.

Hatam

Off Baniyas Square. Daily noon–midnight. One of a lively little trio of Iranian restos just south of Baniyas Square, this simple little restaurant serves up big portions of tasty Persian fare at very modest prices, including a big selection of enormous chicken and lamb kebabs accompanied by huge slabs of flat bread, plus a few, slightly pricier seafood options. *Shiraz Nights* and *Hatam Al Tai* restaurants opposite do a very similar range of food at slightly lower prices and in more cheap-and-cheerful surroundings.

There are other branches of *Hatam* at the BurJuman Centre and Ibn Battuta Mall.

La Moda

Radisson SAS Hotel Dubai Deira Creek, Baniyas Rd ☎04-222 7171. Daily 12.30–3.15pm & 7.30–11.30pm. With its waiters dressed in red mechanics' overalls, modish contemporary decor and a funky pop and chill-out soundtrack, this popular Italian is more urban bistro than traditional trattoria. The food is equally stylish, and good value too, with a wide-ranging menu of flavoursome pastas, risottos and pizzas, plus meat and fish mains and a better-than-average vegetarian selection. Mains from around 40dh.

▲ SHABESTAN

Shabestan

Radisson SAS Hotel Dubai Deira
Creek, Baniyas Rd ☎04-222 7171.
Daily 12.30–3.15pm & 7.30–11.15pm
(Wed & Thurs until 11.30pm).
Entered via a small vestibule
full of fragrant-smelling spices
and intriguing *objets d'art*, this
smart Iranian restaurant remains
enduringly popular with local
Arabs and expat Iranians
thanks to its huge *chelo* kebabs,
fish stews and other Persian
specialities. A resident three-
piece band of violin, drum and
santour performs nightly. Mains
from 68dh.

Shahrzad

Hyatt Regency, Deira Corniche ☎04-
317 2222. Mon–Wed 8pm–midnight,
Thurs–Sat 12.30–3pm & 8pm–
midnight. This picture-perfect
little Iranian restaurant looks
likes it has leapt straight out
of an illustration for the *1001
Nights* (after whose narrator it
takes its name). It also dishes
up probably the best traditional
Persian food in the city, with
delicately spiced *chelo* kebabs

and classic *polos* (rice stews)
such as *zareshk polo ba morgh*
(stewed chicken covered with
rice mixed with barberries and
saffron) – mainly chicken and
lamb, plus a few seafood options.
Live Iranian music nightly from
9pm. Mains from 75dh.

Verre

Hilton Dubai Creek, Baniyas Rd
☎04-227 1111. Daily 7pm–midnight.
Under the management of softly
spoken, triple Michelin-starred
UK chef Gordon Ramsay (who
visits twice a year), *Verre* makes
a strong case to be considered
the best restaurant in Dubai,
constantly wowing diners with
its superb modern European
cuisine, featuring a range of
artfully crafted meat, fish and
seafood dishes. Even if you're
utterly cynical about the whole
celebrity chef industry, it's
difficult not to be impressed by
the heavenly flavours and subtle
culinary combinations which
most other restaurants don't
even begin to imagine, let alone
reach. The smooth but unfussy

modern decor and muted music make sure that attention is firmly focused where it should be – on the food – while an extensive but affordable wine list provides an appropriate accompaniment. It's also significantly less wallet-emptying than you might fear (with mains from 75dh), and when you factor in the additional hors d'oeuvres and between-course "palate cleansers" – some of which virtually amount to fully fledged courses in their own right – a meal here works out at significantly better value than in many of the city's other fine-dining venues. The only negative is the complete lack of vegetarian options, for whom Ramsay maintains a tragically Olympian disregard. Reserve as far in advance as possible, since the restaurant can get booked solid for weeks in advance.

Vivaldi's

Sheraton Dubai Creek, Baniyas Rd ☎04-228 1111. Daily 6.30pm–1.30am. This sedate, old-style Italian restaurant puts the emphasis on comfort over style, and is none the worse for it, with a reasonably priced and well-prepared selection of pizzas, pastas, risottos and other antipasti (from 36dh), plus a selection of hearty, authentic meat and seafood mains (from 55dh). The attractive Creek views are an added bonus.

Yum!

Radisson SAS Hotel Dubai Deira Creek, Baniyas Rd ☎04-222 7171. Daily noon–1am. A sleek, modern cafe-restaurant in the *Radisson*'s shopping arcade, with cool minimalist lines and glassed-in open-plan kitchen. The menu is Southeast and East Asian (predominantly Thai and Chinese), with a good range of tasty, fuss-free offerings, briskly served, including soups, noodles, rice dishes, Thai curries and vegetarian selections, all at very reasonable prices, backed up by a surprisingly extensive wine list. Mains from 30dh.

Bars

Issimo Cocktail Lounge

Hilton Dubai Creek, Baniyas Rd. Daily 7pm–1am. Occupying a corner of the *Hilton*'s ultra-modern, chrome-obsessed ground floor, this chic little cocktail bar has a cute boat-shaped bar and a refreshingly unposey atmosphere – though the drinks list is disappointingly meagre. It's a good spot for an aperitif or digestif before or after a meal at one of the two excellent restaurants upstairs. Occasional live DJs.

Ku Bu

Radisson SAS Hotel Dubai Deira Creek, Baniyas Rd. Daily 7pm–2am. An intimate little drinking hole, tucked away at the rear end of the *Radisson*, with a fancy backlit bar, moody lighting and big comfy sofas and barside perches. It's usually pleasantly chilled early in the evening, though things can get livelier later on when the beautiful people of Deira arrive for cocktails, especially if there's a live DJ on. Tipples include the usual champagnes, cocktails and shots (though the wine list and beer selection is very average), plus various gourmet bar snacks like Beluga caviar and freshly shucked oysters. Best of all, however, is the view from the gents' loos, from where one-way mirrors (at least we hope they're one-way) allow one to spy into

▲ ISSIMO COCKTAIL LOUNGE

the bar whilst going about one's business.

The Pub

Radisson SAS Hotel Dubai Deira Creek, Baniyas Rd. Daily noon–4pm & 6pm–midnight. A spacious and fairly peaceful English-style pub, complete with the usual fake wooden bar and dozens of TVs screening global sports – one of the few good places in Deira for a quiet pint and a break from the cocktail-supping fashionistas who have taken over most of the district's other bars.

Up on the Tenth

Radisson SAS Hotel Dubai Deira Creek, Baniyas Rd. Daily 6.30pm–2am (Thurs until 2.30am). Not the most stylish venue in Dubai – the mirrored Manhattan skyline-effect behind the bar is loved only by the very short-sighted, or the very drunk – but this cosy little tenth-floor bar offers some of the best Creek views to be had in the city centre. Arrive early, grab a windowside seat and watch the city light up. A jazz singer and pianist perform daily (except Fri) from 9.30pm.

The inner suburbs

Fringing the southern and eastern edges of the city centre – and separating it from the more modern areas beyond – are a necklace of low-key suburbs: Garhoud, Oud Metha, Karama and Satwa. This whole area of Dubai has a slightly indeterminate, in-between feel, neither properly part of the city centre, but lacking the modernist pizzazz of the more recently developed areas to the south. Having said that, there's plenty to see and do hereabouts. Garhoud and Oud Metha are home to a good number of shops, restaurants, bars and other attractions, many of them concentrated in two land-mark malls: Oud Metha's upmarket Wafi City and its more downmarket Garhoud cousin, Deira City Centre. Karama and Satwa, meanwhile, are two of the most interesting parts of the city in which to get off the tour-ist trail and see something of local life, with plenty of lively cafés and inexpensive shops for stocking up on designer fakes.

Garhoud

Covering the area between the airport and the Creek, the suburb of Garhoud is an interesting mishmash of up- and downmarket attractions. The Deira City Centre mall (see p.83) is the suburb's main crowd-puller, eternally popular with an eclectic crowd, from Gulf Arabs and Russian tourists to the many expat Indians and Filipinas who live in the down-at-heel suburbs on the far side of the airport.

Just over the road lie the lush green fairways and greens of the Dubai Creek Golf Club, particularly striking when floodlit at night, as is the iconic, modernist clubhouse itself, built in 1993

and still one of the city's most instantly recognizable landmarks, the shape of its uniquely spiky white roofline echoing that of a dhow's sails and masts – like a Dubai remake of the Sydney Opera House.

A short distance down the Creek lies another local landmark, the Dubai Creek Yacht Club, occupying a full-size replica of a ship's bridge, with dozens of beautiful millionaires' yachts moored

▼ WAFI CITY

alongside. There are numerous alluring restaurants (see pp.87–89 for recommendations) in the golf and yacht club buildings, as well as in the recently opened *Park Hyatt* hotel between, whose serene white Moroccan-style buildings, topped with vivid blue-tiled domes, add a further touch of style to the Creekside hereabouts.

Oud Metha

On the opposite side of the Creek from Garhoud, the district of Oud Metha is home to assorted malls, hotels, parks and low-brow leisure attractions. The area's two major landmarks

▲ CHILDREN'S CITY, CREEKSIDE PARK

PLACES The inner suburbs

are the vast *Grand Hyatt Hotel* (see p.174), which stands in majestic isolation at Oud Metha's southern end, its curved, interlocking white wings looking like some kind of giant child's toy, and the wacky Egyptian-themed **Wafi City** shopping and restaurant complex (see listings on pp.84–85), a little slice of Vegas in Dubai, complete with full-size obelisks, pharaohs and gilt columns (even the cubicle doors in the loos are decorated in hieroglyphics).

Flanking the Creek on the eastern edge of Oud Metha between Garhoud and Maktoum bridges, the expansive **Creekside Park** (daily 8am–11pm, Thurs–Sat until 11.30pm; 5dh) serves as one of congested central Dubai's major lungs and is a pleasant place for an idle ramble and some time out from the traffic, with nice views over the Creek towards the golf and yacht clubs

and the *Park Hyatt* hotel. There are lots of playgrounds here, as well as Children's City and the Wonderland theme park (see p.189). You'll also find the Dubai Cable Car (25dh, children 10dh), which offers thirty-five-minute trips above the park and panoramic city views. The park is nicest towards dusk, when the temperature falls and the place fills up a bit; it can be eerily deserted during weekdays.

On the southern edge of Oud Metha, the district of Jaddaf is home to a few traditional dhow-building yards where you can watch local craftsmen at work constructing these magnificent ocean-going vessels using carpenting skills which appear not to have changed for generations. Unfortunately, the whole area is currently in the throes of massive construction work, and finding the yards requires a certain amount of effort and expense. Take a taxi

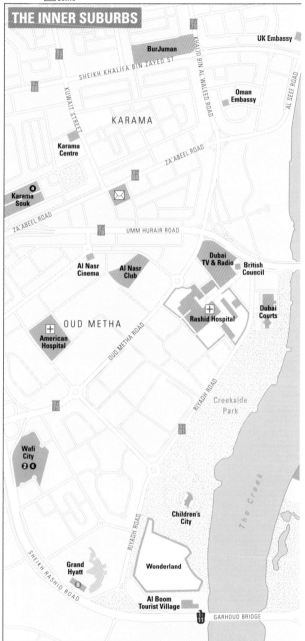

△ Satwa

THE INNER SUBURBS

UK Embassy

BurJuman

SHEIKH KHALIFA BIN ZAYED ST

KHALID BIN AL WALEED ROAD

KUWAIT STREET

Oman Embassy

AL SEEF ROAD

KARAMA

Karama Centre

ZA'ABEEL ROAD

Karama Souk Ⓐ

ZA'ABEEL ROAD

UMM HURAIR ROAD

Al Nasr Cinema

Al Nasr Club

Dubai TV & Radio

British Council

Rashid Hospital

Dubai Courts

American Hospital

OUD METHA

OUD METHA ROAD

RIYADH ROAD

Creekside Park

Wafi City Ⓩ Ⓒ

The Creek

RIYADH ROAD

Children's City

SHEIKH RASHID ROAD

Grand Hyatt Ⓑ

Wonderland

Al Boom Tourist Village

GARHOUD BRIDGE

▽ Jaddaf dhow building yards (500m)

The inner suburbs **PLACES**

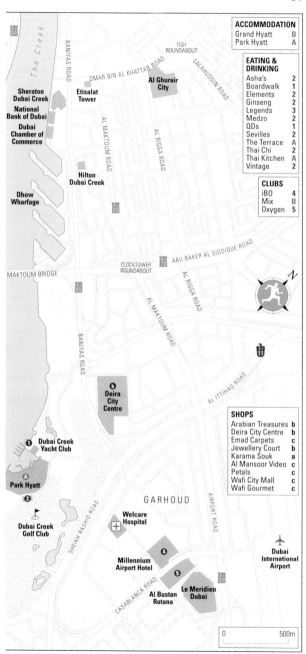

▲ CLOCK TOWER, KARAMA PARK

and Indian pure veg cafés.

Just south of the park is the suburb's main tourist attraction, the Karama Souk, a complex of modest little shops (for more on which see p.84) set in an unprepossessing concrete mall. Although the souk's famous low-quality fakes (featuring a unique array of brands like Colvin Klein and DNKY) have now virtually disappeared following government clampdowns, the market in more upmarket designer rip-offs continues unabated, offering the perfect opportunity to stock up on anything from dodgy D&G to the latest Man Utd football strip.

Satwa

The unpretentious district of Satwa is the southernmost

to Jaddaf, following the road past the *Arabian Park Hotel*, until you reach a large gate signed "Jadaf Dubai, Dubai Ship Docking Yard". Turn left here and try to find someone to give you directions through the mess of building works to the Creekside dhow-building area. And make sure your taxi waits for you, or you'll end up stranded in the middle of nowhere.

Karama

Karama is the classic Dubai inner-city suburb, home to some of the legions of Indian and Pakistani expatriate workers – waiters, taxi drivers, builders and shopkeepers – who supply so much of the city's labour. The district is centred on Kuwait Street and the bustling little Karama Centre, one of the city's pokiest malls; it's nicer to amble around the nearby Karama Park a very modest square of grass – usually busy with a dozen simultaneous cricket matches after dark – surrounded by cheery Pakistani curry houses

▲ SATWA

outpost of Dubai's predominantly low-rise, low-income inner suburbs before you reach the giant skyscrapers of Sheikh Zayed Road and the beginnings of the supersized modern city beyond. It's also one of the few places in Dubai where the city's different ethnic groups really rub shoulders, with a mix of Arab, Indian, Southeast Asian and even a few European residents, reflected in an unusually eclectic selection of places to eat, from cheap-and-cheerful curry houses to Lebanese sweet shops, Persian bakeries and pizzerias. The centre of the district is Satwa Roundabout, overlooked by the *Rydges Plaza Hotel*. The streets south of here are mainly occupied by Indian and Pakistani shops and cafés, such as the well-known *Ravi's* (see p.87). West from the roundabout stretches Satwa's principal thoroughfare, the tree-lined Al-Diyafah Street, one of the nicest streets in Dubai – and one of the few outside the city centre with any real street life – with wide pavements, dozens of restaurants, and an interestingly cosmopolitan atmosphere; it all feels rather Mediterranean, especially after dark, when the cafés get going and the crowds come out, and the low-rise development makes a pleasant change if you've spent some time among the neck-cricking high-rises of nearby Sheikh Zayed Road.

Shops

Arabian Treasures

Level 1, Deira City Centre, Garhoud. A self-contained bazaar inside Deira City Centre mall (see below), housed in its own fake Arabian souk. The bazaar is home to half a dozen carpet shops, plus several handicrafts shops stocked with a vast assortment of artefacts ranging from outright junk (the usual constipated camels and miniature oriental carpet mouse mats) to more unusual and enticing collectables like Hindu bronzes and giant coffee pots – Al Jaber has the best selection, including nice wooden chess sets and pretty inlaid boxes. There's a branch of the Bateel date shop (see p.57) just outside.

Deira City Centre

Garhoud. Daily 10am–10pm (Wed–Fri until midnight). ⓦwww.deiracitycentre .com. Long overtaken in the glamour and glitz stakes by newer shopping centres, this big old mall nevertheless remains the most popular in the city among less image-conscious consumers, and offers a quintessential slice of Dubaian life, attracting everyone from veiled Emirati women to bargain-crazed Russian carpet-baggers – though the crowds can make the whole place rather chaotic and exhausting. The 340-plus outlets here have a largely (though not exclusively) downmarket, bargain-basement emphasis. Pretty much every company that trades in Dubai has a shop here offering every conceivable product. These range from the glittery splendour of the Jewellery Court (see below) to the quaint emporia of the Arabian Treasures souk (see p.83), and there's a vast selection of clothing, perfume and electronics shops, a massive food court, a cinema complex, and big branches of Carrefour (see p.57), Virgin, Debenhams and Woolworths.

Emad Carpets

Wafi City Mall, Oud Metha. Daily 10am–10pm. A very smart carpet and handicrafts shop with a superb array of (expensive) carpets and kilims from Persia, Pakistan, Turkey and Aghanistan (from 800dh and up), plus a classy selection of Arabian and other souvenirs including antique Omani silver, scarves, Pakistani and Kashimiri shawls, and unusual jewellery and beaded pashminas.

Jewellery Court

Level 1, Deira City Centre, Garhoud. The biggest single concentration of jewellery shops in the city outside the dedicated gold souks and shopping malls,

this section of the Deira City Centre mall (see p.83) features an extraordinary collection of jewellery and watch shops selling everything from svelte Italian designs to the most OTT, gem-encrusted Arabian bling imaginable – at equally fabulous prices. Think diamonds. Lots of them.

Karama Souk

Karama. This very basic open-air (it gets unbearably hot in summer) concrete complex in Karama is the place to go for tacky souvenirs and fake watches and designer gear. The little shops here have racks full of reasonable-quality imitation designer clothing and sportswear, while there are also plenty of copy watches and bags to be had – if you don't mind the constant low-level hassle. Trinket shops dotted around the souk sell every kind of desirable and not-so-desirable object imaginable: pashmina shawls, toy camels, mosque-shaped clocks, sand pictures, framed khanjars, perfumes and perfume bottles, Dubai-branded mugs and lighters, wall hangings, framed spiders, slippers, shishas and "genuine fake watches". Much of the stuff is junk, but look hard and you'll find some interesting bits and pieces, and invariably (at least after bargaining) at far lower prices than elsewhere in the city.

Al Mansoor Video

Wafi City, Oud Metha. Sat–Wed 10am–10pm, Thurs & Fri 10am until midnight. A great place to stock up on cheap music and films, with heaps of Arabian, Indian and Western cassettes, CDs and DVDs, usually including lots of discounted items – the cheap cassettes (from as little as

10dh) are particularly good for neophytes exploring the vast wealth of Arabian music for the first time. There are other branches at the nearby Lamcy Plaza and on Al-Esbij Street in Bur Dubai, near the *Astoria Hotel*, though the latter branch sells mainly Hindi music and films, and doesn't carry any Arabic stock.

Petals

Wafi City Mall. This seriously weird shop is all of a piece with the quirky Wafi City Mall. Looking like the ancestral home of an eccentric eighteenth-century aristocrat with a bad opium habit, the interior is stuffed with multicoloured chandeliers, kitsch faux-antique furniture (at very modern prices) plus assorted cheaper knick-knacks like candles and table ornaments.

Wafi City Mall

Al-Qataiyat Rd, Oud Metha. Daily 10am–10pm (Thurs & Fri until midnight). ⊛ www.waficity.com. The centrepiece of the Egyptian-themed Wafi City complex, this medium-sized, upmarket mall makes for a pleasantly superior and laid-back shopping experience, especially when combined with a visit to one of the numerous first-rate restaurants and bars in the mall itself or the adjacent Wafi Pyramids complex. There are plenty of glamorous outlets here including Nicole Farhi, Chanel and Versace, and the mall is particularly good for expensive glittery things like watches and jewellery (including branches of Tiffanys, Chanel Jewellery and Rivoli). There's also an M&S for lovers of sensible underwear and other more down-to-earth products, plus more relatively affordable outlets like Jaeger and Miss Sixty, as well as a large Encounter Zone play area for the kids. The opening of the new Khan Murjan "heritage souk" (due for completion in early 2007) is likely to further bump up the complex's already considerable wow-factor.

Wafi Gourmet

First floor, Wafi City Mall, Oud Metha. Daily 10am–10pm (Thurs & Fri until midnight). The ultimate Dubai deli, this little slice of foodie heaven is piled high with tempting Middle Eastern fare, including big buckets of olives, nuts, spices and dried fruits, and trays of date rolls, marzipan fruits, baklava and fine chocolates. If you can't wait to get stuck in, the café at the back of the shop offers instant gratification with a range of tasty kebabs, mezze and seafood.

▼ WAFI GOURMET

Cafés

Beirut

Al-Diyafah Street, Satwa. Daily
9am–4.30am. One of the most
popular shwarma cafés on
buzzing Al-Diyafah Street, with
plenty of outdoor seating on
the pavement from which to
survey the strip, a chef sawing
away at a pair of kebab stands,
Um Kalthoum on the stereo
and (later at night, at least)
plenty of local atmosphere. Food
is cheap and tasty, with all the
usual mezze and grills, plus huge
fruit juices (but no alcohol).
If it's full, you could try Al-
Mallah, about 50m down the
road, or Sidra, directly opposite,
which offer similar fare and
atmosphere.

Elements

Wafi City Mall, Oud Metha. Sat–Thurs
10am–1am, Fri noon–1am. With its
mix of experimental artwork on
the walls and huge metal pipes
overhead, this funky café looks
like an avant-garde art gallery
inserted into an oil refinery
(there's also a pretty little
tented terrace outside which
is favoured by local shisha-
smokers). The very eclectic
menu includes a decent range
of gourmet sandwiches and

▼ BEIRUT

salads, dim sum, pasta and pizza, plus various meat and fish mains and a bizarre range of so-called "tapas" – meaning anything from falafel to chicken yakitori and samosas. There's also a good selection of shisha (but no alcohol). Mains around 35dh.

Ravi's

Satwa Road, just south of Satwa Roundabout (between the copycat Rawi Palace and Ravi Palace restaurants). Daily 11am–4pm & 6pm–3am. This famous little budget Pakistani café attracts a loyal local and expat clientele thanks to its tasty array of subcontinental standards – veg, chicken and mutton curries, birianis and breads. Most mains are a measly 8dh, though if you go for all the trimmings you might be able to push the bill up to 20dh. The interior is usually packed, and it's more fun, despite the traffic, to sit out on the pavement and watch the street life of Satwa drift by. No alcohol.

▲ ELEMENTS

Restaurants

Asha's

Wafi Pyramids, Oud Metha ☎04-324 4100 ext 121. Daily 12.30–3pm & 7.30pm–12.30am (Wed & Thurs until 1am). Named after legendary Bollywood chanteuse Asha Bhosle (a regular visitor – her favourite recipes feature on the menu), Asha's is a far cry from your average curry house, with sleek modern orange decor, colourful artworks on the walls and the voice of the great lady herself warbling discreetly in the background. The interesting menu features a good selection of traditional Indian favourites – tandooris, thalis, birianis and curries – along with more unusual contemporary dishes such as seared red snapper with lobster basmati, not to mention Mrs Bhosle's own homely culinary contributions. Mains from around 35dh.

Boardwalk

Dubai Creek Yacht Club, Garhoud. Daily noon–midnight. Seemingly always packed, this unpretentious restaurant occupies a spectacular perch on the yacht club's Creekside boardwalk, with stunning city views and cheery international food, ranging from pastas and fajitas to seafood and stir-fries. Reservations aren't accepted, so arrive early or be prepared to wait. Alternatively, head for the slightly more sedate and upmarket *Aquarium* upstairs (daily noon–3pm & 7–11pm; ☎04-295 6000), which has similar Creekside views, a spectacular fish tank and a menu of international and Pacific-rim meat and seafood fusion dishes. Mains at both places run from around 50dh.

Coconut Grove

Rydges Plaza Hotel, Satwa Roundabout, Satwa ☎04-398 2222. Daily noon–3pm & 7pm–midnight. This slightly shabby little restaurant on the ninth floor of the *Rydges Plaza Hotel* doesn't look like much, but remains enduringly popular thanks to its excellent range of Goan, Keralan (Coromandel) and Sri Lankan regional specialites, with authentically fiery chilli-infused coconut sauces. Offerings include numerous spicy seafood options, plus a decent range of meat and veg dishes – from Negombo prawns to Kerala chicken stew – at bargain prices, with most mains at 30dh or under. There's a decent drinks list too, and good views of the Satwa sprawl from the windowside seats.

Legends

Dubai Creek Golf Club, Garhoud ☎04-295 6000. Daily noon–2.30pm & 7–11pm. Set in the golf club's famously futuristic clubhouse, this plush steakhouse serves up a good selection of plump New Zealand and US steaks prepared with a (European) sauce of your choice, as well as a few other meat, seafood and even a couple of cheap vegetarian options. The real draw, however, are the superb Creek views from the restaurant itself and (even better) from the spacious terrace outside. Mains from around 60dh.

Medzo

Wafi Pyramids, Oud Metha ☎04-324 4100. Daily 12.30–3.30pm & 7.30–11.30pm (Fri à la carte brunch 11am–3.30pm). This excellent little restaurant offers top-notch Italian-cum-Mediterranean cuisine in a stylish but laid-back setting with lots of black leather and white linen – although it feels more like a place for a

▼ MEDZO

business lunch than a romantic dinner. Food ranges from pastas, pizzas and risottos through to more substantial meat and seafood mains, all bursting with sunny southern flavours. Mains from around 50dh.

QDs

Dubai Creek Yacht Club, Garhoud. Daily 6pm–2am (no reservations). Fun and good-value restaurant-cum-bar-cum-shisha café in a superb location athwart a large open-air terrace overlooking the Creek. Watch the city lights and the boats plying to and fro while working your way through one of the cheap and well-prepared pizzas, assorted snacks and other light meals (from Lebanese kebabs to fish and chips; mains from around 30dh), or just zone-out with one of the big selection of shishas and/or drinks from the well-stocked bar. It can get surprisingly lively later on, with live DJs occasionally provoking spontaneous outbreaks of dancing.

Il Rustico

Rydges Plaza Hotel, Satwa Roundabout, Satwa ☎04-398 2222. Daily noon–3pm & 6pm–midnight. The homeliest little trattoria in Dubai, with rustic wooden furniture, delicious garlicky smells wafting out of the kitchen and a tasty and reasonably priced selection of

▲ QDS

pizzas, pastas and risottos (from around 40dh), along with meat and seafood mains (from around 50dh).

Sevilles

Wafi Pyramids, Oud Metha ☎04-324 7300. Daily noon–1am (Tues–Fri until 2am). A cosily rustic wood-and-brick Spanish restaurant with a decent spread of traditional tapas such as calamares fritos and patatas bravas, plus meat and fish mains, including paella and Madrid hotpot, along with a few vegetarian options and a decent selection of Iberian wines. A Spanish guitarist strums nightly (except Mon) from 9am. Mains from around 45dh.

Thai Chi

Wafi Pyramids, Oud Metha ☎04-324 4100. Daily noon–3pm & 7pm–midnight. This schizophrenic restaurant offers a mix of contemporary Chinese and traditional Thai cooking, with two kitchens and two dining areas (a pleasantly rustic Chinese-themed space and a more formal Thai room), though you can mix and match cuisines regardless of where you sit. Dishes include solidly prepared takes on all the classic Thai dishes and a slightly smaller but more inventive range of Chinese offerings, marred only by occasionally iffy service. Mains from around 50dh.

Thai Kitchen

Park Hyatt, Garhoud ☎ 04-602 1234. Daily 7pm–midnight, Fri also 12.30–3.30pm. Occupying part of the *Park Hyatt's* lovely Creekside terrace, this smart restaurant dishes up a well-prepared range of traditional Thai fare – salads, claypots, noodles and curries – from its colourful open kitchen. Best of all, food is served in small, mezze-sized portions, meaning that you can work your way through a much wider range of dishes and flavours than you'd normally be able to – although three dishes per person will probably suffice, whatever the waiters may tell you. Dishes from around 20dh.

Bars

Aussie Legends

Rydges Plaza Hotel, Satwa Roundabout. Daily 3pm–3am (Fri & Sat from noon). A popular no-frills Aussie-themed pub with pool tables, sporting memorabilia and real Victoria Bitter. Usually fills up with a very well-watered and voluble crowd of blokes later on. Just don't mention the Ashes.

Ginseng

Wafi Pyramids, Oud Metha. A super-cool bar hidden away right at the back of the Wafi Pyramids complex, with dim red-and-black decor with Chinese touches, flying-saucer lights, a very smooth soundtrack and a dressy young crowd, most of whom can be found behind one of the bar's fancy cocktails. There's good Chinese and Japanese food, too, and regular live DJs. The attached *Blush* (free before 10pm; 60dh after) hosts club nights every Thursday, with leading international DJs on the decks.

The Terrace

Park Hyatt, Garhoud. Daily noon–2am. A seductive waterside bar, with

▼ JADDAF DHOW BUILDING YARD

seating either indoors or outside on the terrace overlooking the Creek and the numerous fancy yachts parked at the adjacent marina. It's all very romantic and mellow, the mood helped along by smooth chill-out music and a reasonable selection of cocktails and other tipples. It also has a good selection of superior bar snacks and meals (from around 90dh), handy if you get peckish and can't be bothered to stagger to the adjacent *Thai Kitchen*.

Vintage

Wafi Pyramids, Oud Metha. Mon–Wed & Fri–Sun 6pm–1.30am, Thurs 4pm–2am. A cosy little wine bar in the heart of the Wafi City action. The wine list isn't particularly huge, but offers a well-chosen spread of international vintages – and with most bottles at under 200dh, it's also refreshingly affordable by Dubai standards. There's also champagnes, beers, spirits and soft drinks, plus a few superior bar snacks and a cheese board to mop it all up with.

Clubs

iB0

Millennium Airport Hotel, Garhoud ☎04-282 1844. Daily 11pm–3am. Stuck out the back of the *Millennium Airport Hotel*, this new and slightly off-the-wall club attracts a very eclectic crowd and plenty of upcoming local DJs along with international guest stars. Entrance fees vary according to who's on deck.

Mix

Grand Hyatt, Oud Metha ☎04-317 1234. Daily except Sat 9pm–3am. One of the oldest and biggest clubs in Dubai, and beginning to show its age a bit, but still good for a night out at weekends, when it continues to see plenty of action. It's split over two floors – one has a techno slant, the other is more R&B – and there are also themed R&B, Indian and Iranian nights. You might have to pay (usually around 30–60dh) to get in if there's a good international DJ playing.

Oxygen

Al Bustan Rotana, Garhoud ☎04-705 4539. Daily 8pm–3am. Another of Dubai's long-running nightspots, and less pretentious than some other places in the city, though the decor is more hotel lobby than urban cool. There's a decent-sized dance floor, and live local and international DJs (and occasional live bands) offer an eclectic spread of music, with themed Iranian, Indian and Filipino nights, and a mix of house and Arabic at other times, while lots of cheap drinks promotions keep things bubbling. Entrance free except on Fri, when single blokes pay a mighty 100dh.

Sheikh Zayed Road

Around three kilometres south of the Creek, the upwardly mobile suburbs of southern Dubai begin in spectacular style with the massed skyscrapers of Sheikh Zayed Road – a vast ten-lane highway flanked by an extraordinary sequence of neck-cracking high-rises, looking like teetering fashion icons in some bizarre postmodern architectural beauty parade. This is the modern city at its most futuristic, flamboyant and inter-nationalist, a million miles away from the cluttered old souks and chuntering abras of the city centre; indeed if you've spent long in the old city, Sheikh Zayed Road's sci-fi architecture, urban chic and five-star pleasures can come as a strange kind of culture shock.

In many ways, Sheikh Zayed Road represents the emblematic heart of modern Dubai and the city's insatiable desire to offer more luxury, more glitz and more storeys than the competition, embodied by the stunning Emirates Towers and the string of top hotels, restaurants and bars that line the strip, not to mention the ever-rising Burj Dubai tower, soon to become the world's tallest building. Not that Sheikh Zayed Road's appeal is exclusively architectural. The real spirit of the road can be found within the towers themselves, in the cavernous interiors of the various five-star hotels, which

▲ SHEIKH ZAYED ROAD

Sheikh Zayed Road runs all the way from Dubai to Abu Dhabi, and forms the principal road link between the two emirates, as well as between the various widely separated areas of southern Dubai. In practice, however, when people refer to "Sheikh Zayed Road" they are usually talking about the section in central Dubai **between Interchange no.1 and the Trade Centre Roundabout** (also known as Za'abeel Roundabout), ie from *Dusit Dubai* hotel to just north of the Emirates Towers, which is home to the strip's densest concentration of hotels, restaurants and shops. This is the sense in which we're using the name. Attractions further south along Sheikh Zayed Road past Interchange no.1 – such as the Mall of the Emirates and the Ibn Battuta Mall – are covered in later chapters.

offer a disorienting snapshot of Dubai's cosmopolitan – but often schizophrenically separated – worlds, from noisy English pubs through shisha-scented Lebanese restaurants to über-cool postmodern bars and clubs – the perfect venue for a quintessentially multicultural Dubaian evening spent hopping between pints of lager, Arabian mezze and swanky cocktails.

Emirates Towers

The soaring Emirates Towers are, after the *Burj Al Arab*, the most iconic symbol of modern Dubai. Opened in 2000, the two towers are the 12th and 27th highest buildings in the world, both topping out at around a third of a kilometre (355m and 309m respectively); the taller of the two towers is currently the loftiest building in the city, at least until the Burj Dubai is completed. The towers are not just impressively large, but also strikingly beautiful. Their unusual triangular ground plan and cutaway summits lend them a futuristic, angular grace, while the constantly changing effects of the strong desert light and shadow on the buildings' sharp edges and highly

▲ EMIRATES TOWERS

reflective surfaces is equally magical.

The taller tower houses the offices of the Emirates airline; the smaller is occupied by the exclusive *Emirates Towers* hotel (see p.175). One curiosity of the buildings is that the taller office tower, despite its considerable extra height, has only two more floors than the hotel tower (56 versus 54). The office tower isn't open to the public, though there are plenty of opportunities

Crossing Sheikh Zayed Road

Dubai's notoriously pedestrian-unfriendly city planners may have succeeded in creating one of the 21st-century's most dramatic cityscapes, but they seem to have completely overlooked one basic consideration: how you get from one side of the road to the other. The situation along Sheikh Zayed Road is particularly frustrating. There are just two ways of getting across. The first is the pedestrian bridge that runs from opposite the *Fairmont* hotel to the World Trade Centre complex. The second, slightly further south, is the pedestrian underpass, which runs alongside the road tunnel from directly outside the *Crowne Plaza* and brings you out just north of the Emirates Towers. Further south, there is simply no way of crossing from one side of the roaring ten-lane highway to the other, unless you have pronounced suicidal tendencies. If you're staying at *Dusit Dubai*, for instance, and you want to have dinner at the *Shangri La*, on the opposite side of the road, there's only one way to reach your destination, and that's to take a cab.

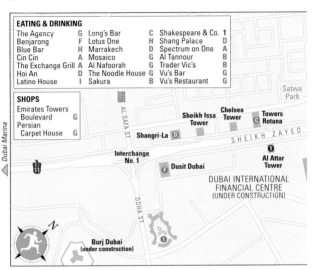

EATING & DRINKING

The Agency	G	Long's Bar	C	Shakespeare & Co.	1	
Benjarong	F	Lotus One	A	Shang Palace	D	
Blue Bar	H	Marrakech	D	Spectrum on One	A	
Cin Cin	A	Mosaico	G	Al Tannour	B	
The Exchange Grill	A	Al Nafoorah	G	Trader Vic's	B	
Hoi An	D	The Noodle House	G	Vu's Bar	G	
Latino House	I	Sakura	B	Vu's Restaurant	G	

SHOPS

Emirates Towers	
Boulevard	G
Persian	
Carpet House	G

Satwa Park

Dubai Marina

AL SAFA ST

Sheikh Issa Tower

Chelsea Tower

Towers Rotana

Shangri-La D

SHEIKH ZAYED

Interchange No. 1

Dusit Dubai

Al Attar Tower

DUBAI INTERNATIONAL FINANCIAL CENTRE (UNDER CONSTRUCTION)

DOHA ST

N

Burj Dubai (under construction)

to look around the hotel tower, most spectacularly from the 50th- and 51st-floor *Vu's* restaurant and bar (see p.103 & p.105).

Around the Emirates Towers

The area surrounding the Emirates Towers is Dubai's international commercial and financial heart – the local equivalent of the City of London or Wall Street. Immediately south of the Emirates Towers stretches the still-evolving Dubai International Financial Centre (due for completion around 2008), its northern end marked by the striking The Gate building (2004), a kind of postmodern Arc de Triomphe-cum-office block which now houses the Dubai Stock Exchange. North of the Emirates Towers extends the sprawling International Exhibition and Conference Centre, in whose cavernous interior you might end up getting lost en route to the two fine bars at the *Novotel* hotel (see p.104), which lies on the Exhibition and Conference Centre's far side. This entire complex forms part of the Dubai World Trade Centre, whose flagship tower rises high above Trade Centre Roundabout. This 39-storey edifice (149m) was the tallest building in the city when completed in 1979, and although it now looks decidedly old-fashioned and unimpressive compared to the more recent buildings along the strip, it still commands a certain nostalgic affection amongst Dubai hands old enough to remember Sheikh Zayed Road back in the old days.

South along Sheikh Zayed Road

South of the Emirates Towers, Sheikh Zayed Road continues in a more or less unbroken line of high-rises. Few are of especial individual distinction

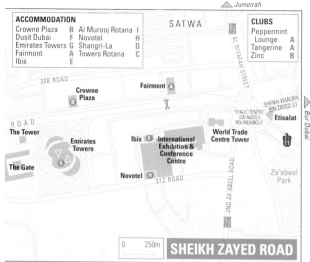

△ Jumeirah

ACCOMMODATION
Crowne Plaza   B   Al Murooj Rotana   I
Dusit Dubai   F   Novotel   H
Emirates Towers G   Shangri-La   D
Fairmont   A   Towers Rotana   C
Ibis   E

CLUBS
Peppermint
Lounge   A
Tangerine   A
Zinc   B

SATWA

AL DIYAFAH STREET

308 ROAD

Crowne
Plaza B

Fairmont A

SHEIKH KHALIFA
BIN ZAYED ST

TRADE CENTRE
(ZA'ABEEL)
ROUNDABOUT

Etisalat

ROAD

The Tower

Emirates
Towers

G

The Gate

Ibis E International
Exhibition &
Conference
Centre

World Trade
Centre Tower

2ND ZA'ABEEL ROAD

Za'abeel
Park

Novotel H   312 ROAD

0   250m

SHEIKH ZAYED ROAD

Bur Dubai

PLACES   Sheikh Zayed Road

(and some are decidedly pedestrian), though, taken together, the effect of the whole – with vast, vertical expanses of plate glass and steel – is vertiginously impressive, and what the buildings lack in style, they make up for with regular blasts of architectural whimsy and playfulness. Immediately south of the Emirates Towers (next to the Dubai International Financial Centre), The Tower is one of the prettiest buildings along the Strip, a vaguely New York-style skyscraper with a faintly Art Deco appearance and stylized palm frond-inspired metal decorations. Further south lies the eye-catching Al Atttar Tower, which appears to have been constructed entirely out of plate glass and enormous gold coins, while over the road are the Chelsea Tower, topped by an enormous toothpick, and, next door, the

Sheikh Issa Tower (above the *Applebees Café*), which looks like it's been built out of giant red and brown Lego bricks. The strip reaches a suitably dramatic end with the iconic Thai-owned *Dusit Dubai* hotel, a towering glass-and-metal edifice built in a shape reminiscent of a gargantuan tuning fork, though the form was actually inspired by the prayer-like wai gesture, a traditional Thai greeting.

Dubai Camel Racecourse

Some 5km inland from Sheikh Zayed Road, the district of Nad Al Sheba (most of it still untouched desert) is home to one of the city's quirkier

▼ RACING CAMELS AT NAD AL SHEBA

Burj Dubai

Given the city's current striving to possess the biggest, priciest, glitziest version of everything – from underwater hotels to mile-long shopping malls – it should come as no suprise that Dubai is currently working on constructing **the world's tallest building**, the Burj Dubai ("Dubai Tower"; ⊛www.burjdubaiskyscraper.com), just south of Interchange 1 on Sheikh Zayed Road. Construction on the tower began in April 2005, under the direction of Chicago firm Skidmore, Owings and Merrill (whose credits include the famous Sears Tower in Chicago, the world's tallest building until 1997). The tower's final dimensions remain a closely guarded secret, lest other countries attempt to trump the building's record-breaking status, though it's thought that it will finally top out at around 800m, with some 160 storeys – dwarfing the current world's tallest building, the 508-metre Taipai 101 tower in Taipei, Taiwan, as well as other proposed buildings including New York's Freedom Tower (the successor to the destroyed World Trade Centers, and another Skidmore, Owings and Merrill project). Due for completion in 2008, the Burj is currently rising at the rate of around one storey per week; as of January 2007 it had already surpassed the hundred-storey mark, and established itself as a major landmark on the city skyline.

Size is not everything, however. The interior of the tower will be designed by Giorgio Armani, who will take possession of the lower 37 floors for the world's first Armani hotel. Floors 45 to 108 will be private apartments (which allegedly sold out within eight hours of going on sale), and there will also be an observation deck, accessed via the world's fastest elevators. In addition, the tower will form the centrepiece of a huge new complex (total cost around eight billion dollars) combining residential apartments and the vast new **Mall of Arabia** (also due for completion in 2008).

Ironically, despite the Burj Dubai headlong race for the skies, it's possible that it might soon be outdone by yet another Dubai mega-development, the **Al Burj** tower at the Dubai Waterfront project (see p.129); rumour has it that it may be the first tower to break the one-kilometre mark.

▼ BURJ DUBAI UNDER CONSTRUCTION

attractions, the Dubai Camel Racecourse. Early-morning camel races (admission free) are held here during the winter months (usually Nov–April), generally on Thursdays and Fridays from around 7am to 8.30pm (call ☎04-338 1168 for information or ask at one of the city's tourist information kiosks). Even if no races are scheduled, you can come and watch the animals being exercised early in the morning (roughly 7–9/10am); it's a captivating sight and one of the classic images of Dubai – against the distant backdrop of skyscrapers on Sheikh Zayed Road, literally hundreds of colourfully dressed beasts and their heavily robed riders amble (and occasionally gallop) across the desert, while their owners charge after them in 4WDs shouting encouragement.

Nad Al Sheba Racecourse

A kilometre or so down the road from the Dubai Camel Racecourse, the more mainstream Nad Al Sheba Racecourse (🅦www .nadalshebaclub.com) has established itself as one of the world's premier horse-racing venues. The racing season (details on 🅦www .emiratesracing.com) runs from November to March, culminating in the dazzling Dubai World Cup, the world's richest horse race, with a massive $6 million in prize money. Races are held nightly from around 7pm. Entrance to the general stands is free; the Gainsborough Lounge (entrance around 75–100dh depending on the night) is licensed and has some surprisingly good places to eat as well, but don't expect to recover your costs at the bookies – betting is illegal in the UAE. Dedicated horseflesh fanciers

Dubailand

The biggest thing yet in a city of increasingly big things, the vast new Dubailand development (🅦www.dubailand.ae) promises to make every other theme park and entertainment complex in the world look like a small kids' playground with an ice-cream van. Occupying a huge swathe of land on the southern side of the city, Dubailand is intended, quite simply, to become the planet's single largest and most spectacular tourist attraction, and to be the engine which drives Dubai's tourist industry forward for the next several decades. The development will comprise a mix of theme parks, shopping malls, sporting and leisure facilities (including vast numbers of new hotels and restaurants) and residential areas, covering a staggeringly large 280 square kilometres – twice the size of the Walt Disney World Resort in Florida, currently the largest amusement park complex in the world – and adding a very significant new chunk to the city's size.

At the heart of the project are a sequence of huge theme parks, including the enormous **Aqua Dubai** waterpark; the **Snowdome** snow and ice leisure park, situated in the world's biggest free-standing dome; **Dubai Sports City**, with state-of-the-art stadiums and other facilities; the **Great Dubai Wheel**, the Gulf's answer to the London Eye (although, naturally, quite a lot bigger); the **Islamic Culture and Science World**; **Fun City**, including a Pharaoh's Theme Park; the **Restless Planet** dinosaur theme park featuring over a hundred animatronic dinosaurs; and the **Falcon City of Wonders**, comprising full-scale replicas of the seven wonders of the world. And of course there will be plenty of shops, including the vast Middle Eastern-themed **Mall of Arabia**, intended to be the largest shopping centre in the world; and the attached **Wadi Walk**, a ten-kilometre canal development lined with shady promenades boasting plenty more places to shop, eat and drink. Also in the pipeline is the **Bawadi** development, which will comprise over thirty hotels (with around 30,000 rooms) including – it goes almost without saying – the **world's largest hotel**, Asia-Asia (6500 rooms), plus reams of other leisure and residential facilities.

The first big attractions are scheduled to open during 2008, with the first section of Bawadi entering service in 2010 and a completion date for the whole project of around 2015–18.

might also relish a chance to go on one of the stable tours (Sept–June Mon, Wed & Sat at 7am; 170dh; bookings on ☎04-336 3666). Founded by the ruling Maktoum family in 1994, Godolphin has rapidly established itself as one of the world's top stables. Tours include a chance to watch early-morning training, a visit to the Godolphin Gallery (with displays on the stable's history and racing exploits) and the grandstand, and a slap-up breakfast in the clubhouse.

Shops

Emirates Towers Boulevard

Emirates Towers. Sat–Thurs 10am–10pm, Fri 4–10pm. On the bottom two floors of the Emirates Towers business tower, this small but very exclusive mall offers the last word in Dubaian ultra-chic – the marbled floor is polished so brightly you could probably fix your make-up in it before sloping off to one of the small but very select number of upmarket outlets which line its soignéed corridors, including Jimmy Choo for sexy shoes, Prada, Emporio Armani, Bulgari, Cartier, Gucci, Yves Saint-Laurent, and the flagship Villa Moda ladieswear store, a work of consumerist art in its own right, its elegantly streamlined racks groaning under the weight of labels such as Alexander McQueen, Miu Miu, Stella McCartney, Marni and Missoni. There's also La Casa del Havana, Dubai's finest cigar shop, and a couple of very smart Iranian carpet shops. The plaza is also home to an excellent range of eating and drinking venues, including *The Noodle House* (p.101), *Al Nafoorah* (p.101) and *The Agency* (p.103), and can be surprisingly lively late at night, particularly at weekends, when

▼ VILLA MODA

▲ EMIRATES BOULEVARD

the place gets overrun with stressed-out expats letting off considerable amounts of steam.

Persian Carpet House

Next to The Noodle House, ground floor, Emirates Boulevard. Sat–Thurs 10am–10pm, Fri 2–10pm. This very superior rug shop (exactly what one would expect in the Emirates Towers Boulevard) stocks superb carpets, plus a few kilims, from Iran, Pakistan, Afghanistan and Kashmir (from 500dh to 500,000dh and up); most are new, though there are also usually a few antique rugs for sale. They also do a sideline in superior arts and crafts, including richly embroidered organza and pashmina shawls from Kashmir, some with fine appliqué beadwork, plus Arabian, Iranian and Pakistani silver antiques, colourful Turkish hanging lights, and other collectables. There's another well-stocked branch in the Holiday Centre mall, next to the *Crowne Plaza* hotel

Restaurants

As well as its enviable string of top-class hotel dining establishments (the best of which are listed below), Sheikh Zayed Road also boasts a healthy roster of more downmarket eating establishments, most of them situated on the ground floors of the various towers and including the usual string of international chains ranging from *KFC* and *McDonalds* through to the recently opened *Wagamama* at the *Crowne Plaza*. There's also a surprising number of clubbable cafés tucked away at street level (such as the engaging *Shakespeare & Co.*, see below), attracting a glamorous expat-Arab crowd who come to chill out over shishas and mezze before heading off to one of the strip's glam bars or nightclubs.

Benjarong

24th floor, Dusit Dubai ☎04-343 3333. Daily noon–3pm & 7–11.30pm. No surprises that the signature restaurant at this excellent Thai-owned hotel offers some of the best Royal Thai cooking in Dubai. Set in a delicately painted wooden pavilion, the stylish restaurant's extensive menu covers pretty much every aspect of the country's cuisine. It's particularly strong on fish and seafood, and does curries in

▲ BENJARONG

all forms and flavours (including refreshingly mild peanut and sweet curries); there's also a big spread of soups, salads and vegetarian offerings, all at surprisingly affordable prices. Mains from 35dh.

The Exchange Grill

Fairmont Hotel ☎04-332 5555. Daily 7pm–midnight. This small and rather exclusive steakhouse feels more like a room in a private club than a public restaurant, with just fourteen tables surrounded by huge leather armchairs. Sink back and choose from filet mignon, New York striploin, T-bone, ribeye and wagyu beef, not to mention Omani lobster and Alaskan king crab legs, then browse the extensive wine list and enjoy the views of the crazy traffic on Sheikh Zayed Road through the big windows. Mains from 135dh.

Hoi An

Shangri-La ☎04-343 8888. Daily 6.30pm–1am. One of the *Shangri-La*'s collection of small but perfectly formed dining establishments, the *Hoi An* specializes in hybrid Vietnamese–French cuisine served in an elegant little wood-pannelled restaurant framed with French-colonial-style latticed and shuttered windows. The menu combines traditional Asian dishes and ingredients with modern Continental cooking techniques to produce a delicate and aromatic range of fusion creations like rice crêpes stuffed with prawns and scallops, wokked and cognac-marinated tournedos of beef, and lemongrass chicken on bamboo pins. Mains from 70dh.

Latino House

Al Murooj Rotana ☎04-321 1111. Daily noon–3pm & 7–11.30pm. Possibly the best of Dubai's very modest selection of Latin American restaurants. The menu mixes juicy steaks (from 115dh; available in suspiciously sexist "Ladies"- and "Gents"-sized portions) along with elaborate takes on traditional Latin fare like the pollo con cacao (chicken stuffed with Mexican mole and chocolate sauce, garnished with black bean tamal), plus a few more unpretentious offerings such as chilli con carne, burritos and tacos. Mains from 75dh.

Marrakech

Shangri La ☎04-343 8888.
Sat–Thurs 6.30pm–1am. Vies with
Tagine (see p.136) for the title
of Dubai's best Moroccan
restaurant. The decor – a subtle
melange of pale-green tiles and
Moorish cusped arches – is
lovely, and the food navigates all
the standard bases of Moroccan
cooking with aplomb, travelling
from harira soup to fish and
meat tagines, kebabs and
couscous dishes. Mains from
70dh.

Mosaico

Emirates Towers ☎04-319 8088. Open
24hr; breakfast and lunch buffets; à la
carte from 7pm. A large and stylish
modern Italian restaurant tucked
away behind the *Emirates Towers
Hotel* lobby, with views through
slatted blinds of the hotel
pool and Sheikh Zayed Road
towers beyond. It's undeservedly
neglected compared to
the other Emirates Towers
restaurants, given the top-notch
food, with a solid selection of
pizzas and meat and fish mains,
as well as inventive and unusual
pasta dishes such as squid-ink
spaghetti with Omani lobster
and Parma ham, or giant penne
with octopus. Mains from 35dh.

Al Nafoorah

Emirates Towers Boulevard ☎04-319
8088. Sat–Thurs 12.30–3.15pm
& 8pm–midnight, Fri 1–3.30pm
& 8pm–midnight. One of the
city's best Middle Eastern
restaurants, this place looks
more like a slightly starchy
Parisian establishment than a
traditional Lebanese eatery, with
floor-length white tablecloths,
flouncy chandeliers and tasteful
old black-and-white photos on
walls. The food is the real deal,
however, from the superb array
of breads and nibbles served on
arrival through the good range
of mezze to a perfectly cooked
array of fish, meat and kebab
mains. It's good value, too, with
mezze from 20dh and mains
from 25dh.

The Noodle House

Emirates Towers Boulevard.
Daily noon–11.20pm. A Dubai
institution, this cheapish and
very cheerful noodle bar
caters to an endless stream of
diners who huddle up on long
communal tables to refuel on
excellent South East Asian and
Chinese fare ranging from curry
laksa and tom yam to Singapore
noodles and Sichuan spiced
beef. No reservations, so you
might have to queue at busy
times. Mains from 35dh. There
are other branches at Madinat
Jumeirah and the BurJuman
Centre, though neither has yet
quite managed to re-create the
atmosphere of the original.

Sakura

Crowne Plaza ☎04-305 6338. Daily
7–11.30pm. This cosy Japanese

▼ THE NOODLE HOUSE

restaurant offers a spread of dining options: either à la carte in the rather staid main restaurant, at the sushi bar, or (most fun) the teppanyaki area, where your food is fried right in front of you by Oscar-winning chefs. The menu covers all the standard Japanese bases, with sashimi, makizushi, sukiyaki, yakimono, menrui, shabu shabu and tempura. Teppanyaki from 50dh, sushi from 10dh, mains from 70dh.

Shakespeare & Co.

Al Attar Business Tower, 37 Street. Daily 7am–12.30am. One of the most appealing of the numerous shisha cafés dotted along Sheikh Zayed Road, with pleasantly offbeat decor and fusty old bits of furniture – some of which looks like it's been stolen from an old people's home. There are good salads, pizzas and sandwiches (from around 30dh), plus a few meat mains to choose from, or you can puff a shisha on the cosy covered terrace outside. The café is easily missed, tucked away around the side of the Al Attar Business Tower on 37 Street (by the HSBC ATM).

Shang Palace

Shangri-La Hotel ☏ 04-343 8888. Daily noon–3pm & 8pm–midnight. This intimate little circular restaurant specializes in top-notch traditional Cantonese cooking, with a decent range of meat and seafood standards, plus plenty of dim sum and a few curiosities like wok-fried minced pigeon (one of several pigeon dishes). There are also set dim sum menus at lunchtime (daily except Fri 11.30am–12.30pm; 68/88dh per person). Mains from around 45dh.

Spectrum on One

Fairmont Hotel ☏ 04-311 8101. Daily 6.30pm–3am, also Fri noon–3pm. This good-looking modern restaurant would be a nice place to eat whatever it was serving up, but also boasts the unique selling point of having no fewer than seven separate kitchens, each specializing in a different cuisine, so you can mix and match from Arabian, Indian, Chinese, Japanese, Thai, European and seafood menus at will. The whole concept is typical of Dubai's more-is-more approach to life,

▼ SPECTUM ON ONE

although the food is actually pretty good – and where else could you experience a meal of sashimi, chicken tikka masala and Italian ice cream, followed by a pot of English breakfast tea accompanied by chocolate-coated dates? Mains from 60dh.

Al Tannour

Crowne Plaza ☎04-331 1111. Daily 8pm–3am. This large and slightly barn-like Middle Eastern restaurant is nothing much to look at, but the atmosphere is comfortable and unpretentious (though service can be shabby) and the food offers a good, if predictable, survey of Middle Eastern standards running through the usual mezze to fragrant fish dishes and kebabs, accompanied by delicious breads made in front of you by a white-robed lady. The place only really gets going late at night, however, when the live music and bellydancing kicks in (nightly 11pm–2am) – earlier in the evening, the nearby *Al Nafoorah* (see p.101) has a better atmosphere.

Trader Vic's

Crowne Plaza ☎04-305 6399. Sat–Thurs 12.30–3pm & 7–11.30pm (Thurs until midnight), Fri 7–11.30pm; bar daily 6pm–1.30am (happy hour daily 6–8pm). This lively Polynesian-themed restaurant is best known for its kick-ass cocktails, party atmosphere and live music (a Cuban band plays 9.20pm–1.30am every night except alternate Sundays). The rather pricey menu comprises an eclectic mixture of grills, seafood and Asian dishes, with filling portions and bright flavours – a bit like very superior pub food, which is kind of what the whole place really is. Mains from 70dh.

Vu's Restaurant

50th floor, Emirates Towers Hotel ☎04-319 8088. Daily 12.30–2.30pm & 7.30–11.15pm. Perched near the summit of the *Emirates Towers Hotel*, this smart and rather formal restaurant is the highest in the city. The view, of course, is a major draw, but the restaurant itself offers one of the city's top international fine-dining experiences, serving up modern European food with a touch of Asian influence – things like cocotte of white asparagus and foie gras with marinated Wagyu salad, or Patagonian toothfish, chorizo, soft parmesan, semolina and shrimp sausage. Visit either for the brisk three-course business lunch (130dh) or for a more relaxed evening à la carte experience. Mains from 90dh.

Bars

The Agency

Emirates Towers Boulevard. Sat–Thurs 12.30pm–1am (Tues–Thurs until 2am), Fri 3pm–1am. A rather sedate-looking wood-pannelled wine bar, quiet enough during the daytime, though it often gets packed out with a noisy expat crowd in the evenings. There's a huge (if pricey) wine list with vintages from all the world's major wine-producing countries by the glass (from around 30dh) or bottle (from 125dh up to a staggering 21,800dh for a 1990 Château Pétrus), including an especially good selection of French brews, plus tasting selections (four 80ml glasses from 85dh), assorted champagnes (from 620dh) and a small menu of fancy bar snacks.

▲ BLUE BAR

Blue Bar

Novotel, World Trade Centre, Sheikh Zayed Rd. Daily 2pm–2am ☎04-332 0000. This stylish but relatively sedate jazz and blues bar is all about soft sofas, smooth sounds and other creature comforts – more the place for a mellow tête-à-tête over one of the bar's good selection of speciality Belgian beers than glam cocktails and party frocks. There's excellent live jazz most Thursday and Friday nights, though even then the atmosphere is pretty low-key.

Cin Cin

Fairmont Hotel. Daily 6pm–2am. This unusual and stylish wine bar meanders around almost an entire floor of the *Fairmont Hotel*, with dim lighting, plush leather sofas and huge racks of bottles to gaze at in alcoholic appreciation, as well as a special rum and cigar bar with walk-in humidor. Choose from 45 wines by the glass plus around three hundred other vintages (bottles from 150dh to 49,000dh). Occasional live chill-out DJs add to the pleasantly crashed-out ambience.

Long's Bar

Towers Rotana Hotel, Sheikh Zayed Road. Daily noon–3am. Proud home to the longest bar in the Middle East, this English-style pub offers one of the strip's more convivial and downmarket drinking holes. There are all the usual tipples, pop-rock soundtrack, TV sports and other Dubai pub essentials, plus a separate dining area serving up basic pub grub and a small dance area which sees action during the intermittent DJ and live music nights, and – in a slightly more spontaneous fashion – towards closing time during the bar's innumerable drinks promotions.

Lotus One

World Trade Centre (next to the Novotel hotel lobby), Sheikh Zayed Road. Daily noon–2am. Newish and very glam bar with a kind of retro-chic decor (fluffy cushions, furry poufs, lotus-shaped candles and a couple of swinging chairs) and a very modish crowd. The place really kicks off during its regular weekend DJ nights, though at other times the atmosphere is fairly laid-back, with discreet modern jazz/chill-out sounds.

▼ LONG'S BAR

There's a huge list of vodkas and other shorts (mainly around 30dh) – everything from vintage rum to absinthe and cherry brandy, though not much beer.

Vu's Bar

Emirates Towers. Daily 5pm–2am. On the 51st floor of the *Emirates Towers* hotel building, this is the highest licensed perch in Dubai currently available. The small, capsule-like bar itself, with floor-to-ceiling windows on one side, feels like the business end of a space rocket, and the muted music, dark decor, dim lighting and rather subdued ambience means there's not much to distract one from wide-eyed contemplation of the endless city lights below – apart from selecting a tipple from the huge drinks list which runs through the complete gamut of cocktails, mocktails, shorts, beers, wines and champagnes, all at slightly less stratospheric prices than one might expect. Arrive at 5pm and watch the lights go on.

Clubs

Peppermint Lounge

Fairmont Hotel ☎04-311 8101. Fri 10pm–3am. Held in the rather unlikely setting of the *Fairmont Hotel*'s Barjeel Ballroom, this was Dubai's biggest club night at the time of writing, attacting top international DJs alongside residents MaDJam and Afroboogie playing to the city's posiest crowd. Entrance charges vary – usually around 60–120dh for blokes but generally free for women.

Tangerine

Fairmont Hotel ☎04-311 8101. One of the city's longest-established

and most chichi clubbing venues, this place was closed at the time of writing, but slated to reopen sometime during 2007, probably under a new name, though most likely with its crowd-pulling roster of live DJs and glam expat-Lebanese clientele intact.

Zinc

Crowne Plaza ☎04-331 1111. Daily 8pm–3am. One of the mainstays of the Dubai clubbing scene, now back after an expensive facelift, with a roster of international guest DJs performing on Tuesday nights (including the popular Kinky Malinki London House night) and resident DJ Greg Stainer at other times. Expect a mix of house and hip-hop and one of the city's dressier crowds (plus lots of visiting air-crews). Entrance free most nights (men pay 50dh on Tues).

▼ VU'S BAR

Jumeirah

A couple of kilometres south of the Creek, the beach-side suburb of Jumeirah (or Jumeira) marks the beginning of southern Dubai's endless suburban sprawl. The area's swathes of chintzy low-rise villas are home to many of the city's European expats and their wives – immortalized in Dubai legend as the so-called "Jumeirah Janes" – who (the stereotype runs) spend their days in an endless round of luncheons and beach parties, while their hard-working spouses slave away to keep them in the style to which they have very rapidly become accustomed.

The suburb is strung out along the Jumeirah Road, which arrows straight down the coast and provides the area with its principal focus, lined with a long string of shopping malls and cafés, most of them fairly low key, apart from the bizarre, Italian-themed Mercato mall. The suburb also offers a handful of modest attractions, ranging from the traditional Jumeirah Mosque and Majlis Ghorfat Um Al Sheef to the more hedonistic Jumeirah Beach Park, the city's most attractive public beach.

Jumeirah Mosque

Jumeirah Rd. Tours Tues, Thurs & Sun 10.15–11.15am (additional tours are sometimes organized during Ramadan). 10dh. Under-5s not allowed. Rising proudly above the northern end of the Jumeirah Road, the stately Jumeirah Mosque is one of the largest and most attractive in the city. Built in quasi-Fatimid (Egyptian) style, the mosque is reminiscent in appearance (if not quite in size) of the great mosques of Cairo, with a pair of soaring minarets, a roofline embellished with delicately carved miniature domes and richly decorated windows set in elaborate rectangular recesses – though as with many of Dubai's more venerable-looking buildings, appearances are deceptive, since it was actually built only in 1979. It also has the added attraction of being the only mosque in Dubai that can be visited by non-Muslims thanks to the

▼ JUMEIRAH MOSQUE

thrice-weekly tours run by the Sheikh Mohammed Centre for Cultural Understanding (☎04-353 6666, ⓦ www.cultures.ae). Entertaining and informative guides explain some of the basic precepts and practices of Islam before throwing the floor open for questions on any subject – a rare chance to settle some of those perplexing local conundrums, whether it be a description of the workings of the Islamic calendar or an explanation of exactly what Emirati men wear under their robes.

Iranian Hospital and Mosque

Al Wasl Rd. Standing on either side of Al Wasl Road, a ten-minute walk inland from the Jumeirah Mosque, the striking Iranian Hospital and Mosque add a welcome splash of colour to the pasty concrete tints which rule in this part of the city. The hospital is a large and rather functional-looking modern building improbably covered in vast quantities of superb, blue-green tiling in the elaborate abstract floral patterns beloved of Persian artists. The mosque is even finer, its sumptuously tiled dome and two minarets particularly magical, especially in low light early or late in the day. Unfortunately, the mosque is walled off and you can only see it from a certain distance – the best view is from the small residential side street which runs around the back of it, rather than from Al Wasl Road itself.

Green Art Gallery

Villa 23, 51 St, just off Jumeirah Rd by Dubai Zoo. Daily except Fri 9.30am–1.30pm & 4.30–8.30pm. ⓦ www.gagallery.com. The small independent Green Art Gallery keeps the creative flicker burning amidst the cultural wasteland of the Jumeirah Road, staging excellent shows of works by leading artists from the Middle East, as well as from parts of Asia. If you're inspired to buy, you can expect to pay from around 5000dh and up for original works, but there's also a selection of much more modestly priced prints and fine-art photos for sale (from around 500dh).

Dubai Zoo

Jumeirah Rd. Daily except Tues 10am–6pm. 2dh. The Dubai Zoo was founded in 1967 – the first on the Arabian peninsula – and has acquired a wide range of animals since, almost all of them taken from smugglers apprehended by UAE customs officials. The resultant mishmash of haphazardly aquired animals includes giraffes, tigers, lions, chimps and brown bears, as well as smaller mammals such as Arabian wolves and oryx, plus assorted birds, though it's difficult to see very much thanks to the ugly cages, covered in thick wire-mesh (installed, ironically, to protect the animals from visitors, rather than the other way around – when the zoo first opened, locals would turn up armed with sticks to prod the animals into action, and sadly the behaviour of many of today's visitors is little better). Unfortunately, the whole place has now become severely overcrowded and rather depressing, a situation that will thankfully be remedied when the zoo moves into spacious new safari-park-style premises on the edge of the city near Mushrif Park in 2008.

EATING & DRINKING		SHOPS		ACCOMMODATION	
Boudoir	B	Beach Centre	b	Dubai Marine Beach Resort	B
Japengo	1	Jumaira Plaza	c	Regent Beach Resort	A
Lime Tree Cafe	2	Magrudy's	d		
Malecon	B	Mercato	a		
Al Qasr	B	Red Sea Exhibitions	b		
Sho-Cho	B				

JUMEIRAH ROAD

Jumeirah
Beach Park

**Majlis Ghorfat
Um Al Sheef**

AL ATHAR ST

AL WASL ROAD

AL HADIQA ST

Safa Park

Mercato mall

Jumeirah Rd. Sat–Thurs 10am–
10pm, Fri 2–10pm. ⓦwww
.MercatoShoppingMall.com. About
halfway down Jumeirah Road,
the eye-popping Mercato mall
ranks as one of the area's leading
tourist attractions and is well
worth a visit even if you've no
intention of actually buying
anything in it. Looking like
a kind of miniature medieval
Italian city rebuilt by the Disney
Corporation, the mall comprises
a series of brightly coloured
quasi-Venetian-cum-Tuscan
palazzi arranged around a huge
central atrium overlooked by
panoramic balconies, while
side passages lead to miniature
piazzas on either side – a
memorable example of the sort
of brazen but enjoyable kitsch

that Dubai seems to do so well.
Not surprisingly, it's all proved
immensely popular, and the
fake-Florentine thoroughfares
are thronged most hours of
the day and night by a very
eclectic crowd, with Jumeirah
Janes ducking in and out of the
mall's designer boutiques and
crowds of white-robed Emirati
men lounging over coffee in
the ground-floor *Starbucks* while
their veiled wives and Filipina
maids take the kids upstairs for
burgers and fries at *McDonalds*
– a picture-perfect example of
the multicultural zaniness of
modern Dubai. For more on the
mall's shops, see p.110.

Jumeirah Beach Park

Jumeirah Rd. Daily 7am–10.30pm,
Thurs–Sat until 11pm; Mon ladies
only. 5dh. Squeezed in between
the sea and Jumeirah
Road near the
suburb's southern end,
Jumeirah Beach Park
is easily the nicest
park and public beach
in Dubai – wildly
popular both with
city residents and with
sand-starved tourists
staying in city-centre

▼ MERCATO MALL

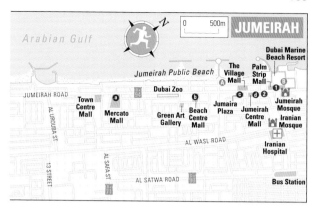

hotels. The beach itself is large enough to soak up the crowds, a fine, wide swathe of white sand manned with lifeguards and equipped with loungers and parasols, while the pleasantly wooded strip of park behind has lots of shaded grass for picnics, barbecue facilities, a couple of cafés, and a well-equipped kids' play area. On the downside, swim-suited females (whether accompanied or not) are often the victims of persistent staring and surreptitious photography by sex-starved gangs of Indian and Pakistani voyeurs; Mondays, when only ladies are admitted to the park, offer welcome respite.

Safa Park

Al Wasl Rd. Daily 8am–11pm, Thurs–Sat until 11.30pm. 3dh. Flanking Al Wasl Road, a couple of blocks inland from the coast, Safa Park offers a refreshing expanse of grassy parkland impressively backdropped by the skyscrapers of Sheikh Zayed Road. The park is well supplied with children's attractions, including numerous play areas, a boating lake and a miniature fairground area

▼ JUMEIRAH BEACH PARK

featuring a merry-go-round, a (small) big wheel, dodgems, games arcade, trampolines and a giant slide (although some of these attractions only operate in the evenings).

Majlis Ghorfat Um Al Sheef

17 Street, off Jumeirah Rd. Sat–Thurs 8.30am–1.30pm & 3.30–8.30pm, Fri 3.30–8.30pm. 1dh. Tucked away down a side street near the southern end of Jumeirah Road, the modest little Majlis Ghorfat Um Al Sheef offers a touching memento of old Dubai, now incongruously marooned amidst a sea of chintzy modern villas. Built in 1955 when Jumeirah was no more than a small fishing village, this modest little traditional house was used by Sheikh Rashid, the inspiration behind modern Dubai's spectacular development, as a summer retreat and hosted many of the discussions about the city's future which led to its dramatic economic explosion

▼ MAJLIS GHORFAT UM AL SHEEF

during the 1960s and 1970s. The two-storey building serves as a fetching reminder of earlier and simpler times: it's a sturdy coral-and-gypsum structure topped by a pair of wind towers and embellished with fine doors and windows of solid teak, the whole enclosed in an old-fashioned Arabian garden complete with date palms and *falaj* (irrigation) channels. The *majlis* (meeting room) itself is on the upper floor, with cushions laid out around its edges and the walls and floor adorned with a modest selection of household objects – an old-fashioned European radio and clock, plus rifles, oil lamps and coffee pots – which in 1950s Dubai were considered all the luxury necessary even in a residence of the ruling sheikh – a far cry from the seven-star amenities enjoyed by today's Emiratis.

Note that the *majlis* is a bit tricky to find (and taxi drivers are unlikely to know it). Look for the HSBC Bank and BinSina Pharmacy on the corner of 17 Street and Jumeirah Road. Turn down 17 Street for about 50m; the *majlis* is on your left.

Shops

Beach Centre

Jumeirah Rd. Daily 10am–1pm & 4.30–9.30pm. One of the more rewarding of the endless malls strung out along Jumeirah Road thanks to the interesting clutch of craft and curio shops located upstairs, including Red Sea Exhibitions (see opposite), Moroccan Treasures, Barcelona Shoes and Abdul Ghani Sharaf Novelties. There's also a branch of the *Lebanese Automatic* restaurant chain here (see p.61).

▲ JUMEIRA PLAZA

Jumaira Plaza

Jumeirah Rd. Sat–Thurs 6am–midnight, Fri noon–midnight.
This glittery pink mall is the biggest and best of the various shopping centres on the northern end of the Jumeirah Road. Outlets include Damascus Palace (selling pretty Arabian lamps, and so on), the well-stocked Kashmir Crafts, stuffed with all sorts of collectables, and the smart Wajahat and Sujhat Carpets. The well-run little House of Prose secondhand bookshop, next to Wajahat and Sujhat Carpets, usually has a few worthwhile titles, though it's mainly full of the sort of bodice-ripping schlock with which bored local expat housewives fill the empty hours between beach outings and cocktail parties. There's also a welcome branch of the excellent *Dôme* café (see p.59).

Magrudy's

Magrudy's Centre, Jumeirah Rd. Sat–Thurs 9am–9pm, Fri 4.30–9pm. A small but (by Dubai standards) well-stocked bookshop with a fair range of Middle Eastern-related titles, plus a reasonable array of fiction and other English-language titles. There are other branches at Deira City Centre, BurJuman and Ibn Battuta malls, and in the Spinneys at Jumeirah and in the Mercato mall.

Mercato

Jumeirah Rd. Sat–Thurs 10am–10pm, Fri 2–10pm. This kitsch Italian-themed mall (see p.108) is relatively small compared to many others in the city, but packs in a good selection of rather upmarket outlets, particularly strong on mainstream designer clothes (including Boss, Armani and Diesel), as well as some interesting little ladies' boutiques like Fleurt and Moda Brazil. There's also a big Virgin Megastore, a handful of upmarket carpet shops and a fair range of places to eat and drink.

Red Sea Exhibitions

Beach Centre, Jumeirah Rd. Sat–Thurs 9am–1pm & 4–10pm, Fri 4–10pm.
Classy but well-priced selection of carpets and kilims from all the main rug-producing countries, including a few antiques, as well as pure silk carpets and wool–silk mixes. You can pick up small rugs here from as little as 150–200dh, though you'll probably be tempted by something bigger than that.

Cafés

Japengo

Palm Strip Mall, Jumeirah Rd. Daily 11.30–1am, Fri & Sat until 2am. The original branch of this lively Dubai chain of café–restaurants, with chic decor, jazzy music and a fun atmosphere. The menu is the most shamelessly eclectic in town, based around a longish list of Japanese standards (sushi, sashimi, noodles) spliced together with Middle Eastern mezze, Southeast Asian stir-fries, Italian pizzas and pastas, plus sandwiches, salads and a range of Japengo "specials" (meaning anything from yakitori to lamb chops). The end result of this very Dubaian culinary free-for-all is much tastier and more consistent than you might fear, and prices are a snip – just a shame they don't serve alcohol. Mains from around 35dh. There are other branches in Wafi City, BurJuman, the Oasis Tower on Sheikh Zayed Road, Madinat Jumeirah and Ibn Battuta Mall.

Lime Tree Café

Jumeirah Rd. Thurs–Sat 7.30am–1am, Sun–Wed 7.30am–11pm. Sitting in this funky little green and orange café amidst the local community of expat ladies-who-lunch you have to pinch yourself to remember that you're actually in Dubai, rather than in some upwardly mobile suburb of London or Melbourne. The place stays perpetually busy thanks to its utterly moreish – but quite reasonably priced – wraps, focaccias, panini, quiches, salads, and fat cakes, as well as tasty fruit juices. There's another branch at the Ibn Battuta Mall (see p.133).

Restaurants and bars

Al Qasr

Dubai Marine Beach Resort ☎04-346 1111. Daily 12.30–3.30pm & 7pm–3am. This soothing restaurant offers an oasis of old-fashioned Arabian calm amidst the sometimes unruly nightlife of the *Dubai Marine Beach Resort*. The food runs through all the usual Middle Eastern staples with aplomb, from perfectly cooked *shish taouk* to crisp *fatayer* and fragrant *kibbeh*, and the setting on a balcony above the floodlit hotel pool and palms is lovely, albeit rather more Barbados than Beirut. Mains from around 45dh.

Boudoir

Dubai Marine Beach Resort ☎04-346 1111. Daily 7pm–3am. This sultry restaurant-cum-bar looks like the apartment of an upper-class nineteenth-century Parisian courtesan, with plush red drapes, chintzy chandeliers and an indecent number of mirrors. The restaurant (mains from around 50dh) specializes

▼ BOUDOIR

▲ MALECON

in contemporary European cuisine, with a mix of seafood and meat dishes such as pot-roasted chicken with truffle and herbs, and pan-fried red snapper. The small bar area tends to be a bit more sedate and attracts a slightly older crowd than the hotel's other drinking spots, although it can feel oddly sleazy (think Emile Zola with tequila slammers) – or maybe that's just the decor. A DJ spins his discs nightly from midnight until 3am.

Malecon

Dubai Marine Beach Resort ☏ 04-346 1111. Daily 7pm–3am. This restaurant-cum-bar has live Latin bands nightly from 9am till 1am, followed by a late-night DJ, helped along by a good drinks list including plenty of mojitos and rum-based cocktails to help bring out the inner *salsero* in you. Food is contemporary Latino, with a mix of seafood and meat dishes (not to mention the "Cuban Smokeless Cigar", a cigar-shaped chocolate mousse complete with ice-cream ashtray). Mains from around 70dh.

Sho-Cho

Dubai Marine Beach Resort ☏ 04-346 1111. Daily 7pm–3am. This very chic little restaurant dishes up a reasonably priced and prepared list of Japanese standards (mains from 40dh), though it's best known for its cool little outside terrace bar, one of the posiest spots to sup a cocktail in Dubai. Most nights see a cast of confirmed fashionistas ranging from freshly tanned tourists to Lebanese pop stars slumming around in expensive scraps of Armani and Chanel. Dress to impress (or alternatively go and buy some fake labels in Karama), though you'll have to arrive unfashionably early if you want to get a seat. Regular live DJs add to the very cool ambience.

▼ SHO-CHO

The Burj Al Arab and around

Some 10km south of the Creek, the southern end of the Jumeirah Road runs through the district of Umm Suqeim, a long and anonymous swathe of Dubai-style suburban sprawl, with huge millionaire's villas cloistered behind high walls and ranged along endless deserted streets, the silence broken only by the occasional Land Cruiser or Mercedes sidling discreetly past. This seemingly unpromising district is, however, home to a trio of famous Dubaian landmarks which rise spectacularly out of the low-rise suburban desert: the Jumeirah Beach Hotel, the Madinat Jumeirah hotel and shopping complex, and, most famously, the iconic Burj Al Arab, the sail-shaped hotel which has probably done more than anything else in the city to put Dubai on the global map. There are further attractions at the wacky Wild Wadi waterpark and at Ski Dubai, the Middle East's first ski-slope, while more sedentary pleasures can be found at the adjoining vast new Mall of the Emirates.

The Burj Al Arab

Lying just off the coast, the spectacular *Burj Al Arab* ("Arabian Tower") has done more than anything else to stamp Dubai on the international consciousness. Although still less than ten years old, the *Burj* has already become as emblematic and instantly recognizable a symbol of Dubai as the Eiffel Tower, Empire State Building and Big Ben are of their respective cities, featuring on the number plates of the city's cars, on endless

▼ THE BURJ AL ARAB AND JUMEIRAH BEACH HOTEL

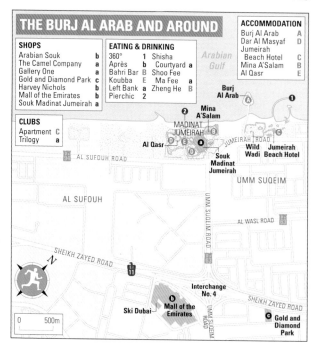

tourist souvenirs (from T-shirts and postcards to Burj-shaped paperweights and perfume bottles) and on virtually every guidebook or piece of promotional literature about the city published in the past eight years. Even the top-floor helipad has acquired celebrity status: Agassi and Federer played tennis on it; Tiger Woods used it as a makeshift driving range (before ringing room service for more balls); and Ronan Keating shot a music video on it.

The *Burj* is home to the world's first so-called "seven-star" hotel, having awarded itself two extra stars to emphasize the unique levels of style and luxury offered within (even though, officially, such a category doesn't actually exist – technically it's a five-star-luxury hotel, but the fact that so few people quibble over the extra stars is a measure of the *Burj's* distinction). Staying here is a very expensive pleasure, and even visiting it presents certain financial and practical challenges (see the box on p.116 for more). Fortunately the exterior of the building can be enjoyed for free from numerous vantage points nearby.

Designed to echo the shape of a dhow's sail, the *Burj* forms a kind of maritime counterpart to the adjacent *Jumeirah Beach Hotel's* "breaking wave" (see below), offering a contemporary tribute to Dubai's historic seafaring traditions – its sail-like shape (not to mention its very exclusive aura) enhanced by its location on a specially reclaimed island some 300m offshore. The building was constructed between 1993 and 1999 at a still undisclosed (but presumably staggering) cost by UK engineering and architectural firm W.S. Atkins under lead designer Tom Wills-Wright and interior designer Kuan Chew. The statistics alone are impressive. At 321m, the *Burj* is the tallest dedicated hotel in the world (and the twenty-first-highest building full stop). The spire-like superstructure alone, incredibly, is taller than the entire *Jumeirah Beach Hotel*, while the atrium (180m) is also the world's loftiest – and capacious enough to swallow up the entire Statue of Liberty or, for that matter, the 38-storey Dubai World Trade Centre (see p.94). The sheer scale of the *Burj* is overwhelming, and only really appreciated in the flesh, since photographs of the building, perhaps inevitably, always seem to diminish it to the size of an expensive toy. The *Burj*'s scale is tempered by its extraordinary grace and the sinuous simplicity of its basic design, broken only by the celebrated cantilevered helipad and (on the building's sea-facing side) the projecting *Al Muntaha* ("The Highest") restaurant. The hotel's shore-facing side mainly comprises a huge sheet of white Teflon-coated fibreglass cloth – a symbolic sail which is spectacularly illuminated from within by night, turning the entire building into a magically glowing beacon. Less universally admired is the building's rear elevation, in the shape of a huge cross, a feature that caused considerable controversy amongst Muslims at the time of construction, though it's only visible from the sea, and (significantly) is almost never photographed.

Most of the interior is actually hollow, comprising an enormous atrium vibrantly coloured in great swathes of red, blue, green and gold. It's like the bastard architectural lovechild of an Art Deco skyscraper

Visiting the Burj

Non-guests are only allowed into the *Burj* with a prior reservation at one of the hotel's bars, cafés or restaurants. Many visitors come in for a cocktail at the 27th-floor **Al Muntaha Skyview Bar** (attached to the restaurant; see below), perhaps the best way of getting a good look at the hotel without going bankrupt, with drinks from around 60dh (although it often gets booked solid, so reserve as far in advance as you can). Alternatively, a visit for afternoon tea at the **Sahn Eddar** atrium lounge will cost around 250dh. If you want to go the whole hog, you could dine at one of the *Burj*'s two restaurants, among the city's most spectacular. The first is the brightly coloured 27th-floor **Al Muntaha Sky View Restaurant** – *Al Muntaha* means the "ultimate" or the "highest", which describes equally well both the restaurant's spectacular location near the top of the *Burj* and the equally spectacular prices (with veg mains from 195dh, and meat and seafood mains from around 300dh). The menu features a range of Mediterranean-style fine dining creations. At the other end of the hotel (and at similar prices), the **Al Mahara** seafood restaurant is actually located below the waterline, approached via a three-minute simulated submarine ride and surrounded by enormous fish tanks, complete with resident sharks.

For more on staying at the *Burj*, see p.177.

and a James Bond movie set, the chez Blofeld extravagance of it all encapsulated by the enormous fish tanks that flank the entrance staircase and which are so deep that cleaners have to put on diving suits to scrub them out (a performance you can witness daily from 2pm to 4pm). The interior is often dismissed as a classic example of garish opulence gone mad (that's not gold paint on the walls, incidentally, but genuine 22ct gold leaf), but this doesn't really do justice to *Burj's* unique aura, and the huge expanses of vibrant primary colours, the elegantly curved tiers of balconied floors rising far overhead and the massive bulbous golden piers that support them possess a strange, sculptural beauty, as much a work of visual art as a piece of traditional architectural, and a fittingly original, sequel to the remarkable exterior.

Jumeirah Beach Hotel

On the beach right next to the *Burj* sits the second of the area's classic buildings, the huge *Jumeirah Beach Hotel*. Designed to resemble an enormous breaking wave (although it could just as easily be the dorsal fin of some enormous sea creature rising above the surface), and rising to a height of over 100m, the hotel was considered the most spectacular and luxurious in the city when it opened in 1997. Although it has since been overtaken on both counts, and now caters to a cheery and relatively downmarket package crowd, it remains a fine sight, especially when seen from a distance in combination with the *Burj*, against whose slender sail it appears (with a little

imagination) to be about to crash.

Wild Wadi

Directly behind the Burj Al Arab and Jumeirah Beach Hotel. Daily 11am–6pm (Sept, Oct & March–May until 7pm; June–Aug until 9pm; Thurs June–Sept park closes 1hr early for ladies night). All-day admission 150dh, children (under 1.1m tall) 125dh. ☎04-348 4444, ⊛www.wildwadi.com.
Modelled on a Sinbad-inspired fantasy tropical lagoon, with cascading waterfalls, whitewater rapids, hanging bridges and big piles of rocks, the spectacular Wild Wadi waterpark offers a variety of attractions to suit everyone from small kids to physically fit adrenalin junkies. Get oriented with a circuit around the edge of the park on the Whitewater Wadi ride (MasterBlaster), during which you're squirted on powerful jets of water up and down eleven long, twisting slides before being catapulted down the

▼ JUMEIRAH SCEIRAH, WILD WADI

darkened Tunnel of Doom. Dedicated thrill-seekers should try the Wipeout and Riptide Flowriders, simulating powerful surfing waves, and the park's stellar attraction, the Jumeirah Sceirah (the tallest and fastest speed slide outside North America), during which you're likely to hit around 80kph and experience temporary weightlessness. There are also less demanding attractions such as gentle tube-rides down Lazy River, family-oriented water games in Juha's Dhow and Lagoon or the chance to bob up and down in the big simulated waves of Breaker's Bay. Many

people make a day of it, and you can buy food and drinks inside the park using money stored on an ingenious waterproof wristwatch. Note that as well as the basic entrance charge, you'll also have to pay a rather steep additional 20dh to get a locker to leave your stuff in, as well as an exorbitant 20dh if you need to hire a towel – much better to take your own.

Madinat Jumeirah

Ⓦ www.madinatjumeirah.com. The huge new shopping and hotel complex of Madinat Jumeirah is, in its own kitsch way, almost as astonishing a sight as the *Burj Al Arab*. The entire complex, containing the *Mina A'Salam* and *Al Qasr* luxury hotels (see p.178) and the labyrinthine Souk Madinat Jumeirah bazaar (often referred to, especially by taxi drivers, as the "Medina Jumeirah"; see p.121), is built in the form of a self-contained Arabian-style city, with towering sand-coloured buildings, embellished with Orientalist decorative touches and topped by an extraordinary quantity of wind towers (best viewed from the entrance to the *Al Qasr* hotel), the whole arranged around a meandering lagoon system along which hotel guests are chauffeured in replica abras.

There's an undeniable whiff of Disneyland about the entire complex, and the whole place, despite its "authentic" Arabian architecture, bears about as much relation to an old-time

▼ SOUK MADINAT JUMEIRAH

▲ MALL OF THE EMIRATES

Dubaian settlement as London's Houses of Parliament do to a medieval English parish church. Nevertheless, the sheer scale of the place, with its relentlessly picturesque array of wind towers, wood-framed souks and palm-fringed waterways, is strangely compelling, and a perfect example of the kind of thing – mixing unbridled extravagance with a significant dose of surreal kitsch and a healthy disregard for all notions of received taste – that Dubai seems to do so well. The Madinat also offers some of the most eye-boggling views in Dubai, with the sinuous, futuristic outlines of the *Burj Al Arab* surreally framed between medieval-looking wind towers and Moorish arcading. The fact that the fake medieval city is actually newer than the ultra-modern *Burj* is, by Dubai's standards, exactly what one would expect.

The obvious place from which to explore the complex is the Souk Madinat Jumeirah, though it's well worth investigating some of the superb restaurants and bars in the *Al Qasr* and *Mina A'Salam* hotels (see listings on pp.122–124), several of which offer superlative views over the Madinat, *Burj Al Arab*

and coastline, as well as offering a peek into the extravagantly designed interiors of these two sumptuous hotels.

Mall of the Emirates

Interchange 4, Sheikh Zayed Rd. Daily 10am–10pm (Thurs–Sat until midnight). ⓦ www.malloftheemirates .com. The largest mall in Dubai (at least for the time being), this enormous new shopping complex, packed with some five hundred shops, has already proved immensely popular with locals and tourists alike, despite being more or less in the middle of nowhere – unless you consider Interchange 4 on the multi-lane Sheikh Zayed Road a place you would ordinarily consider worth visiting. Centred around a huge, glass-roofed central atrium, the mall is spread over three levels, criss crossed by escalators and little wrought-iron bridges, and topped by the large, pink, five-star *Kempinski Hotel*. There's also the added bonus of surreal views of the snow-covered slopes of Ski Dubai through huge glass walls at the western end of the mall, or from one of the various restaurants and bars overlooking the slopes, such as *Après* (see p.122). For more on the mall's shops, see p.120.

Ski Dubai

Interchange 4, Sheikh Zayed Rd, next to the Mall of the Emirates. Daily 10am–11pm (Thurs–Sat until midnight). ☎04-409 4000, ⊚www .skidxb.com. Snow park: adult 60dh, child 50dh; ski slope (2hr) adult 140dh, child 120dh; ski slope day pass adult 230dh, child 180dh. Prices include clothing, boots and equipment but not hats and gloves, though these can be purchased at the attached ski shop.

The huge indoor ski resort of Ski Dubai is unquestionably one of Dubai's weirder ideas. The sight of a huge indoor snow-covered ski slope (the first in the Middle East), complete with regular snowfall, is strange enough amidst the sultry heat of the Gulf, while the spectacle of robed Emiratis skiing, snowboarding or just chucking snowballs at one another adds a decidedly surreal touch to the already unlikely proceedings (and can be enjoyed for free from the viewing areas at the attached Mall of the Emirates). The complex contains the world's largest indoor snow park, comprising a huge 3000-square-metres of snow-covered faux-Alpine mountainside, complete with chair-lift. Accredited skiiers and snowboarders (you'll need to undergo a brief personal assessment to prove you possess the necessary basic skills to use the main slope) can use five runs of varying height, steepness and difficulty, ranging from a beginners' track through to the world's first indoor black run, as well as a "freestyle zone" for show-off winter sports aficionados. There's also a Snow School ski academy for beginners and improvers (both adults and kids, from 120dh per hour), as well as a twin-track bobsled ride, a snowball-throwing gallery, snow cavern, adventure trail, tobogganing, and snowman-building opportunities.

Shops

Arabian Souk

Mall of the Emirates. Daily 10am–10pm (Thurs–Sat until midnight). A themed section within the Mall of the Emirates with fake Moorish architectural touches and a good selection of Arabian curio, carpet and handicrafts shops, including Al Jaber Gallery, Aminian Persian Carpets, Pride of Kashmir and branches of the Camel Company (see below) and Gallery One (see opposite).

The Camel Company

Souk Madinat Jumeirah. Daily 10am–11pm. This dromedary-obsessed shop stocks Dubai's cutest selection of stuffed toy camels (from 20dh) – vastly superior to the usual hump-backed horrors on offer elsewhere in the city

▼ SKI DUBAI

– plus camel mugs, camel cards, camel T-shirts . . . in fact, pretty much everything apart from Camel cigarettes. There's another branch in the Mall of the Emirates.

Gallery One

Souk Madinat Jumeirah. Daily 9.30am–11pm. ⓦ www.galleryonestore.com.
Sells a good range of superb, limited-edition photographs of Dubai – expensive, but not outrageous – as well as other fine-art photography and a gorgeous (but pricey) selection of postcards. There's another branch at Mall of the Emirates.

Gold and Diamond Park

Sheikh Zayed Rd between interchanges 3 and 4. Daily 10am–10pm. This low-key little mall is the place to come if you want diamonds, which generally retail here for around half the price you'd expect to pay back home. The mall's seventy-odd shops are stuffed full of diamond-encrusted jewellery; most is made according to European rather than Arabian designs, with a good range of pieces in classic Italian styles. You'll also find a few other precious stones and platinum jewellery for sale, plus a small amount of gold.

Harvey Nichols

Mall of the Emirates. Daily 10am–10pm (Thurs–Sat until midnight).
The flagship store of one of Dubai's flagship malls, this suave, minimalist three-storey department store offers a vast array of fashion classics like Armani and Thomas Pink, as well as more contemporary designers such as Ozwald Boateng and (ahem) Victoria Beckham. There's also a big range of designer scents in the ground-floor perfumeries,

plus superior homeware and the shop's signature range of upmarket food and drink – essential fare for all expats slumming it in their Jumeirah villas.

Mall of the Emirates

Interchange 4, Sheikh Zayed Rd. Daily 10am–10pm (Thurs–Sat until midnight). ⓦ www.malloftheemirates .com. This swanky new megamall's vast array of five hundred-odd stores (as ever, it pays to pick up a map at the entrance) has a rather upmarket emphasis, exemplified by the ab-fab flagship branch of UK department store Harvey Nichols (see opposite), which fills three floors with a superb range of designer clobber in a memorably chic setting. There's also a massive new Borders, which promises to add a welcome new dimension to Dubai's moribund array of bookshops, and a big Carrefour hypermarket (see p.57), while kids will enjoy the big Toy Store, scattered with giant stuffed animals and selling everything from Thomas the Tank Engines to Tamagotchis, as well as the adjacent Magic Planet play area. Also home to the Arabian Souk (see opposite) handicrafts and carpet bazaar.

Souk Madinat Jumeirah

Madinat Jumeirah. Daily 10am–10pm. ⓦ www.madinatjumeirah.com.
At the heart of the Madinat Jumeirah, this superb re-creation of a "traditional" souk (though it's naturally far smarter, cleaner and more picturesque than any real-life old-time souk ever was) serves up a beguiling mix of shopping, eating and drinking opportunities either within the souk's narrow, wood-framed

passageways or on the lagoon-facing terraces outside. Like all good bazaars, the layout is mazy and disorienting – you can pick up a map at the entrance, though it's more fun to get lost and just wander at random; the place isn't so big that you'll ever be far from where you want to be. The souk's shops are mainly concerned with traditional arts and crafts, a veritable Aladdin's cave stuffed with a superb array of curio and carpet shops including well-established Dubai names like Al Jaber, Pride of Kashmir and the Persian Carpet House – as well as more unusual outlets like The Camel Company and Gallery One (see above) – serving up anything from ouds and embroidered slippers to Moroccan hanging lamps and tagine pots.

Restaurants

As well as the restaurants listed below, there are plenty of comparatively inexpensive eating options scattered around the Souk Madinat Jumeirah, including branches of *The Noodle House* (p.101), *Dôme* (p.59), *Left Bank* (see p.125), *Trader Vic's* (p.111) and *Japengo* (p.125), to mention just a few. The last three are all ranged along the souk's beautiful waterfront terrace, which gets very lively after dark and makes a superb spot to take in the souk's cosmopolitan nightlife, with its eclectic mix of tourists, Emiratis and expat Arabs.

Après

Mall of the Emirates ☎ 04-341 2575. Daily noon–1am. This chic bar-restaurant offers a perfect lunch stop during a long shop in the Mall of the Emirates, with wonderful views over the slopes of Ski Dubai through its big picture windows and a good selection of unpretentious, well-prepared food, including burgers, fish and chips, and excellent thin-crust pizzas (from 45dh). The long mirrored bar also makes it a good place for drink; from the vast selection of backlit bottles staff conjure up a big range of classic and contemporary cocktails, plus draught and bottled beers.

Pierchic

Al Qasr ☎ 04-366 8888. Daily noon–2.45pm & 7–11.30pm. One of the city's most spectacularly situated restaurants, perched at the end of a breezy pier jutting out in front of the grandiose *Al Qasr* hotel, of which it offers magnificent views, while the nearby *Burj* adds a further splash of eye-popping magic. The largely seafood menu has prices to match the location, with a selection of globally acquired fish dishes featuring sea bass, dorada, turbot, Atlantic lobster, Dover sole and Gulf prawns, plus a few meat options and a couple of token vegetarian choices. The food doesn't always quite live up to the setting, but when the setting's this good, you might not care. Mains from 90dh.

Shoo Fee Ma Fee

Souk Madinat Jumeirah ☎ 04-366 6730. Daily 7pm–12.30am (Fri from 4pm). One of the liveliest of the new Madinat Jumeirah restaurants (the chatty name translates as "What's Up?"), this vibrant Moroccan establishment comes complete with cheery jellaba-clad waiters, a good live Moroccan band (from 9pm), and an upbeat and informal atmosphere backed up by a range of excellent authentic fare including palate-teasers like mokh magli (fried lamb's brains) and pigeon pie, plus the usual lamb, chicken and vegetarian tagines and couscous dishes. Mains from 65dh.

Zheng He

Mina A'Salam ☎04-366 6730. Daily noon–3pm & 7–11.30pm. This classy Chinese restaurant – generally reckoned one of the best in the city – offers a superbly cooked and beautifully presented range of Chinese veg, meat and seafood standards alongside more innovative European-cum-Chinese fusion dishes, with classic Asian flavours cleverly combined with ingedients ranging from pesto and pine nuts to tenderloin steak. The food doesn't come cheap, however, and service can be surprisingly hit and miss given the prices. Seating is either inside the svelte restaurant itself or outside on the beautiful *Burj*-facing terrace. Mains from around 90dh.

▲ ZHENG HE

Bars and shisha

360°

Jumeirah Beach Hotel. Daily 5pm until late (Thurs & Fri from 4pm). The ultimate Dubaian chill-out bar, spectacularly located at the end of a long breakwater which arcs out into the Gulf opposite the *Jumeirah Beach Hotel* and *Burj Al Arab*, and offering sublime views of both, particularly when

▼ 360° BAR

the illuminations come on after dark. White sofas and beanbags lie scattered around the circular open-air terrace, filled most nights with a very mellow crowd of tanned tourists and expat Arabs who lounge in attitudes of fashionable insensibility over cocktails, Coronas and shishas, while resident and visiting DJs pump hypnotic house out into the night.

Bahri Bar

Mina A'Salam. Daily noon–2am. This superb little Arabian-style outdoor terrace is deservedly popular, liberally scattered with canopied sofas, Moorish artefacts and Persian carpets, and offering drop-dead gorgeous views of the Burj and Madinat Jumeirah (there's also attractive indoor seating around the cocktail bar, prettily inserted into a kind of Bedouin tent – good

for the hot summer months). It's particularly lovely towards sunset, though once you've got stuck into the long list of cocktails, vodka martinis and wines (plus relatively affordable draught beer) you might find the time passing more quickly than you anticipated. If hunger strikes, there's a good selection of quirky international snacks ranging from sushi to "South Indian tapas".

Koubba

Al Qasr. Daily noon–2am. One of the most memorable of the many idyllic drinking holes scattered about the Madinat Jumeirah complex, this superb Arabian-themed bar offers jaw-dropping views over Al Qasr and the Burj Al Arab from its spacious terrace and can prove remarkably difficult to leave once you've settled down on one of its comfy sofas scattered with piles

▼ BAHRI BAR

▲ KOUBBA

of brightly coloured cushions. There's a good list of classic and contemporary cocktails, a small wine list and – bliss for beer drinkers – draught pints at (considering the setting) quite reasonable prices.

Left Bank

Souk Madinat Jumeirah. Daily noon–2am. Jostling for elbow room amongst the string of incredibly popular eating and drinking spots along the Souk Madinat Jumeirah waterfront, this suave but unpretentious modern bar offers a good spot to watch the passing scene if you can bag a table on the outside terrace (although the indoor section is pleasantly convivial as well). There's a reasonably priced list of draught beers and a passable wine list, plus spirits and cocktails, as well as a good selection of simple but tasty bar meals.

Shisha Courtyard

Souk Madinat Jumeirah. Daily 11am–12.30am. The picturesque central courtyard of the Madinat Jumeirah offers a captivating place to kick back over a shisha (albeit an expensive one, at 30–45dh) or a beer, wine or cocktail from the modest drinks list and watch the engaging night-time life of the souk – from sunburnt tourists to robed Emiratis and their *abbeya*-clad wives – roll past.

Live music

Jambase

Souk Madinat Jumeirah. Daily 7pm–2.45am. Dubai's premier dedicated live-music venue, this cool modern underground establishment hosts a stomping resident Brazilian band who rock the floor most nights, along with visiting acts; the dance floor usually kicks off towards midnight, while earlier on it's a good place for a drink and something to eat. There's a good, if relatively pricey bar, and a surprisingly extensive and classy menu of steaks, seafood and other mains from around 90dh.

Clubs

Apartment

Jumeirah Beach Hotel. Tues–Sat 8pm–3am. Tucked away around the back of the *Jumeirah Beach Hotel*, this stylish and intimate little place is one of Dubai's more sophisticated dance venues – just the place to show off that newly acquired tan and Chloe handbag. The club divides into two sections: the larger club area (with dance floor) and the more chilled-out lounge, with different music in each. The resident DJ and international guest artists play a mix of R&B, house and trance, except on ladies' night (Wed), when 80s music rules the dance floor. Entrance fees (around 70dh) sometimes apply, depending on who's manning the decks.

Trilogy

Souk Madinat Jumeirah. Daily except Sun 9pm–3am (Rooftop Bar from 7pm). ⓦwww.trilogy.ae. Dubai's most eye-catching club, Trilogy serves up a potent combination of cool music in an even cooler setting, with a roster of big-name international guest DJs spinning a heady mixture of R&B and house tunes to one of the city's most glam crowds. The club spreads over three levels (though not all are open every night). The bottom two flank a cavernous Arabian-style internal courtyard-cum-dance floor – it feels a bit like clubbing in medieval Morocco – while the top level is occupied by a gorgeous little rooftop bar with superb views over the Madinat, well worth a visit for a pre-dinner aperitif. Entrance charges vary according to the nightly acts: some nights are free, at other times you'll have to fork out up to 100dh.

Theatre

Madinat Theatre

Souk Madinat Jumeirah ☎04-366 8888, ⓦwww.madinattheatre.com. The recent opening of the modern and well-equipped Madinat Theatre at the Souk Madinat Jumeirah, the only purpose-built performance venue in the city so far, has come as a much needed shot in the arm to Dubai's lacklustre cultural scene. Not that the Madinat Theatre has so far blazed many cultural trails, hosting a range of mainstream drama, dance and light entertainment shows (think Neil Simon romantic comedies or *100% Kylie*). Though it's a start, at least.

Dubai Marina

Nowhere is the scale of Dubai's explosive growth as apparent as in the far south of the city. Barely five years ago the lower reaches of the emirate south of the Burj Al Arab were largely desert, untouched apart from a discreet string of luxury hotels lining the coast. Now, virtually from nothing, an entire new city is under construction, stretching for the best part of ten kilometres from just south of Madinat Jumeirah down to the industrial zone and port at Jebel Ali. At the heart of this new urban explosion is the Dubai Marina development – centred around the existing beachside hotels, which have now been engulfed in a rash of new high-rises – and the adjacent dedicated business zones of Dubai Media City and Dubai Internet City, while offshore the huge new Palm Jumeirah artificial island will soon open for business. Future developments include the new Jebel Ali Airport, slated eventually to become the world's largest airport, and yet more developments further south, around the so-called Dubai Waterfront, which will ultimately extend Dubai city all the way to the border with Abu Dhabi.

There's no real precedent anywhere in the world for urban growth on this scale or at this speed, and when complete the huge new residential districts and commercial and tourist facilities of Dubai Marina and surrounding areas will undoubtedly shift the focus of the entire emirate decisively southwards, and perhaps in time even eclipse the old city centre itself. For the time being, however, Dubai Marina is still very much a work-in-progress, although even in a place in which the most extravagant building projects have become commonplace, the sight of the fledgling city is astonishing, with the skeletons of literally hundreds of thirty- and forty-storey skyscrapers in various stages of completion stretching as far as the eye can see.

▼ SKYSCRAPERS AND BILLBOARD, DUBAI MARINA

The Palm, Jumeirah, The World, and other islands

One of the most striking features of Dubai's recent development is its obsession with artificial islands. The reasons for this are obvious: in its natural state, the diminutive emirate of Dubai boasts a mere 70 kilometres of coastline, totally insufficient to service the needs of its rocketing number of beach-hungry tourist visitors and residents (at present the city boasts only around fifteen genuine beach hotels, which are usually booked solid more or less throughout the year). The solution has been to inaugurate the construction of a series of four enormous man-made islands off the coast – the largest in the world – creating at a stroke an additional 520km of coastline, as well as huge new swathes of valuable commercial land surrounded by the calm blue waters of the Arabian Gulf. The islands are being constructed by the government but are being sold on to private developers, who will be free to develop them as they see fit, meaning that exact details about what will actually be on them remain to be finalized.

The oldest of these four developments is **The Palm, Jumeirah**, a huge palm-shaped island linked to the mainland by a causeway off the coast just north of Dubai Marina, which opened for business at the beginning of 2007, when the first private residential apartments entered service (tenants include several members of the England football team, among them David Beckham, and a raft of other celebrities). The palm's "branches" will be given over to residential areas, while the palm's "trunk" and outer beaches will host public leisure facilities (scheduled to open gradually for business from 2007 to 2010), including around thirty new hotels, plus myriad luxury holiday apartments, restaurants and shops.

Following hot on the heels of The Palm Jumeirah is the even more extravagant **The World**, due to open in stages from 2008 onwards. Lying a couple

▼ MODEL OF DUBAI MARINA DEVELOPMENT

Dubai Marina beach

Pending the completion of Dubai's new urban dream, the Dubai Marina's attractions are largely confined to the string of luxurious beachside hotels which have been a long-established feature of the city's tourist credentials, and staying within the confines of one of these five-star sanctuaries – and keeping your eyes on the sea – it's easy to almost completely ignore the building bonanza going on just a few yards inland. If you want a holiday combining sun, sea and sand, and you don't mind spending most of your time cloistered within one of the spectacular beachside hotels, the marina area remains as appealing as ever. And if you do venture outside, the sight of a unique piece of of kilometres off the coast (access by boat only, unlike the three palm developments, all of which will be connected directly to the mainland), this vast complex of artificial islands has been planned with characteristic Dubaian theatricality, being constructed in the shape of a map of the world (not that you'll notice from ground level, although it's weirdly impressive when seen from the air). Many of the world's nations are represented by their own islands within the map (although the state of Israel is notably absent), while larger countries have been subdivided into several islands. It's hoped that developers will buy up individual islands and create themed tourist developments, perhaps based on the island that they occupy (again, exact details have yet to be confirmed, although Richard Branson has already announced his intention of buying up the island of Great Britain).

Not that this is the end of Dubai's offshore reclamation projects. Two further palm-shaped islands are already in the pipeline. These are **The Palm, Jebel Ali** (this one complete with an enclosing string of islands in the shape of a line of Arabic verse by Sheikh Mohammed himself), due for completion sometime around 2009; and the gargantuan **The Palm, Deira**, easily the largest of the three palms, right next to the city centre itself, with a proposed opening date sometime around 2010, which will be (it is claimed) larger than Paris. Again, it's expected that these developments will comprise a mix of residential and tourist facilities, as and when they are released onto the market. And finally, and perhaps biggest of all, is the massive **Dubai Waterfront** project, which will comprise a huge new semicircular arc of land enclosing The Palm Jebel Ali and add the final flourish to Dubai's ever-expanding coastline.

urban history in the making is undeniably fascinating – and also means that you'll be able to come back in a few years' time and reminisce about how different it all looked back in the good old days.

The beach itself comprises a fine wide swathe of golden sand (for details of how to get onto it if you're not staying at one of the local hotels, see the box on p.130), though the beaches at the lower-end hotels can get very crowded. Watersports companies operate out of all of the beachside hotels, offering all sorts of activities like windsurfing, sailing, kayaking, water skiing, wake boarding and parasailing, while roving pseudo-Bedouin roam the beach with colourfully upholstered camels offering rides.

▼ DUBAI MARINA BEACH

Marina beaches

All the marina beach hotels apart from the *Royal Meridien* allow non-guests to use their beaches, swimming pools and other facilities for a fee. Some are open daily; others only open to outsiders when occupancy levels fall below a certain level (it's best to ring in advance to check the latest situation wherever you're planning to go).

Habtoor Grand Daily; 325dh, including 100dh food voucher (children 225dh, including 50dh food).

Hilton Jumeirah Beach Daily except Fridays; 110dh.

Le Meridien Mina Seyahi Opens to outsiders depending on levels of hotel occupancy; around 150dh.

Oasis Beach Sat–Thurs, 140dh; Fri & public holidays, 200dh. Price includes BBQ lunch.

One&Only Royal Mirage Opens to outsiders depending on levels of hotel occupancy; 175dh.

Ritz-Carlton Opens to outsiders depending on levels of hotel occupancy; Sun–Wed, around 200dh; Thurs–Sat, around 300dh.

Sheraton Jumeirah Beach Sun–Wed, 100dh; Thurs–Sat, 125dh.

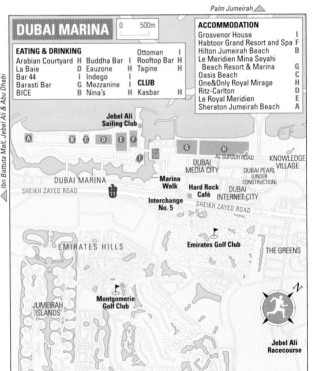

Palm Jumeirah

DUBAI MARINA

0   500m

EATING & DRINKING

Arabian Courtyard	H	Buddha Bar	I
La Baie	D	Eauzone	H
Bar 44	I	Indego	I
Barasti Bar	G	Mezzanine	I
BICE	B	Nina's	H

Ottoman I
Rooftop Bar H
Tagine H

CLUB

Kasbar H

ACCOMMODATION

Grosvenor House	I
Habtoor Grand Resort and Spa	F
Hilton Jumeirah Beach	B
Le Meridien Mina Seyahi	
Beach Resort & Marina	G
Oasis Beach	C
One&Only Royal Mirage	H
Ritz-Carlton	D
Le Royal Meridien	E
Sheraton Jumeirah Beach	A

Jebel Ali Sailing Club

Ibn Battuta Mall, Jebel Ali & Abu Dhabi

AL SUFOUH ROAD

DUBAI MEDIA CITY

KNOWLEDGE VILLAGE

DUBAI PEARL (UNDER CONSTRUCTION)

DUBAI MARINA

Marina Walk

Hard Rock Café

DUBAI INTERNET CITY

SHEIKH ZAYED ROAD

Interchange No. 5

SHEIKH ZAYED ROAD

EMIRATES HILLS

Emirates Golf Club

THE GREENS

JUMEIRAH ISLANDS

Montgomerie Golf Club

Jebel Ali Racecourse

N

Marina Walk

Amid the endless cranes and half-finished high-rises of the Dubai Marina development, the attractive new Marina Walk – the only section of the project to have been finished at the time of writing – gives an intriguing idea of what this entire part of the city might look like when finally completed. Tucked away at the back of the *Grosvenor House* hotel, the pedestrianized walkway runs around the start of the broad inland waterway that will eventually form the nucleus of the marina proper, with a string of low-key cafés and restaurants dotted along the waterfront and dozens of luxury yachts and fancy speedboats moored up alongside. It's proved particularly popular with locals and expat Arabs, and is best after dark, when the cafés fill up, the air mists over with fragrant clouds of shisha smoke and the surrounding towers light

▲ CONSTRUCTION WORK, DUBAI MARINA

up in a modest blaze of neon – an appealing (and blessedly traffic-free) blend of traditional and futuristic Dubai. The Walk is surprisingly tricky to find: walk or take a taxi north from *Grosvenor House* to the end of the block, turning inland at the first main road. The entrance to the development (easily missed) is on your right after a couple of hundred metres.

Sleeping with the fishes

Slated to open sometime in 2008 or 2009, **Hydropolis** is, even by Dubai standards, a rather startling concept: the world's first **luxury underwater hotel** (though not the world's first underwater hotel, which is *Jules' Undersea Lodge* at Key Largo in Florida – although unlike *Hydropolis* it lacks an access tunnel from ground level, so you need to put on a diving suit to reach it). Costing a reputed $500 million and using technologies employed in submarines and offshore oil rigs, *Hydropolis* will be located about 300m off the coast opposite Dubai Marina. The hotel will comprise a land-based, wave-shaped reception area and a connecting 1700 feet tunnel, along which a train will run to the main underwater section of the hotel, boasting 220 bubble-shaped suites set 20m beneath the waterline and walled with clear plexiglass. And if the thought of sleeping below the waves makes you feel nervous, the hotel has a reassuring array of security features to protect against typhoons, missile strikes and terrorist attacks – and will even manufacture its own clouds to protect its glassed-in guests from sunstroke.

▲ DUBAI MARINA AND MARINA WALK

Dubai Internet and Media cities

At the north end of Dubai Marina lie the twin business areas known, matter-of-factly, as Dubai Internet City and Dubai Media City. These two districts are typical of the way the Dubai government has encouraged foreign firms to set up offices in designated areas of the city under preferential commercial terms, obviating the bundles of red tape that have traditionally stood in the way of foreign investment in other parts of the Gulf (and, indeed, in other parts of Dubai). There's nothing really to see here, though travelling down the coastal road you'll notice an impressive number of large signs advertising the offices of international corporate heavyweights such as Microsoft, CNN and Reuters, along with numerous other overseas and local businesses (though the area's major landmark is actually the bizarre *Hard Rock Café* – a kind of miniature Gotham City-style skyscraper fronted by an enormous guitar – which sits next to Sheikh Zayed Road on the district's inland side). Occasional big-name rock concerts are held here at the Media City Amphitheatre.

Ibn Battuta Mall

Between interchanges 5 and 6, Sheikh Zayed Rd. Daily 10am–10pm (Wed–Fri until midnight). ⓦwww.ibnbattutamall.com. Situated way down along Sheikh Zayed Road south of the main marina area, the extraordinary new mile-long Ibn Battuta Mall is worth the trip out to the furthest reaches of the city suburbs to sample what is undoubtedly Dubai's wackiest shopping experience (which is saying something). The mall is themed in six different sections after some of the countries – Morocco, Analucia, Tunisia, Persia, India and China – visited by the famous Arab traveller Ibn Battuta, with all the architectural kitsch and caprice you'd expect. Highlights en route include a life-size elephant complete with mechanical mahout, a twilit Tunisian village and a full-size Chinese junk, while the lavishness of some of the decoration would seem more appropriate on a Rajput palace or a Persian grand mosque than a motorway mall. As so often in Dubai, the underlying concept may be naff, but it's carried through with such extravagance, and on such a scale, that it's difficult not to be at least slightly impressed – or appalled. In addition, the walk from one end of the elongated mall to the other is the most pleasant stroll you can have in Dubai's pedestrian-hating suburbs, especially in the heat of summer. For more on the mall's shops, see below.

Shops

Ibn Battuta Mall

Between interchanges 5 and 6, Sheikh Zayed Rd. Daily 10am–10pm (Wed–Fri until midnight). ⓦwww.ibnbattutamall.com. The Ibn Battuta-inspired decor at this new mall (see above) is so attention-grabbing that it's easy not to even notice the shops en route, though the three hundred-plus outlets cover all the usual retail bases, with plenty of fashion, jewellery and perfume outlets (wannabe

▼ LEGO SHOP, IBN BATTUTA MALL

Bollywood filmstars should check out the superb, if pricey, Indian designs at Mumbai Sé). Kids will enjoy the branch of the Toy Store (see p.121) located here, as well as the eye-catching little Lego Shop, with lots of games laid out to play, plus fun pick 'n' mix Lego pots for sale. There's also one of the city's best branches of the Magrudy's bookstore chain, plus an unusually good selection of places to eat and drink, including branches of Hatam (see p.74), the Lime Tree Café (p.112) and Japengo (p.111).

Restaurants

La Baie

Ritz Carlton ☎04-399 4000. Mon–Sat 7–11pm. This decidedly formal, old-school French-style restaurant would feel very odd in most parts of Dubai, but works well in the context of the *Ritz Carlton*'s rather patrician setting. The fine-dining menu features a very small range of so-called "progressive" European dishes, meaning things like fillet of cod with chorizo red wine compote and confit of fennel or eucalyptus-smoked Victorian lamb (but no vegetarian options). Beautiful food, though with mains from

145dh it's about twice the price of Gordon Ramsay's *Verre*.

BICE

Hilton Jumeirah Beach ☎04-399 1111. Daily noon–3pm & 7–11.30pm. Smooth modern Italian restaurant, generally reckoned the best in the southern city (although closed for refurbishment at the time of writing). Food includes tasty pizzas and pastas bursting with fresh ingredients and flavours (try the penne with sautéed chicken, shrimps, bell peppers julienne and creamy curry sauce), plus a mix of meat and seafood *secondi piatti*. Mains from around 60dh.

Buddha Bar

Grosvenor House ☎04-317 6000. Daily 7.30pm–2am (Thurs until 3pm). Modelled after the famous Parisian joint, this superb bar-restaurant is a sight in its own right: a huge, sepulchral space hung with dozens of red-lantern chandeliers and presided over by an enormous golden Buddha, with classic Buddha Bar soundtracks murmuring away in the background. The menu features a fine array of Japanese and pan-Asian cooking, with sushi and sashimi plates alongside Thai- and Chinese-inspired meat, seafood and vegetarian mains (from 90dh). Even if you don't eat here, it's worth coming in for a drink to sample the atmosphere and one of the bar's long, minty cocktails.

Eauzone

Arabian Courtyard, One&Only Royal Mirage ☎04-399 9999. Daily noon–3.30pm

▼ BUDDHA BAR

& 7–11.30pm. Arguably the most romantic restaurant in Dubai, with Arabian-tented tables dotted on miniature islands amidst the beautifully floodlit waters of one of the Royal Mirage's various swimming pools – which seems to transform by night into a luminous, palm-studded lagoon. The menu offers a fairly conservative, but generally well prepared, array of internationally themed meat and seafood dishes (plus a few vegetarian options), with mains like salt-roasted cornfed chicken or king prawns in chilli sauce. The only problem is getting a reservation. If you can't, you can always console yourself with a drink at the beautiful attached bar – just make sure you don't fall into the water on your way out. Mains from 85dh.

Indego

Grosvenor House ☎ 04-317 6000. Daily except Sat 7.30pm–midnight (Thurs until 1am). A super-stylish Indian restaurant under the stewardship of Michelin-starred chef Vineet Bhatia. Food comprises a spread of traditional and contemporary subcontinental cuisine, ranging from novelties like asparagus and goat's cheese samosas to more mainstream concoctions like malai kofta, lamb biriyani and chicken tikka, all superbly prepared and presented. Mains from around 80dh.

Mezzanine

Grosvenor House ☎ 04-317 6000. Daily except Fri 7pm–midnight (Thurs until 1am). Opened in 2006 under the management of Gary Robinson (former chef to Prince Charles), *Mezzanine* has rapidly established itself as the nearest challenger to Gordon Ramsey's *Verre* in Dubai's fine-dining stakes – and rather more interesting to look at too, with a quirkily designed pure-white interior dotted with brightly coloured armchairs. Robinson has now gone and his place taken (as of early 2007) by UK celebrity chef Gary Rhodes, whose seasonally changing menu of inventive modern European cuisine promises to uphold the restaurant's growing culinary credentials (as well as providing Dubai with yet another top chef with the initials GR). Mains from 100dh.

Nina's

Arabian Courtyard, One&Only Royal Mirage ☎ 04-399 9999. Mon–Sat 7–11.15pm. Dubai's most innovative Indian restaurant, this place gives a wonderful contemporary twist to the classic flavours and dishes of the subcontinent – and indeed sometimes seems to leave them behind completely. The

▼ ONE&ONLY ROYAL MIRAGE

menu ranges from traditional curries and tandooris to thoroughly outré concoctions like lamb dumplings and celery alongside frogs legs with rambutan, green peppercorn and basil, all delicately prepared and discreetly spiced so that the whole experience is more European fine dining than curry house blow-out. The sumptuous orange decor, complete with oddly mismatched chandeliers, red chinese lanterns and quasi-Moroccan arches, adds its own curious touch of hybrid magic. Mains from 55dh.

Ottoman

Grosvenor House ☎ 04-317 6000. Mon–Sat 8pm–1am. A slick Turkish restaurant offering an intriguing little bit of culinary time-travelling, using ancient recipes from Ottoman palace kitchens fine-tuned for contemporary tastes. Choose from a range of hot and cold starters such as stuffed grape leaves and pistachio-crusted shrimps before launching into an unusual list of mains stretching from vegetable-stuffed cabbage and swordfish kebab to pan-roasted boneless quail and Turkish *bouillabaisse*. Mains from 75dh.

Tagine

The Palace, One&Only Royal Mirage ☎ 04-399 9999. Tues–Sun 7–11.15pm. This sumptuous little Moroccan restaurant is a feast for both the eye and taste buds, the beautiful Moorish decor complemented by rich cooking ranging from starters including spicy harira soup, lamb's brain and pigeon pie, through to a delicious selection of tagines, sweetly flavoured with ingredients like honey, crushed almonds, lemon, red olives, raisins and apricot, plus a few kebabs and seafood options. There's also good live music, and friendly service from fetchingly jellaba'd waiters. Mains from 75dh.

Bars and shisha

Arabian Courtyard

Arabian Courtyard, One&Only Royal Mirage. Daily 7pm–12.30am. A beautiful Moroccan-style courtyard with fairy-lit palms and seating in pretty little open-side tented pavilions provides the magical setting for one of Dubai's most romantic shisha venues. Choose from sixteen varieties of hubbly-bubbly (around 35dh), plus simple Middle eastern snacks and mezze and a small selection of beers and cocktails. The Palace Courtyard, in the same hotel's The Palace wing, is very similar.

▼ ARABIAN COURTYARD

PLACES · Dubai Marina

Bar 44

44th floor,
Grosvenor House.
Daily from 6pm.
Perched atop
the soaring
Grosvenor House
hotel, this svelte
contemporary
bar offers
peerless
views of the
entire Marina
development,
with twinkling
high-rises
stretching
away in every
direction – as
memorable a
view of the
modern city
as you're likely

▲ ROOFTOP BAR

to get, short of climbing in a
helicopter. The drinks list is as
upmarket as the setting, with a
big selection of wallet-emptying
champagnes alongside cool
cocktails and other designer
tipples.

Barasti Bar

Le Meridien Mina Sehayi. One of
the Marina's most beguiling
spots for a drink and/or shisha
during the cooler winter
months, set on a terrace around
the hotel's floodlit pool, with
views out to sea. Closed at the
time of writing, but should have
reopened by the time you read
this.

Rooftop Bar

Arabian Courtyard, One&Only Royal
Mirage. Daily 5pm–1am. The most
romantic bar in the southern
city, this seductive, Arabian-
themed rooftop bar offers one
of Dubai's ultimate orientalist
fantasies, with Moroccan-
style pavilions scattered with
cushions, silver-tray tables and

other assorted ethnic artefacts,
while vaguely psychedelic
lighting and a smooth live
DJ add to the 1001 Nights
ambience. The downstairs
indoor bar is lovely too,
although the Arabian style is
slightly neutered by the banks
of TVs dotted about the place
catering to visiting footie fans.

Clubs

Kasbar

The Palace, One&Only Royal Mirage.
Daily except Sun 9pm–3am. 50dh,
hotel guests free. This very
superior-looking club shares
the opulent Moroccan styling
of the rest of the *Royal Mirage*
complex, spread over three
large floors, with the resident
DJ serving up a mixed menu of
house, techno, R&B, hip-hop
and Arabian fusion. Sometimes
lively, but at other times there's
more of a crowd and a better
atmosphere at the hotel's *Rooftop
Bar* (see opposite).

Sharjah

Just 10km down the coast from Dubai, the emirate of Sharjah seems at first sight like simply an extension of its more famous neighbour, with whose northern suburbs it seamlessly merges in an ugly concrete sprawl. The two cities may physically have fused into one, but culturally they remain very separate. Sharjah has a distinctively different flavour from Dubai, and the entire emirate has clung much more firmly to its traditional Islamic and Arabian culture, with none of Dubai's free-wheeling glitz and tourist fleshpots – and precious few tourists either, for that matter.

Sharjah's traditional Arabian values lie at the heart of the city's modest appeal. Self-styled "cultural capital" of the UAE, Sharjah compensates for its puritanical regime (see box on p.142) with a splendid array of museums devoted to various aspects of Islamic culture and local Emirati life, most of them housed in the so-called Heritage Area right in the city centre. These include the outstanding **Islamic Museum**, the excellent **Sharjah Art Gallery** and the quaint little **Al Hisn Fort**, along with more modest, but still interesting, exhibits at the **Bait Al Naboodah**, the **Calligraphy Museum** and

Transport to and around Sharjah

Regular **minibuses** (5dh) connect Deira's Gold Souk and Bur Dubai's Al Ghubaiba bus stations with the main bus terminal in Sharjah on Al Burj Avenue (just south of Al Hisn Fort), with departures roughly every 15–20min from early morning until late at night. Alternatively, a **taxi** from central Dubai to Sharjah will cost around 40–50dh. If you're staying outside central Dubai, you may as well catch a cab direct to Sharjah, since you won't save that much money (or any time) by taxi-ing to one of the bus stations and then picking up a minibus.

The main highway between Dubai and Sharjah is notorious for its massive **traffic jams**. Significantly lower rents in Sharjah mean that many people commute daily from Sharjah to Dubai, resulting in daily gridlock travelling into Dubai from around 7 to 10am and again from around 5 to 8pm travelling back to Sharjah. As a tourist, you'll be travelling in the opposite direction to most of the traffic, but the roads can still be horribly congested, and it's worth avoiding the peak hours, if possible, perhaps travelling to Sharjah mid-afternoon and returning in the evening.

A convenient alternative to travelling under your own steam is to take a **tour** of Sharjah. These are offered by most of the companies listed on p.187 and cost around 130–150dh, sometimes including a brief visit to the neighbouring emirates of Ajman as well.

There are plenty of **taxis in Sharjah** for short hops around the city. These are (or should be) metered, and slightly cheaper than those in Dubai, with a basic flag fare of 2.5dh.

Sharjah museum practicalities

Admission to Sharjah's various museums and Al Hisn Fort costs 5dh per museum; an alternative (and much better value) option is to purchase a **combined ticket** covering all these sites for just 15dh. Technically, you should be able to buy this ticket at any of the museums or the fort, though it's most easily done at the Islamic Museum, given that the other museums are often staffed by local Emiratis who may not speak any English. Museum **opening times** seem to change erratically. In theory, they're all meant to be open Saturday to Thursday from 8am to 8pm (Fri 5–8pm only); in practice, however, at the time of writing all but Al Hisn and the Islamic Museum were closed from 1pm to 5pm. This irritatingly long and inconvenient afternoon closure means that you'll either have to arrive early or stay late if you want to do the museums any sort of justice, and even then you'll be pressed for time.

the **Museum of Sharjah Heritage**. Other attractions include the sprawling **Blue Souk**, one of the largest in the UAE, and the **Souq Al Arsah**, one of the prettiest.

Al Hisn Fort

Al Burj Ave. Daily 8am–8pm (Fri 5–8pm only). 5dh. At the very heart of Sharjah on Al Burj Avenue, the modest little Al Hisn Fort is one of the traditional symbols of old Sharjah, formerly home to the ruling Al Qassimi family and the rallying-point in days gone by for all important city gatherings – though the low-lying fort is now rather ignominiously hemmed in by rows of unforgiveably ugly apartment blocks. The fact that the fort exists at all is entirely due to the current ruler of Sharjah, Sheikh Sultan Bin Mohammad Al Qassimi. In 1969, the young sheikh (then crown prince) was studying in Cairo when he heard that the fort was being demolished. Al Qassimi jumped onto the first available plane and returned to Sharjah post-haste to halt the destruction, only to discover that he had arrived too late to prevent most of the fort from being demolished, apart from a single tower.

Nothing daunted, he ordered the immediate rebuilding of the fort, whose reconstruction he personally supervised, using old photos and plans, and salvaging as much of the material of the demolished building – including its fine old wooden doors – as was possible.

The fort now houses an interesting museum devoted to the history of the emirate. There are a few displays in the rooms in the section of the fort around the entrance – including absorbing old film footage of

▼ AL HISN FORT

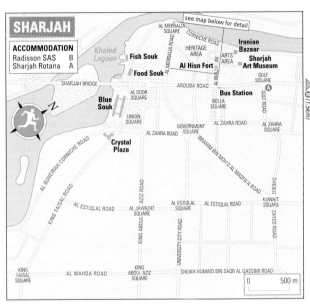

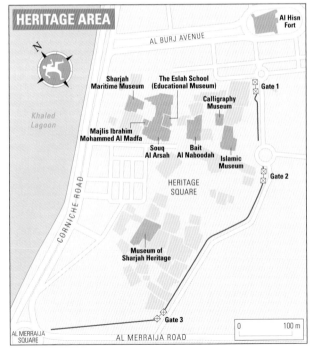

the fort and city – but most exhibits are housed in the rooms around the edge of the large central courtyard. These include the usual old coins, rifles and swords, along with a fascinating sequence of old photographs of Sharjah in the 1930s, among them shots of the Al Qassimi family, plus some wonderfully atmospheric pictures of camel trains, dhows and the old fish market – a reminder that, up until World War II, it was Sharjah, rather than Dubai, that was the leading commercial player in this part of the Gulf.

Heritage Area

Heading due west from Al Hisn Fort brings you to a long section of reconstructed old city wall marking the edge of Sharjah's extensive Heritage Area. This is where you'll find all the city's myriad museums (apart from the Art Museum), but even if you don't go into a single museum, the district is worth a visit for its attractively old-fashioned architecture, with dozens of meticulously restored traditional Emirati buildings scattered around expansive pedestrianized squares. Although not that large, the quarter can be suprisingly disorienting; there's a very useful large-scale map of it in the little brochure which you should be given when you buy a ticket to the museums. The entire area is nicest towards dusk and after dark; during the day, the lack of shade and wind means that it can get oppressively hot.

Islamic Museum

Heritage Area. Daily 8am–8pm (Fri 5–8pm only). 5dh. Easily the finest of the Heritage Area's many museums, the Islamic Museum offers a superb collection of world-class artefacts from around the Islamic world, beautifully displayed and backed up by excellent interpretive panels. The Islamic theme is most obvious in the museum's opening section, devoted to a fascinating (if slightly baffling) explanation of the complicated rituals performed by pilgrims to Mecca, along with a huge curtain, intricately worked in gold and silver thread on black cloth, which formerly shrouded the Ka'bah itself.

Next follows (walking anticlockwise) a huge and beautifully presented selection of coins from the early Islamic Umayyad (labelled "Ommid") and Abbasid dynasties through to the Ottoman era – much more interesting than it sounds, and impressive proof of the wide-ranging commercial contacts that even this relatively

▼ ISLAMIC MUSEUM

▲ BAIT AL NABOODAH

far-flung outpost enjoyed with the central lands of the Islamic caliphate. Beyond here, further rooms are devoted to beautifully crafted items of metalware, glassware and old wooden furniture, plus intricate astrolabes, weapons, armour, and some magnificent manuscripts including old Korans and copies of letters written by the prophet Mohammed himself. Look out, too, for the first-ever map of the then known world (ie Eurasia), created by Moroccan cartographer Al Shereef Al Idrisi in 1099 – a surprisingly accurate document given its very early date, although slightly baffling at first sight since it's oriented upside down, with south at the top.

Bait Al Naboodah

Heritage Area. Daily 8am–1pm & 5–8pm (Fri 5–8pm only). 5dh.
Situated in an atmospheric old traditional house opposite Souq Al Arsah, the Bait Al Naboodah (also known as the Sharjah Heritage Museum, but not to be confused with the Museum of Sharjah Heritage – see p.144) offers an interesting re-creation of life in a traditional family house in Sharjah in years gone by. The main attraction is the rambling two-storey building itself, flanking a spacious central courtyard, its exposed coral-brick walls and wooden verandahs supported by incongruous Greek-style wooden Ionic columns. Only the rooms on the ground floor

Sharjah's Islamic laws

Sharjah is infamous amongst expats for its hardline Islamic stance on matters of dress, alcohol and the relationship between the sexes. Alcohol is banned (making it the only dry emirate in the UAE); the wearing of tight or revealing clothing in public areas is likely to get you into trouble with the locals or police; while couples "not in a legally acceptable relationship" are (according to the emirate's so-called "decency laws" of 2001) not even meant to be alone in public together. In practice, unmarried Western couples behaving in a respectable manner are extremely unlikely to experience any hassle, though there have been reports of relatively powerless Asian expat workers being reported for alleged indiscretions by the city's moral mafia and being carted off into police detention – in 2005 an unmarried Indian couple were sentenced to a year's imprisonment for the "crime" of kissing in the back of a taxi.

are open, each furnished in traditional Gulf style, with a string of bedrooms featuring the usual old-fashioned wooden beds and piles of cushions, the walls decorated with rifles and old radios, along with a couple of rustic kitchens, a small *majlis* (with a few pictures of the Al Naboodah family who once lived here) and a traditional games room with quaint local toys.

Souk Al Arsah

Heritage Area. Shops open daily from around 9am to 9pm or later. Immediately north of the Bait Al Naboodah, the Souk Al Arsah (or Souq Al Arsa, according to the sign) is far and away the prettiest souk in Sharjah, if not the whole of the UAE. The souk is centred around an atmospheric central pillared courtyard, flanked by carpet shops and the quaint little *Al Arsaha Coffee Shop* (see p.145), beyond which radiates an intriguing tangle of alleyways – surprisingly disorienting, despite their miniature scale. The coral-stone buildings are stuffed with all sorts of colourful local handicrafts, from Persian rugs and Omani silver to Indian textiles and stuffed camels.

Tucked away around the back (north) side of the Souq Al Arsah, the **Majlis Ibrahim Mohammed Al Madfa** (according to the sign – or the Majlis Ibrahim Al Midfaa,

according to the tourist brochure) is one of the prettiest buildings in the Heritage Area. You can't go inside, but it's worth having a look at the building itself, topped by a quaint little round wind tower, said to be the only one in the UAE.

Calligraphy Museum

Heritage Area. Daily 8am–1pm & 5–8pm (Fri 5–8pm only). 5dh. The attractive but rather enigmatic Calligraphy Museum (officially called the Museum for the Art of Arabic Calligraphy and Ornamentations) houses a huge collection of Arabic calligraphic artworks, including outstanding examples of traditional and contemporary calligraphic design, from lines of blocky Kufic script to extravagantly florid rosette patterns and modern renderings in acrylic on canvas, all consumately executed and beautifully displayed. Sadly, the total lack of signage or any kind of guide or guidebook means that the exhibits' meaning, function and provenance remains a complete mystery, at least for non-Arabic speakers.

▼ CALLIGRAPHY MUSEUM

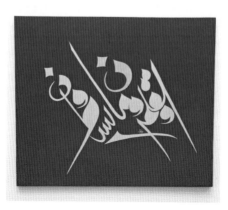

▲ SHARJAH ART MUSEUM

Museum of Sharjah Heritage

Heritage Area. Daily 8am–1pm &
5–8pm (Fri 5–8pm only). 5dh. The
Museum of Sharjah Heritage
(not to be confused with the
Bait Al Naboodah, see above)
offers a comprehensive overview
of the culture and commerce
of traditional Sharjah, the
wide-ranging displays backed
up by interesting interpretive
panels (although the English
translations are amusingly
erratic). The museum comprises
a sequence of rooms each
focusing on a different subject
of local interest, and although
it's all a bit didactic and school-
mistressy compared to other
museums in the city, serious
students of Gulf history will
find much of interest. Exhibits
include a display of the coins
and banknotes used before
the establishment of a unified
UAE currency in 1973 (mainly
Indian rupees issued under
British rule); a big array of
unusual and colourful colonial-
era stamps (Sharjah didn't issue
its own stamps until 1963, and
didn't even have a post office
until 1965); a room showing
the items used in a traditional
Gulf classroom; a folk arts
room with musical instruments
including drums, ouds and
strange wind instruments; plus
rooms devoted to popular
medicine (with displays of herbs
and descriptions of their uses),
perfumes, cosmetics, clothing
and textiles.

Sharjah Art Museum

Heritage Area. Daily 8am–1pm &
5–8pm (Fri 5–8pm only). 5dh. The
excellent Sharjah Art Museum
is one of the city's highlights
– albeit one that seems totally
incongruous in the context
of this apparently provincial
and Islamic-leaning emirate
(especially so given traditional
Islamic strictures against
the painting of humans and
animals). The first section of the
museum (upstairs) is devoted to
a stunning collection of painting
by nineteenth-century European
artists' depicting life in Islamic
lands. The centrepiece of this
section is a wonderful selection
of lithographs by Scottish artist
David Roberts (1796–1864),
whose celebrated *Sketches
in the Holy Land and Syria*,
based on a journey Roberts
made through the Middle
East in 1838–39, remains one
of the quintessential pictorial
expressions of Orientalism,
with picturesquely robed and
turbaned natives reclining in
carefully staged postures amidst
even more picturesque mosques,
forts and assorted Arabian ruins,
all executed with a mix of
immaculate draughtsmanship
and romantic whimsy.

At the back of the ground
floor, the **Sharjah Museum**

of Contemporary Arab Art houses an extensive collection of works by artists from across the Arab world since 1975 in a wide variety of media and styles – an impressively large collection, even if most of the works on display are competent rather than memorable. There are also assorted unlabelled contemporary pieces (including some quirky installations) on the opposite side of the top floor, while temporary exhibitions are held downstairs.

The museum is tucked away in the backstreets east of Al Hisn Fort. From the fort, head north to the waterfront, then turn right and continue for around 250m, past a small Iranian market and the *Fen Restaurant* until you reach a sign pointing inland to the Arts Area; head about 50m inland from here to reach the gallery, a large building topped by wind towers.

Blue Souk

A kilometre west of the city centre along the Corniche, the huge Blue Souk (officially known as the Central Market) is Sharjah's most visited and photographed attraction, occupying an enormous, eye-catching and ungainly pair of buildings which – despite the myriad wind towers, blue tiling and other Arabian decorative touches – look like nothing so much as a large railway station. The souk is best known for its numerous carpet shops, which stock a vast range of Persian and other rugs at prices that are generally significantly cheaper than in Dubai. If you're not after rugs, there are plenty of electronics, clothes, jewellery and handicrafts shops (although Souq Al Arsah has a better selection of Arabian souvenirs) to browse, though the quality and range of goods on offer is fairly underwhelming compared to Dubai.

Restaurants and cafés

Al Arsaha Coffee Shop

Souq Al Arsah. Daily 9am–9pm. At the heart of the pretty Souq Al Arsah, this quaint little café offers a beguiling window on local life, with rattan-covered walls, old wooden doors and windows and colourful tables covered in big Lipton's tea logos. It's a good place to grab a glass of mint tea or a cup of coffee,

▼ BLUE SOUK

▲ KORAN ROUNDABOUT, SHARJAH

and there's also a small range of simple birianis and meat dishes at lunchtime and after dark.

Crystal Plaza

Corniche Road, immediately south of the Blue Souk. Sharjah's fanciest mall, set in eye-catching pyramidal glass-covered towers, the Crystal Plaza offers a range of low-key eating options, including a ground-floor pizzeria, ice-cream parlour and coffee shop, as well as a rather moribund food court upstairs centred around the *Danial Restaurant*, which offers a mix

of Middle Eastern and buffet fare. It's all pretty unexciting compared to the big Dubai malls, but given that there's nowhere to eat or drink in the Blue Souk itself (bar a few modest coffee stalls), it offers a convenient pit stop, if not much else.

Radisson SAS

Corniche Rd ☎06-565 7777, ⓦwww.sharjah .radissonsas.com. A ten-minute taxi ride east of the city centre, the *Radisson* has Sharjah's best selection of eating outlets, including the *China Garden*, *Shahzadeh* (Persian and Moroccan) and the *Café at the Falls* (international), located in the hotel's striking, tropical-rainforest-themed atrium.

Sharjah Rotana

Al Arouba St ☎06-563 7777, ⓦwww .rotana.com. In a conveniently central location about 500m east of the centre, this run-of-the-mill business hotel has several passable (if not particularly inspiring) places to eat, including the *Al Dar* restaurant, with international buffet and à la carte option, plus a lobby café and the *Aquarius Snack Bar*.

Al Ain

For a complete change of pace and scenery, a day-trip out to the desert city of Al Ain, some 130km inland from Dubai on the border with Oman, offers the perfect antidote to the rip-roaring pace of life on the coast. The only large inland settlement in the UAE, Al Ain – and the twin city of Buraimi, on the Omani side of the border – grew up around the extensive oasis that still forms one of the modern city's most attractive features. It served as an important staging post on trading routes between Oman and the Gulf, a fact attested to by the numerous forts that dot the town and its hinterland, and by the rich archeological remains found in the vicinity, evidence of continuous settlement here for perhaps as much as four thousand years.

Al Ain is actually part of **Abu Dhabi Emirate**, and celebrated as the birthplace of the UAE's much-loved ruler, Sheikh Zayed Bin Sultan Al Nahyan (d.2004). The modern city is sprawling, disorienting and largely featureless, but if you've spent long in Dubai you might enjoy Al Ain's rather somnolent atmosphere – which can seem either pleasantly crashed out or maddeningly provincial, depending on your mood – and verdant, palm-fringed streets, evidence of Sheikh Zayed's well-known obsession with "greening" the desert. The city's slightly elevated position also makes it a popular summer retreat for wealthy Emiratis on account of its slightly cooler temperatures (though, in truth, you're unlikely to notice much

Transport to and around Al Ain

Minibuses (20dh) run hourly between Al Ain's bus station and Al Ghubaiba Bus Station in Bur Dubai; the journey takes around 1hr 30min, unless you get stuck in the Dubai morning or evening rush hours, in which case it'll take more like 2hr.

Al Ain is quite spread out, so you're likely to have recourse to **taxis** to get around (there are plenty on the streets, and you'll probably be hooted at constantly by the drivers of empty cabs). Taxis in Al Ain are painted gold and white, with quaint Islamic-style green-pointed signs on top; they're metred (or should be), with a flag fare of 2.50dh. Taxis in Oman are orange and white and are unmetred, so you'll have to agree a fare before setting off, which can be difficult, since few of the drivers speak English. Taxi drivers aren't usually willing to take you across the border, so if you're heading out to Buraimi you'll probably have to pick up one cab to the border, and another one on the far side. Or just walk (which takes around 30min).

A convenient alternative is to take a **tour** to Al Ain. These are offered by virtually all the operators listed on p.187 and cost around 200–250dh.

Getting oriented in Al Ain

Al Ain can be a remarkably disorientating place at the best of times, especially when you've just arrived and haven't yet got your bearings. Having alighted at the bus station, turn to face the long low line of sheds housing the vegetable market (see p.151) and then head right, walking for around 100m until you see a large roundabout, adorned with a big coffeepot sculpture, ahead. Just before reaching this roundabout, veer right, across a dusty car parking area, past the entrance to the Al Ain Oasis (see p.151), immediately past which are the Al Ain Museum and Livestock Market (see p.150).

difference). There are plenty of low-key attractions here to fill up a day. The **Al Ain Museum** is one of the best in the region, while the nearby **Al Ain Oasis**, the **livestock and camel markets** and the **Al Ain Souk** all merit a look. You can also hop across the border with Oman to visit the city of Buraimi, home to the fine **Al Khandaq fort**, while the largely unspoilt desert scenery that surrounds the town is home to a further smattering of attractions including the **Hili Archeological Park** and the craggy summit of **Jebel Hafeet**.

Camel Souk (3 km), Hili Gardens (6 km) & Dubai (123 km)

Jebel Hafeet (30 km)

0   500m

AL AIN & BURAIMI

OMAN

EATING & DRINKING	
Al Mallah	3
Mandarin	2
Pizza Hut	1
The Hut	1

Buraimi Souk

Al Khandaq Fort

BURAIMI

N

Border Checkpoint

SHAKHBOOT BIN SULTAN ST

ALI IBN ABI TALEB ST

GLOBE R/A

BURAIMI R/A

SA'ARIDEEN AL AYYUBI ST

ABU BAKR AL SIDDIQ ST

AL AIN

KHALIFA IBN ZAYED ST

CLOCK-TOWER SULTAN ST

ZAYED BIN R/A

Al Ain Souk

COFFEEPOT R/A

OTHMAN BIN AFFAN ST

OMAR BIN AL KHATTAN ST

Bus Station

Al Ain Oasis

AL AIN ST

Al Ain Rotana

Jahili Fort & Park

Al Ain Museum & Sultan Bin Zayed Fort

ZAYED BIN SULTAN ST

AL SALAM ST

SULTAN BIN ZAYED AL AWWAL ST

U.A.E.

Livestock Market

Hilton Al Ain

ACCOMMODATION	
Al Ain Rotana	A
Hilton Al Ain	B
Intercontinental Al Ain	C

KHALID BIN SULTAN ST

/2 km

Al Ain Museum

Al Muraba Roundabout. Tues–Thurs, Sat & Sun 8.30am–7.30pm, Fri 3–7.30pm, Mon closed. 3dh. ®www.aam.gov.ae. The Al Ain Museum is one of the more rewarding in the UAE, and makes a logical starting point for any tour of the city. The museum is in two parts. The first has extensive displays covering various aspects of local life, with a diverse collection of exhibits including curiosities such as implements used during circumcisions and the shoulder bones of cows, used by school pupils as writing slates, along with a more predictable selection of old Korans, fine antique silver jewellery (including an interesting necklace made from Austrian Maria Theresa silver thalers, once the standard currency in this part of the Gulf), perfume bottles, farming and cooking equipment, weapons (including fine old khanjars) and some

PLACES

▼ AL AIN MUSEUM

marvellous photos of Abu Dhabi Emirate in 1960s. There's also a mishmash of gifts presented to Sheikh Zayed over the years by luminaries including Eygyptian president Gamal Nasser (a pair of large embossed plates) and the celebrated female Palestinian freedom fighter Lyla Khaled (a bullet).

The second section offers a comprehensive overview of the archeology of the UAE, including extensive artefacts from the main archeological sites such as Umm an Nar, near Abu Dhabi, and Jebel Hafeet and Hili (see p.153), just outside Al Ain. Most of the exhibits are fairly unexciting – pots, seals, fragments of arrow heads and other stone fragments – but they're well displayed and explained, offering an interesting picture of local cultural and commercial links right back to the Sumerian era.

▼ LIVESTOCK MARKET

Sultan Bin Zayed Fort

Right next to the museum (same hours and ticket), the Sultan Bin Zayed Fort (or Eastern Fort) is one of the eighteen or so forts scattered around Al Ain and the surrounding desert. The picturesque three-towered structure is best known as the birthplace of Sheikh Zayed Bin Sultan Al Nahyan (ruled 1966–2004), the much-loved ruler of Abu Dhabi and first president of the UAE, who oversaw the transformation of the emirate from impoverished Arabian backwater into today's oil-rich contemporary city-state. The fort houses a superb collection of 1960s and 1970s black-and-white photos from around the Gulf, while the picturesque little courtyard at its centre is dotted with a trio of trees and a couple of little traditional palm-thatched *barasti* huts – humble beginnings for the sheikh who would subsequently become one of the world's richest men.

Livestock Market

Immediately behind the museum lies the city's rough-and-ready Livestock Market, an attractively rustic-looking place, with plaintively mooing, bleating and clucking livestock penned up in the backs of long lines of collapsed pick-up trucks. It's liveliest in the early morning, up to around 9am, when locals come to haggle over anything from chickens to cows. At other times things can be pretty sleepy, though it's still worth a quick look.

▲ AL AIN OASIS

Al Ain Oasis

Daily 24hr. Free. On the other side of Al Ain Museum on the way back into town, a large arch – signed "Welcome to the Al Ain Oasis (no entry except for owners and tourists)" – leads into the beautiful Al Ain Oasis. This is easily the most idyllic spot in town, with a tangle of little walled lanes running between densely planted stands of date palms, their roots fed with traditional *falaj* irrigation channels (though they're only filled with water during the hot summer months) – a wonderfully peaceful little spot, the silence only broken by the calls to prayer from the two mosques nestled amongst the palms, and pleasantly cool as well.

Al Ain Souk

Immediately in front of the bus station, the Al Ain Souk is home to the city's main meat, fruit and vegetable market. Housed in a long, functional warehouse-style building, the souk is stocked with the usual picturesque piles of produce (along with the dangling carcasses of animals in the meat section), prettiest at the west end of the souk, where Indian traders sit enthroned amidst huge mounds of fruit and veg. The souk attracts a colourful

▼ AL AIN SOUK

cast of characters, including striking Emirati and Omani men with splendid beards and big white turbans, while heavily veiled and Bedouin women are also often seen – a much more authentically Arabian spectacle compared to the meat and vegetable souk in Dubai.

Buraimi

The border with Oman lies about 1km north of central Al Ain, beyond which lies the contiguous Omani city of Buraimi. You're allowed to cross the border freely – there are no visa requirements if you're just going into Buraimi – though pedantic UAE border officials may ask you to explain your movements; just say you're visiting Al Khandaq Fort, be as polite as possible and try to remember to take your passport with you (though even without it you shouldn't be stopped from entering Oman). The Omani side of the border is not that obviously different from the UAE – less green and a bit more run-down, perhaps, though the endless concrete ribbon development is pretty much identical with that in Al Ain. The most striking difference between the two countries is the sight of Omani men performing the sort of jobs – like driving taxis and working in restaurants – that are usually carried out by expat Indians and Pakistanis in the UAE. If you're expecting Oman to arrive in a blaze of picturesque Arabian splendour, however, you'll be disappointed.

Easily the most impressive sight in Buraimi is the immaculately restored **Al Khandaq Fort**, about 1km beyond the border. Dating back to at least 1788, perhaps earlier, this is a relatively large and complex structure compared to the forts on the UAE side of the border, with a wide moat (dry), a double set of enclosing bastions and finely carved turrets and battlements. The fort is apparently sometimes opened to visitors, but exactly when this might happen is unclear.

A couple of hundred metres past the fort, the so-called **Buraimi Souk** occupies a pair of buildings both built

▼ AL KHANDAQ FORT, BURAIMI

▲ UAE BORDER SIGN, AL AIN

to vaguely resemble Omani forts. The one nearest to Al Khandaq is manned exclusively by Indian traders selling fruit and veg, and there's a low-key string of craft shops by the entrance, though the whole place is usually pretty comatose. Just beyond here, a second building attracts a more mixed crowd: veiled local women sell spices and Omani men haggle over rifles in its central courtyard, while Indian traders flog low-grade household items out of the string of small shops in the aisles to either side.

The Camel Souk

On the edge of Al Ain, the atmospheric Camel Souk (actually just a series of pens in the open desert) is one of the city's most evocative Arabian sights, with dozens of dromedaries lined up for sale and a lively crowd of local camel-fanciers haggling over the beast of their choice. Unfortunately, most of the action happens early in the morning (before 9am), meaning that if you're day-tripping from Dubai you're unlikely to arrive early enough to get a real flavour of the place, although some very low-key trading continues until around noon.

Jahili Fort

Near the *Al Ain Rotana* hotel on the west side of town, the Jahili Fort, built in 1898, is one of the finest traditional buildings in the Al Ain area, with an impressively battlemented main tower. You can't go in, but you're free to explore the verdant surrounding gardens (daily 9am–10pm; 1dh).

Hili Gardens and Archeological Park

Daily 9am–10pm. 1dh. Further afield, the Hili Gardens and Archeological Park, about 8km north of the city, is the site of one of the most important archeological finds in the UAE (many finds from here are displayed in the Al Ain Museum, which also provides a good explanation of their significance). The main surviving building is the so-called Great Hili Tomb (though it may actually have been some kind of temple), dating from the third century BC, a diminutive little circular structure decorated with a quaint primitive carving of animals and humans. The adjacent Grand Garden Tomb yielded over two hundred skeletons when excavated.

Jebel Hafeet

If you have your own vehicle (or are prepared to stump up the taxi fare), the soaring 1180-metre summit of Jebel Hafeet (or Hafit), 30km south of Al Ain on the Omani border, offers peerless views over the surrounding Hajar mountains and is a popular local retreat with Emiratis wanting to escape the heat of the desert below.

Restaurants and cafés

Eating in Al Ain is basically a choice between the numerous unpretentious cafés in the city centre and the various restaurants in the city's three five-star hotels. Many of the city-centre restaurants are run by and cater to Al Ain's sizeable Pakistani community, serving basic north Indian staples and breads at rock-bottom prices.

There's also a good cluster of slightly more upmarket places around Globe Roundabout, on the northern edge of the city centre. These include *Al Mallah*, a simple little shwarma joint which serves up good-sized portions of tasty Lebanese fare, and the nearby *Mandarin* coffee shop and *The Hut* café, both cosy spots for a (non-alocholic) drink and a snack or light meal. All these places are open daily for lunch and dinner.

For something a bit smarter you'll need to head out to one of the city's trio of five-star hotels. The **Al Ain Rotana**, about 1km west of the city centre, hosts a branch of the ever-popular *Trader Vic's* (see p.103) and the better-than-average *Min Zaman* Lebanese restaurant, while the **Hilton Al Ain**, 1km south of the Al Ain Museum, is home to the stylish *Al Khayam* Persian restaurant (closed Sun). Further afield, the **InterContinental** hotel, about 4km east of the city centre, is home to various restaurants, including the chic Italian *Luce*, probably the most stylish venue in town. Mains generally run around 40–50dh at all these places, and all serve alcohol.

Abu Dhabi

The capital of the UAE, Abu Dhabi is the very model of a modern Gulf petro-city, thoroughly contemporary, shamelessly wealthy and decidedly staid. Abu Dhabi's lightning change from obscure Arabian fishing village into modernist city-state within the past thirty years is perhaps the most dramatic of all the stories of oil-driven transformation that dot the region, and although the city's endless glass-fronted high-rises and multi-lane highways can seem fairly uninspiring on first aquaintance, locals take understandable pride in their home town's remarkable recent metamorphosis.

For the casual visitor, modern Abu Dhabi is mainly interesting for the contrasts it presents with its more famous neighbour – an Arabian Washington versus Dubai's Las Vegas. Many visitors enjoy the city's far more laid-back and traditional way of life, and even as a day-tripper you're likely to sense something of Abu Dhabi's very different cultural flavour. Specific sights are relatively thin on the ground, it must be said, and much of the pleasure of a visit lies in wandering through the city centre and along the handsome waterfront Corniche and getting a feel for a city which is, in many ways, far more representative of

▲ STREET SCULPTURES, AIRPORT ROAD

Transport to and around Abu Dhabi

Regular (cramped) **minibuses** and more comfortable **express buses** run between Abu Dhabi's main bus station, about 3km inland from the Cultural Foundation, to Al Ghubaiba Bus Station in Bur Dubai from early in the morning until late at night. The journey costs 30dh in both buses and minibuses and is meant to take just 1hr 30min, but can easily stretch up to 2hr, or longer if the traffic is bad.

Abu Dhabi's various attractions are very spread out. There are plenty of **taxis** around town; they should all be metred (flag fare 2.50dh), although drivers are sometimes reluctant to switch them on, in which case it's best to find another cab.

A convenient alternative is to take a **tour** from Dubai. Many of the companies listed on p.187 offer Abu Dhabi day-trips, generally costing around 200–250dh.

ABU DHABI

EATING & DRINKING
Art Cauldron Café	4
Beach Rotana Hotel	3
Delma Café	2
Hilton Abu Dhabi	1

the contemporary UAE than Dubai. The city's **Cultural Foundation** and adjacent **Al Hosn Fort** are worth a quick look, however, as is the fine **UAE Heritage Village**, offering superb views of Abu Dhabi's sprawling waterfront. Perhaps the city's most memorable attraction is the vast new **Emirates Palace Hotel**, intended to provide Abu Dhabi with an architectural icon to rival Dubai's *Burj Al Arab* – although the contrast between the *Burj*'s futuristic fantasy and Abu Dhabi's far more conservative, quasi-Arabian new landmark speaks volumes about these two very different cities.

The Cultural Foundation

Corner of Hamdan St and Sheikh Rashid St. Sun–Thurs 8am–3pm & 5–10pm, Fri & Sat 9am–noon & 5–9pm. ℡02-621 5300, ⊛www.cultural.org.ae/e. More or less at the very centre of Abu Dhabi, the city's sleek modern Cultural Foundation hosts various collections including the National Library and Archives and offers a pleasantly cool and peaceful retreat from the city outside. Casual visitors will usually find something going on here: regular (free) temporary exhibitions, usually with a local or Islamic theme, are held downstairs, while there are a few other exhibits dotted around the corridors, and artisans can often be found working upstairs by the pleasant *Delma Cafe* (see p.161). There are also regular film screenings and classical music concerts in the evening.

Qasr Al Hosn

Right next to the Cultural Foundation sits the venerable old Qasr Al Hosn fort of 1793, the oldest building in Abu Dhabi, and formerly home to the city's rulers. The large and rather plain whitewashed structure is of no particular architectural distinction, though the rambling battlemented walls, dotted with a few quaint watchtowers, are modestly pretty, as are the surrounding palm-studded gardens. You can sometimes go inside the fort (if someone's left the front door open), though there's not really much to see apart from a rather unprepossessing cluster of modern-looking buildings.

Immediately north of the Cultural Foundation, Sheikh Rashid Street (also known as Airport Road) is home to an arresting sequence of oversized **sculptures**, including a vast canon, enormous perfume bottle and gargantuan coffee pot – an endearingly quirky contrast to the drab surrounding architecture.

▼ VIEW FROM THE CULTURAL FOUNDATION

▲ WATERFRONT

The Corniche

Driving through the modern city's suburban sprawl, it's easy not to notice the fact that Abu Dhabi is actually built on an island, rather than on the mainland itself. The city's location amidst the balmy waters of the Gulf is best appreciated from the waterfront Corniche, which runs for the best part of 5km along Abu Dhabi's western edge. It's lined by a long line of glass-clad high-rises and five-star hotels, which encapsulate the modern city's internationalist credentials and provide Abu Dhabi with its most memorable views (although the entire waterfront is perhaps best appreciated from the UAE Heritage Village or Marina Mall on the opposite side of the waters). The Corniche is also a popular spot with local residents catching (or shooting) the breeze, particularly towards dusk, when its Gulf-side walkways fill up with a diverse crowd of promenading Emiratis, jogging Europeans and picnicking Indians – a perfect snapshot of modern Abu Dhabi in miniature.

The Louvre and the Guggenheim in Abu Dhabi

Though it may currently be playing second-fiddle to neighbouring Dubai in the global tourism stakes, Abu Dhabi has recently announced bold plans to make up lost ground on its rival emirate in the race to become one of the world's must-visit destinations in the 21st century. At the centre of Abu Dhabi's strategic vision is the new $27 billion cultural district to be developed on the currently uninhabited island of **Saadiyat** ("Isle of Happiness"), a few kilometres offshore. The complex will comprise a mix of luxury hotels, the inevitable golf courses and (yet another) "iconic seven-star hotel". The most exciting aspect of the scheme, however, are the plans for a string of top-notch international **museums** to be located on the island – a rather more high-brow alternative to the fun-focused pleasuredromes which are likely to form the mainstay of Dubai's future development.

Abu Dhabi's new plans have already resulted in two spectacular cultural coups, unveiled at the end of 2006. The first was the announcement that the **Guggenheim Foundation** had signed a deal to build an enormous new museum, due to open in 2012 and designed by stellar architect Frank Gehry, the creative brains behind the celebrated Guggenheim Museum in Bilbao. News of the Guggenheim scoop, however, was rapidly overshadowed by the even more spectacular announce-ment that a new branch of **The Louvre** would be opening on the island, housed in a huge flying saucer-shaped museum designed by acclaimed French architect Jean Nouvel, and slated to open at around the same time as the Guggenheim.

▲ EMIRATES PALACE HOTEL

Emirates Palace Hotel

Corniche West Street ☎02-690 9000, ⓦwww.emiratespalace.com.

At the far western end of the Corniche lies the city's newest and perhaps most spectacular tourist attraction, the *Emirates Palace Hotel* (opened in 2005), built to rival Dubai's *Burj Al Arab* and provide Abu Dhabi with a similar iconic architectural signature – it even claims the same "seven-star" rating as the Burj, although with rather less conviction. In fact, the *Emirates Palace* is a far more traditional and less original beast than its Dubaian rival – a sprawling, sand-coloured quasi-Arabian complex that is more kitsch Hollywood film set than architectural marvel. And although it's undeniably impressive, if only for its sheer size (it's 1km long) and opulence (114 domes, 140 elevators, 2000 members of staff, and so on), it lacks the charm and style of similar Arabian-themed places in Dubai, while much of the exterior looks strangely plain and even a little bit cheap – ironic, really, given that the hotel is believed to have

Abu Dhabi will pay an estimated $1.3 billion for rights to the Louvre's collection, parts of which will be shipped out on a temporary basis to fill the new museum – it's estimated that around three hundred French works will be loaned out during the museum's first year of opening, a figure that is likely to shrink over time as the museum acquires its own collection. French officials have promised that the Paris Louvre is not about to sell any of its 35,000-piece collection, though it's also worth remembering that the Louvre currently owns around ten thousand Islamic artefacts, most of which are now in storage because of a lack of exhibition space. It's also worth noting that potential curators at both museums have been at pains to emphasize that they will not be exhibiting pictures of nudes or religious subjects that might inflame local cultural sensibilities.

Many commentators have claimed that the new museum has less to do with cultural issues than with France's desire to buttress its political and economic interests in the Arab world, though no less a figure than Jacques Chirac has sought to underline the project's transcontinental cultural significance, stating that the museum is a symbol of a "world which considers the clash of civilizations the most dangerous trap of our time". Whatever the underlying philosophy, both the Guggenheim and the Louvre promise to add a fascinating new cultural incentive to visitors to the Gulf – and perhaps even to threaten Dubai's so-far unchallenged touristic hegemony.

been the most expensive ever built (at a rumoured cost of US$3 billion or so). The interior is all gold-leaf, chandeliers and European-style chintz – incredibly lavish, though hardly original. Non-guests can usually pop in for a meal at one of the hotel's numerous restaurants or cafés (see the website for details) without a booking, though it may be best to make a reservation in advance; alternatively, drop in for one of the hotel's sumptuous afternoon teas (120–260dh).

UAE Heritage Village

Sat–Wed 8am–1pm & 5–9pm, Thurs 5–9pm. Dramatically situated on the Corniche-facing side of the Breakwater – a small protuberance of reclaimed land jutting out from the southern end of the Corniche – the UAE Heritage Village offers a well-presented look into the traditional customs and cultures of the region, although there's little to surprise you if you've already visited similar places elsewhere in the Emirates. The "village" occupies a quaint little development with plenty of picturesque little *barasti*

▼ TRADITIONAL SHOP, HERITAGE VILLAGE

huts and illuminated palm trees – particularly pretty at night – while the views over the water to the Corniche are spectacular. There's a decent little **museum** here, housed in a miniature replica fort, with displays of traditional dress and a fine collection of old silver jewellery, along with more mundane items including cooking and agricultural implements, weaponry, currency, pearling equipment and a few curios ranging from a camel harnesss to a stuffed puffer fish. Opposite the museum is a string of **workshops** where local artisans practise traditional skills such as carpentry, glassworking, pottery and brass-working; the so-called "old market", however, is basically just a few ladies flogging cheap handicrafts out of a line of *barasti* huts.

The Heritage Village is right next to the enormous **flagpole**, which can be seen for miles around; at 123m, this was until quite recently claimed to be the tallest in the world, until topped by one in Jordan in 2003 (which, ironically, was actually made in Dubai) – although in fact there's another one in North Korea that outstrips both of them by over 30m.

Marina Mall

Sat–Thurs 10am–10pm (Wed & Thurs until 11pm), Fri 2–10pm. On a small headland facing the southern end of the Corniche, the large modern Marina Mall is the city's top shopping destination. Although pretty uninspiring compared to any of the top Dubai malls, it does offer sweeping views over to the Corniche and its long line of glittering, glass-faced high-rises (while its food court offers a useful pit stop before or after a visit to the UAE Heritage Village). For a bird's-eye view, head up to the new *Burj Al Marina* tower (free) at the back of the mall (under construction at the time of writing, though it should have opened by the time you read this), complete with viewing platform and the obligatory revolving restaurant on top.

Restaurants and cafés

Art Cauldron Café

Al Falah St, opposite the Navy Gate. Daily 11am–midnight. This funky little basement café offers a rare splash of bohemia in po-faced Abu Dhabi, with quirky decor, a good range of international food – pastas, salads, sandwiches and the like (mains from around 35dh) – and a huge range of coffees. It's a bit tricky to find, however. Head to Navy Gate on Al Falah Street, then walk round the back of the building opposite and head down the stairs.

Beach Rotana Hotel

Tourist Club Area ☎ 02-644 3000. This huge, swanky beachfront hotel on the northern side of town has perhaps the best spread of restaurants in the city, with eleven contrasting eating and drinking venues to choose from. Many people head for the perenially popular *Prego's* (daily noon–midnight), which serves seasonal Italian fare either in its stylish wood-pannelled interior or on a beautiful terrace overlooking the Arabian Gulf. There's also a branch of the lively *Trader Vic's* chain (see p.103; daily noon–3.30pm & 7–11.30pm), the sleek *Behihana* Japanese restaurant (daily noon–3pm & 7pm–midnight), and the cosy *Rodeo Grill* steakhouse (daily noon–3.30pm & 7–11.30pm). Mains from around 50–70dh.

Delma Café

First floor, Cultural Foundation. Sun–Thurs 8am–10pm, Fri & Sat 10am–10pm. This quaint little flower-filled café offers an excellent, low-key lunch option if you're in the vicinity of the Cultural Foundation. The simple café menu features cheap and tasty sandwiches and salads, all at bargain prices (from around 10dh). Popular with Abu Dhabi's older female expat set.

Hilton Abu Dhabi

The Corniche ☎ 02-681 1900. This low-key five-star rivals the *Beach Rotana Hotel* for its spread of in-house bars and restaurants – and in a more convenient location, close to the Marina Mall and Corniche. The laid-back *Jazz Bar* (Sun–Fri 7pm–11.45pm) is one of the most popular spots in town amongst expats, with live jazz, tempting cocktails and excellent contemporary European cuisine. The hacienda-style *Hemingway's* bistro (daily noon–1am) is another long-standing favourite for after-dark carousing, serving tasty Latin American food and more-ish margheritas. Other options include the well-regarded *Vasco's* (daily noon –11pm), with a good selection of fusion food ranging from freshly made tagliatelli to Indian tandooris; the *Royal Orchid* (daily noon–11.45pm), rolling out classy Thai, Chinese and Mongolian cuisine; and the *Mawal* (daily 12.30pm–1.30am), one of the top Lebanese restaurants in town, with the inevitable live singer and belly dancer in the evening. Mains at all these places run at around 60–70dh.

PLACES

The east coast

The east coast of the UAE is almost the exact opposite of the west. Compared to the country's heavily developed Arabian Gulf seaboard, the Indian Ocean-facing east is only thinly settled and still relatively untouched, thanks largely to the rocky and barren **Hajar Mountains** which occupy much of the region. Somnolent and scenic, the east is a popular weekend destination for visitors from Dubai, just two hours' drive away, who come to loll around on the relatively empty beaches that dot the coast, and even a day-trip around the region is an easy way to get a feel for what makes the rest of the UAE tick.

▲ HAJAR MOUNTAINS

The Hajar Mountains

One of the major attractions of a trip out to the east coast is the chance to get a look at the magnificent Hajar Mountains, which run down the eastern side of the UAE and on into Oman. Bare and craggy, the UAE section of the Hajar rise to a highest point of 1527m at Jebel Yibir, inland from Dibba in the far north of the country, and provide a scenic backdrop to the length of the eastern coast, changing in colour from slate grey to deep red as the light alters through the course of the day and picks out the different red, yellow, grey and green mineral strata of the rock. On a less picturesque note, you're also likely to see long lines of lorries laden with stones quarried from the Hajar being shipped west to Dubai, where they are used to built the huge new offshore islands

Visiting the east coast

Most of the tour operators listed on p.187 offer **day-tours** of the east, usually costing around 200–250dh. **Renting your own vehicle** is another possibility, and once you've managed to get out of Dubai, the roads in the east are some of the emptiest and driver-friendly in the country. **Public transport** around the east is fairly sketchy, however, and won't really get you very far in a day.

PLACES The east coast

The many emirates of the east

The division of the tip of the Arabian peninsula between the seven emirates of the UAE and Oman is remarkably convoluted – a complicated little jigsaw puzzle with different segments of territory owing allegiance to different emirates. The borders were drawn up by British colonial officials who simply wandered around the peninsula for months enquiring in each village as to which sheikh they owed allegiance to, and drawing up the boundaries accordingly. Travelling around the east you'll pass through a surprising number of emirates. Most of the area falls within Fujairah Emirate, though Masafi belongs to Ras Al Khaimah and Khor Fakkan to Sharjah, while Dibba is divided into three districts: Dibba Muhallab, ruled by the Emirate of Fujairah, Dibba al Hisn, ruled by the Emirate of Sharjah, and Dibba Bayah, which belongs to the Sultanate of Oman.

described on p.128, with as yet uncatalogued environmental consequences.

Masafi

Most tours to the east coast stop en route at the small town of Masafi, the western gateway to the Hajar Mountains. Masafi is famous for two things. The first is mineral water – this is where the eponymous Masafi mineral water, sold all over the Emirates, is bottled. The second is the town's so-called Friday Market (open daily from around 8am to 10pm,

despite its name). Strung along either side of the busy main road, this heavily touristed and unatmospheric highway bazaar survives largely on passing coach-party trade. It's best for fruit and veg, plants, low-grade souvenirs and, especially, carpets. You can occasionally unearth a few decent items here (and at cheaper prices than in Dubai), but most of the stock is kitsch factory-made tat – if you ever wanted a rug embellished with an enormous portrait of Sheikh Zayed, for example, now's your chance.

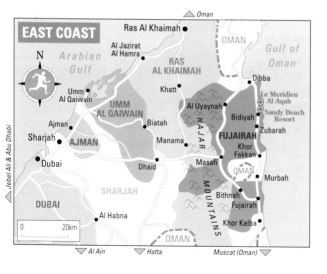

▲ DIBBA

Dibba

From Masafi, a road heads north to the somnolent coastal town of Dibba. Surprisingly, this sleepy little spot was the site of one of the major battles of early Islamic history, when in 633 AD, a year after the Prophet Mohammed's death, the forces of his successor, the caliph Abu Bakr, defeated those of a local ruler who had renounced Islam. A large cemetery outside town is traditionally believed to house the remains of the apostates killed in the battle. Despite its illustrious past, there's nothing much to see here apart from the town's fine main mosque, topped by four soaring minarets, but the setting on a broad bay, backed by the dramatic Hajar mountains is breezy and scenic, and the town itself is about as pretty as any in the UAE, with low-slung little houses, many of them embellished with brightly painted metal doors.

Al Aqah Beach

Dibba is also the jumping-off point for the lovely Al Aqah Beach, a fine stretch of golden sand with a pair of hotels – the low-key *Sandy Beach Motel* and the more upmarket *Le Meridien Al Aqah Beach Resort* – either of which makes a good spot for lunch and some down-time on the sand. The waters around the curiously shaped rock – popularly known as "Snoopy Island" – directly offshore, opposite the *Sandy Beach Motel*, are a popular spot for diving and snorkelling.

Bidiya

A couple of kilometres south of Snoopy Island, the small fishing village of Bidiya is famous as the site of the UAE's oldest mosque (and, for once, "old" doesn't mean 1975), dating back to the fifteenth century, a rustic little structure made of mud brick and gypsum, topped by four

▼ BIDIYA MOSQUE

very flat small domes; visitors are sometimes allowed into the small and dimly lit interior, supported by a single column. Behind the mosque, steps lead up to the top of the hill behind, studded with a couple of watchtowers and offering superb views over the Hajar mountains.

Khor Fakkan

Around 10km further down the coast, the sizeable town of Khor Fakkan sprawls round a superb bay – one of the loveliest in the UAE – though as the town is part of the booze-free and ultra-conservative Sharjah emirate, it hasn't enjoyed the tourist boom its location would otherwise have suggested. It's a pleasant spot for a brief visit though, with a fine seafront corniche complete with fish market, a tempting stretch of beach and views of Sharq Island offshore (another popular diving spot), sometimes mistranslated as the rather alarming "Shark Island", although *sharq* is in fact simply the Arabic for "east".

Fujairah

Another 20km down the coast brings you to Fujairah city, the largest settlement on the east coast, whose modest high-rises and urban sprawl come as something of a surprise after the unspoilt surrounding countryside. The city has recently enjoyed something of a minor boom, mainly on the back of economic developments in neighbouring emirates, especially Dubai. The focus of much of this new economic activity is the massive oil-refuelling, or "bunkering", port, the world's second largest (after Singapore), at the southern end of town. This is where most of the UAE's oil is exported from (the east coast location saves shipping from making a time-consuming two-day dog-leg around the tip of the Arabian peninsula) and there's usually a line of tankers several kilometres long lined up offshore waiting for their turn at the pumps.

Altogether more picturesque is **Fujairah Fort**, perhaps the most attractive in the UAE, on the northern edge of the city centre. Dating back to the sixteenth century, the fort is unusually well fortified, set atop a large plinth and with high, bare walls rising to a pretty cluster of towers and battlements, dramatically posed against the backdrop of the

▼ FORT, FUJAIRAH

Hajar Mountains. The fort was closed for restoration at the time of writing, although it may open to the public when this work is finished. The area around here was formerly the heart of Fujairah's old town, and a few old-fashioned, low-lying mud-brick buildings remain amidst patches of thorny scrub and piles of building materials. Nearby, the rather pedestrian **Fujairah Museum** (Sun–Thurs 8.30am–1.30pm & 4.30–6.30pm, Fri 2–6.30pm; 1dh) houses a run-of-the-mill collection of local weaponry, jewellery and archeological displays.

Restaurants and cafés

The best place for lunch during a tour of the east coast is one of the beachfront hotels between Dibba and Bidiyah. The dramatic **Le Meridien Al Aqah** is the obvious target, though its two best restaurants (the Southeast Asian *Taste* and the Indian *Swaad*) only open in the evenings, so for lunch you're limited to the hotel's (albeit pleasant enough) *View* coffee-shop-cum-restaurant. The new **Fujairah Rotana Resort** nearby (under construction at the time of writing, though it should have opened by the time you read this) is likely to be a better bet, with a trio of all-day eating options including the *Waves* beachfront restaurant, *Al Falaj* café lounge and *Mozaique* restaurant. Coach parties normally head for the **Sandy Beach Resort** – a nice little hotel, but the buffet lunches are pretty awful.

Accommodation

Accommodation

Dubai has a vast range of accommodation. At the **top end** of the market, the city boasts one of the planet's finest array of five-star stunners, and (if you can afford it) a stay in one of these contemporary Arabian palaces is likely to prove a highlight of your visit to the city. Many of the top hotels are ranged along the beach in Jumeirah and Dubai Marina, but note that the overall shortage of beachside accommodation means that these places tend to get booked solid way in advance, especially during the winter months (even in the stifling summer months, occupancy levels remain remarkably high). There are also several excellent top-end city-centre hotels, mainly concentrated along the Creek in Deira, as well as a string of top-notch designer hotels on Sheikh Zayed Road.

Mid-range options are more limited – the city as a whole suffers from a distinct lack of really appealing three- and four-star options, with a few notable exceptions (and if you want to stay on the beach without forking out loads of cash, your only option is the rather unexciting *Regent Beach Resort*). Having said that, there are plenty of comfortable, reasonably priced places scattered around Bur Dubai and Deira, though don't expect any frills, or any particular character.

There's no real **budget accommodation** in Dubai, unless you can get a bed at the city's youth hostel. You won't find a double room anywhere in the city for less than about 250dh (except in summer, when rates in some places fall to around 150dh, though even then

these are hard to find). The good news is that stringent government regulations and inspections mean that standards are good even at the cheapest hotels – all are scrupulously clean and fairly well maintained, and come with en-suite bathroom, plenty of hot water, satellite TV and fridge – although noise from the street or from in-house nightclubs can be a problem in some places.

Hotels in all price ranges chop and change their **room rates** constantly according to the time of year and demand, so a hotel may be brilliant value one week, and a rip-off the next. It's worth shopping around (and having a look at the Internet too, which often throws up good deals). Prices usually (but not always) depend on **the season**. In general, prices are highest during the cool winter months from November to February (especially during the fantastically popular Dubai Shopping Festival) and cheapest in high summer (June to August), when rates at some places, especially away from the beach) can tumble by as much as 75 percent. **Taxes** are sometimes included in the quoted price, but not always, so check when booking or you might find yourself suddenly having to cough up an extra twenty percent (ten percent service charge and ten percent municipality tax). The rates quoted in the following reviews are **inclusive of tax**. All the prices given in the reviews below are for the **cheapest double room in high season** (inclusive of all taxes) – though note that due to constantly fluctuating rates, these are only a guide.

Bur Dubai

The listings below are shown on the map on p.48.

Central Bur Dubai has a reasonable spread of budget accommodation (though less than Deira, and usually at fractionally higher prices); look out for in-house nightclubs in this part of town, which can often make otherwise good hotels (such as the *Hyde Park* and *Sun City* hotels) unbearably noisy. There are also a few decent mid-range options. More upmarket places (mainly four stars) are strung out along Khalid Bin Al Waleed Road, though most are fairly uninspiring, with a couple of honourable exceptions.

Admiral Plaza Al Nadha St ☎04-393 5333, ⊛www.admiralplazahotel.com. This appealing lower mid-range option offers a good central location and bright, modern rooms at fairly reasonable prices. Facilities include the inevitable English-style *Victory Pub* and Indian and international restaurants, plus a health club and indoor

▼ ARABIAN COURTYARD HOTEL

pool. Around 500dh, including breakfast and airport transfers.

Ambassador Al Falah St ☎04-393 9555, ⊛www.astamb.com. Similar to its sister hotel, the nearby *Astoria*, though slightly more sedate, this is a well-run and centrally located three-star, close to the Textile Souk. Rooms are modern and reasonably smart. There's a swimming pool, a couple of in-house restaurants (Indian and international) and the lively English-style *George & Dragon* pub. Around 500dh.

Arabian Courtyard Al Fahidi St ☎04-351 9111, ⊛www.arabiancourtyard.com. This newish four-star is a distinct cut above the other mid-range places in Bur Dubai (albeit a touch more expensive, too). In an excellent location opposite the Dubai Museum, the hotel is modern with stylish Arabian touches, including attractive wood-furnished rooms. Among the facilities on offer are a jacuzzi, a small gym, health club and the attractive little Zaiton Spa, though the pool is disappointingly tiny. There's also a couple of passable Indian and Asian restaurants and the *Sherlock Holmes Pub* – one of the better English-style drinking holes in the city centre. Around 1500dh.

Astoria Al Fahidi St ☎04-353 4300, ⊛www.astamb.com. One of the oldest hotels in Bur Dubai, this place still pulls in a lively and cosmopolitan crowd ranging from Russian housewives to Indian tourists. Rooms are fairly modern and run-of-the-mill, but decent value at the price, though it's not the most peaceful place in town thanks to its big selection of in-house restaurants and bars, including the famous old *Pancho Villa's* Tex-Mex restaurant and pub, which has a good resident Latino band and an even more eye-catching troupe of resident Thai hookers. Approach with caution. Around 550dh.

Dallas Hotel Al Nadha St ☎04-351 1223, ✉siavash2@emirates.net.ae. One of the cheaper places in Bur Dubai, on a side street just off Khalid Bin Al Waleed Road, this acceptable two-star has pleasantly spacious rooms, though with a rather dreary mishmash of recycled furniture. There's an in-house restaurant, but no bars or nightclubs, so it's all reasonably peaceful. Around 300dh.

Four Points Sheraton Khalid Bin Al Waleed Rd ☎04-397 7444, ⊛www.fourpoints.com/burdubai. One of the classiest hotels in Bur Dubai (if you ignore the dull exterior), this understated but very comfortable four-star is a cut above most of the local competition. Rooms are nicely furnished in simple international style, and there's also a gym, sauna, beauty salon, a (smallish) swimming pool, plus a handful of restaurants and bars including the excellent *Antique Bazaar* (see p.60) and the cosy *Viceroy Bar* (see p.61). Rates vary according to demand, but can be surprisingly good value. From around 700dh.

New Penninsula Hotel Al Raffa St ☎04-393 9111, ⊛www.newpenninsula.com. One of the better-value lower mid-range hotels in Bur Dubai (despite their dodgy spelling), well run and in a very central location next to the bus station. Rooms, set around a cool white atrium, are comfortably old-fashioned, with slightly chintzy decor, and there's a good range of in-house entertainment, including a Mughal-style restaurant and a couple of Indian-themed bars. Around 400dh.

Regent Palace Hotel Sheikh Zayed Rd ☎04-396 3888, ⊛www.ramee-group.com. This big old concrete box looks fairly dour from the outside, but has a certain amount of chintzy, old-fashioned charm once you're through the doors, with an intimate atrium festooned in dangling vines and stuffed with leather armchairs, and cosy rooms sporting copious quantities of plush, blood-red fabrics (although with twin beds only). Facilities include a gym, small pool, Keralan and Asian restaurants and the *Rock Bottom Café*, a notorious late-night pick-up joint. Around 1100dh.

Royal Ascot Hotel Khalid Bin Al Waleed Rd ☎04-355 8500, ⊛www.royalascothotel-dubai.com. This swanky faux-Georgian-style hotel is one of the nicer-looking places along this strip (although service can be dreadful). Rooms in the huge new section of the hotel are plush and chintzy (there are also a few plainer but much cheaper rooms in the old wing), and there are several decent in-house restaurants, including the excellent *Yakitori* (see p.61), plus pool, spa and gym.

Popular with air crews. New wing around 1500dh, old wing 850dh.

Time Palace Hotel Al Fahidi St ☎04-353 2111, ⊛www.time-palace.com. The best cheapie in Bur Dubai, in an unbeatable location just 50m up from the main entrance to the Textile Souk, though it's surprisingly quiet given how central it is (only the local mosque disturbs the peace). Rooms are spacious, cool and well maintained, and there's a simple in-house Indian café, but no other facilities. It often gets booked up well in advance, so reserve early if you can. Around 300dh.

XVA Bastakia ☎04-353 5383, ⊛www.xvagallery.com. A refreshing change from Bur Dubai's usual run-of-the-mill accommodation, this atmospheric gallery-cum-café (see p.53 and p.60) has three guest rooms in its fine old Bastakia house. Rooms are small but brimful of character, with Arabian furnishings, slatted windows and four-poster beds, plus captivating views over the surrounding wind towers. There are no in-room facilities, though there's a TV lounge and WiFi access downstairs in the beautiful courtyard café. Rates are a bargain, but you'll need to book well in advance. Standard room 650dh, deluxe room 750dh.

Deira

The listings below are shown on the map on p.64, unless otherwise indicated.

Deira easily has the city's biggest selection of budget hotels and cheapest room rates, as well as plenty of mid-range options and a few excellent top-end establishments located along the side of the Creek, and offering marvellous views of it. Staying here puts you right in the heart of the city centre action, but, equally, means that you're a longish taxi ride from other parts of the city and the beach.

Carlton Tower Hotel Baniyas St ☎04-222 7111, ⊛www.carltontower.net. Opened in 1977, this cosy four-star is one of oldest hotels in Dubai, and retains a slight but pleasing old-fashioned ambience, as well as an excellent location right in the thick of the city. Rooms are comfortable, if dated; some boast fine Creek views (others have city vews), though road noise can be slightly intrusive on lower floors. Facilities include Iranian and international restaurants, a rooftop pool, and the usual English pub. There's also a free shuttle to the public beach at Jumeirah. Around 1200dh.

Dubai Youth Hostel Al Nahda Rd, Al Qusais ☏04-298 8151, ⓦ www.uaeyha .com. See map on back outside flap. The cheapest accommodation in Dubai, although it's a considerable distance from the centre, way out en route to Sharjah in the suburb of Al Qusais, so unless you're really counting the pennies it's preferable to base yourself in a cheap city-centre hotel, since the hostel's doubles aren't an awful lot cheaper than those in some Deira budget hotels (and you might spend the difference in taxi fares just in getting to and from the hostel anyway); there's also a maximum three-day stay. Having said that, facilities are excellent for the price, with bright, clean a/c singles and doubles plus cheap dorm beds, a pool, gym, sauna and spa (accommodation in the slightly more expensive new wing is much nicer than in the old wing). The hostel is a bit tricky to find; try asking for the Al Ahli Club on Al Nadha Rd, just south of the junction with Al Ittihad Rd, the main highway to Sharjah – the hostel is 100m further south along the same road. Buses #3, #17 and #31 run right past the hostel en route to and from the city centre. Dorm beds 60–85dh/75–100dh per person, doubles 150–170dh/170–200dh (YHA member/non-members). If you're not already a YHA member, you can join up at the hostel for 150dh.

Florida Hotel Al Sabkha Rd ☏04-226 8888, ⓦ www.florahotels.ae. Not to be confused with the rather more upmarket *Hotel Florida International* down the road, this is one of Deira's smarter-looking budget options, with small but nicely furnished rooms overlooking Al Sabkha Street (though slight street noise occasionally intrudes) and friendly staff. Around 320dh.

Gold Plaza Guesthouse Sikkat Al Khail ☏04-225 0240. A long-standing cheapie almost next door to the Gold Souk entrance (and popular with African traders visiting it). Rooms are nothing special, but inexpensive, reasonably quiet, and acceptable at the price. It also boasts a few ultra-cheap singles (125–175dh), if you can manage to get one. Around 250dh.

Al Hijaz Heritage Motel Next to Al Ahmadiya School ☏04-225 0085, ⓦ www.alhijazmotel.com. A Somali-run place occupying a lovely old traditional house right next to Al Ahmadiya School. Rooms are nicely done up and filled with lovely chunky antique wooden furniture – a bargain at the price. Not much English is spoken, however, and the courtyard café is usually full of Somali men lounging around the television over cups of Lipton's tea, adding a lively splash of local colour to the boutique ambience. Around 420dh.

Hilton Dubai Creek Baniyas Rd ☏04-227 1111, ⓦ www.hiltondubaicreek .com. The most striking hotel in the city centre, the *Hilton Dubai Creek* is all about slick contemporary style, from the Carlos Ott interior designs to the in-house Gordon Ramsay restaurant, *Verre* (see p.75). The striking decor mixes industrial-chic with designer-Zen, from the in-your-face foyer, twinkling with huge quantities of reflective metal fittings, to the mirrored lifts and soothing wood-panelled corridors with blue floor lights. Rooms are exceptionally well equipped (fax machines, foot massagers and DVD players come as standard) and stylishly decorated in minimalist whites and creams; some also have grand Creek views, framed by floor-to-ceiling windows. There's a health club and a small rooftop pool with spectacular views (though no sauna or spa). Given the style, it's generally

▼ HILTON DUBAI CREEK HOTEL

surprisingly good value, especially in summer. Around 1500dh.

Hotel Florida International Opposite Al Sabkha Bus Station, Al Sabkha Rd ☎04-224 7777, ⓦwww.florahotels.ae. One of Deira's more upmarket and appealing budget hotels, right in the heart of the downtown action. Service is good, and rooms, though rather small, are neat and nicely furnished; decent soundproofing also means that they're reasonably quiet despite the location on a busy main road (though you might prefer to sacrifice the street views for a more peaceful room around the back). Around 500dh.

Hyatt Regency ☎04-209 1234, ⓦwww .dubai.regency.hyatt.com. A gargantuan five-star standing in monolithic splendour on the northern side of Deira, conveniently close to the Gold Souk and city centre. Inside, this is a very polished offering – literally so, in the case of the shiny white marbled atrium – with spacious rooms attractively decorated in pine-and-white minimalist style. All have views – spectacular from the higher floors – and all come with five-star mod-cons. There's also a pool, health club, and a good selection of in-house restaurants (see pp.73–75). From around 1500dh.

Al Karnak Hotel Naif Rd ☎04-226 8799, ⓔalkarnakhotel@hotmail.com. One of the cheapest of the Deira cheapies, right in the thick of things. Rooms look a bit past it, but are pleasantly spacious, and at the price you can't really complain. Popular with Africans visiting the nearby Gold Souk. Around 220dh.

Al Khayam Hotel Near the entrance to the Gold Souk, almost opposite the Gold Plaza Guesthouse ☎04-226 4211, ⓔkhayamh@emirates.net.ae. Another of the various guesthouses dotted around the Gold Souk, this one has a mix of averagely furnished and priced "modern" rooms and a few "old" singles and twins – a tad shabby, but perfectly OK, and as cheap as anywhere in Deira. 200–300dh.

La Paz Near the entrance to the Gold Souk, a few doors down from the Gold Plaza Guesthouse ☎04-226 8800, ⓔhotellapaz@hotmail.com. This "family hotel" (so no alcohol or disreputable ladies) is perhaps the quietest of the guesthouses clustered around the entrance to the Gold Souk. Rooms look a bit shabby, with mismatched bedcloths and worn furniture, but are perfectly clean and comfortable. Around 300dh including breakfast and airport transfer.

Radisson SAS Hotel Dubai Deira Creek (still widely referred to as the InterContinental, as it was named until late 2006) Baniyas Rd ☎04-222 7171, ⓦwww .deiracreek.dubai.radissonsas.com. The first five-star in the city, this grand old lady of the Dubai hotel world still has plenty going for it, including an extremely central location, an outstanding array of restaurants (see pp.72–76) and a scenic position right on the Creek – and the fact that all rooms have a view of it, which get better the higher up the building you go. The style is engagingly old-fashioned and European, with rather chintzy public areas and plush rooms (but small bathrooms) and a certain understated swankiness which even extends to providing miniature TVs above each of the gents' urinals. There's also a pool and a good range of health and fitness facilities. Around 1900dh, though check the website for special deals.

Sheraton Dubai Creek Baniyas Rd ☎04-228 1111, ⓦwww.sheraton.com/dubai. This attractive five-star enjoys a good central location, a scenic setting right on the Creek, and swanky public areas with lots of shiny white marble and an unusual wedge-shaped atrium dotted with palm trees. Roughly half the rooms have Creek views (increasingly splendid the higher you get), though decor is disappointingly dated and dull compared to the public areas, and the bathrooms are small. There's a decent range of leisure facilities, including sauna, well-equipped gym and pool, and a trio of nice in-house restaurants (the *Ashiana*, *Creekside* and *Vivaldi*'s – see pp.72–76). Rates can be excellent value, and significantly lower than at nearby five-stars. Around 1000dh.

St George ☎04-225 1122, ⓦwww .stgeorgedubai.com. Set on the Creek near the tip of the Deira peninsula, this biggish three-star offers spacious and nicely furnished rooms, most with good Creek and city views, and an unbeatable location very

ACCOMMODATION

▲ PARK HYATT HOTEL

close to the souks and abras, all at a very reasonable price. The only minus points are the lack of a pool, while the Iranian and Arabian nightclubs and bar on the top floor can be noisy if you're in a room nearby. Around 850dh.

The inner suburbs

The listings below are shown on the map on pp.80–81, unless otherwise indicated.

There aren't many stand-out places to stay in Dubai's inner suburbs, though the three places listed below all compensate in different ways for their slightly out-of-the-way locations.

Grand Hyatt Al Qataiyat Rd, Oud Metha ☎04-317 1234, ⊛www.dubai.grand .hyatt.com. This colossus of a hotel – the biggest in Dubai, with 674 rooms spread over sixteen floors – is grand in every sense. The vast atrium alone could happily swallow two or three smaller establishments and is home to a big array of shops, cafés and restaurants, plus a substantial patch of fake tropical rainforest, with the wooden hulls of four large boats poking out of the ceiling above. Rooms are larger than average and have grand views either towards the Creek or Sheikh Zayed Road through big picture windows (though the decor itself is uninspiring) and there's a vast range of facilities: four pools (including a nice indoor pool with underwater music), spa, jacuzzi, steam bath, sauna, kids' club, a large gym, several good restaurants and the *Mix* nightclub (see p.91). Rates are generally relatively good value for money. The hotel's only real drawback is its

middle-of-nowhere location – though, equally, its strategic position close to Garhoud Bridge and assorted major highways puts it within a fairly short taxi ride of pretty much anywhere in the northern half of the city. From 800–1200dh.

Park Hyatt Dubai Creek Golf and Yacht Club, Garhoud ☎04-602 1234, ⊛www .dubai.park.hyatt.com. Dubai's most appealing city centre hotel, this alluring new five-star, situated between the Dubai Creek Golf and Yacht club, occupies a sprawling, low-rise complex of white-walled, blue-domed buildings in quasi-Moroccan style surrounded by extensive grounds and plenty of palm trees – a beguiling mixture of golf and Gulf. Rooms (some with beautiful Creek views) are unusually large, with cool white and cream decor and spacious bathrooms, and facilities include a large pool and excellent spa, gym and other health and relaxation facilities, plus the good *Thai Kitchen* restaurant and the attractive *The Terrace* marina-side bar. Around 1800dh.

Rydges Plaza Al Diyafah St, Satwa ☎04-398 2222, ⊛www.rydges.com. See map on p.82. If you want to stay in this part of town, this unpretentious four-star-deluxe overlooking Satwa Roundabout is the place to be. Rooms are comfortable (although those overlooking the roundabout suffer from slight road noise) and facilities include a smallish pool, plus gym, health club and twice-daily free transfers to Jumeirah Beach Park. There are also some excellent in-house eating and drinking options, including *Il Rustico* (see p.89) and *Coconut Grove* (see p.88), plus the enduringly popular *Aussie Legends* pub (see p.90). Around 1000dh.

Sheikh Zayed Road

▲ ATRIUM, EMIRATES TOWERS HOTEL

The listings below are shown on the map on p.94.

Room rates in the stylish hotels along Sheikh Zayed Road are as sky-high as the towers themselves, although the superb views and classy facilities make up for the financial pain. The area's only non-luxury option is the excellent, mid-range *Ibis*.

Crowne Plaza Sheikh Zayed Rd ☏04-331 1111, ⊛www .crowneplaza.com. One of the cheapest five-stars on the strip, the *Crowne Plaza* is a haven of old-world chintz amidst the modernist establishments lining Sheikh Zayed Road. It's all rather dated but still engaging, with a distinctly European-style ambience, from the cluttered but convivial foyer and public areas to the cosy rooms, complete with abundant quantities of plush fabrics and slightly naff furnishings, as well as all the usual five-star mod-cons. There's also a decent range of in-house eating and drinking establishments (see pp.101–105), plus a passable range of leisure facilities including pool and gym – though they don't compare with other places along the road. From 825dh.

Dusit Dubai Sheikh Zayed Rd ☏04-343 3333, ⊛www.dusit.com. This *wai*-shaped

▼ DUSIT DUBAI HOTEL

Sheikh Zayed Road landmark (see p.95) is one of the nicest and best-value five-stars hereabouts. Thai-owned and -style, the whole place has a distinctive ambience which combines serene interior design and ultra-attentive service. Rooms are stylishly decorated in soothing creams and browns (and cleverly designed so that you can even watch TV from the bath), and there are all the usual five-star facilities, including the excellent *Benjarong* restaurant (see p.99). Rates are good value considering the standard of the place. Around 1500dh.

Emirates Towers Sheikh Zayed Rd ☏04-319 8760, ⊛www .jumeirahemiratestowers.com. Occupying the smaller of the two iconic Emirates Towers, this exclusive establishment is generally rated the top business hotel in the city, catering mainly to senior execs on very generous expense accounts. Rooms are tailored to match, with rather austere decor and severe grey furnishings calculated to avoid ruffling the nerves of busy CEOs – if you're not here to work, you might find the set-up a bit spartan. Out-of-office hours can be spent in the larger-than-average swimming pool, and there's also a health club and the men-only H20 spa, as well as all the many shops, restaurants and bars of the Emirates Boulevard close by. Around 3200dh.

▲ ATRIUM, FAIRMONT HOTEL

Fairmont Sheikh Zayed Rd ☎04-332 5555, ⊛www.fairmont.com. A Sheikh Zayed Road landmark, instantly recognizable after dark thanks to its four luridly illuminated turrets. Inside, the hotel is one of the most stylish on the road, huddled around a soaring, rather futuristic-looking glass-and-steel atrium done up in muted greys with splashes of multicoloured lights. Rooms are beautifully furnished, with soothing cream decor, huge TVs and all the usual mod-cons, plus larger-than-average bathrooms. The whole of the ninth floor is given over to leisure facilities, including the sumptuous Willow Stream Spa and sunset and sunrise pools on opposite corners of the building. Bags of class, though at a very hefty price. Around 3000dh.

Ibis World Trade Centre ☎04-318 7000, ⊛www.ibishotel.com. This unpretentious and excellent-value establishment is the only refuge in this part of town for those without sheikh-sized wallets. Rooms are small but attractively furnished, and the higher ones have nice views. There are no in-house facilities apart from a couple of decent restaurants and bars, but guests can use those at the adjacent *Novotel* for a very modest 20dh. Around 350dh.

Al Murooj Rotana Doha St ☎04-321 1111, ⊛www.rotana.com. This sprawling new hotel is unforgiveably ugly on the outside, but fortunately things get much better once you're through the front door,

with tastefully furnished modern rooms (some with excellent Burj Dubai views) and a decent range of amenities, including the *Latino House* restaurant (see p.100) and *Double Decker* pub. Usually one of the cheaper of the Sheikh Zayed Road five-stars. Around 1450dh.

Novotel World Trade Centre ☎04-318 7000, ⊛www.novotel.com. Cheaper and less obviously flash than other five-stars further down Sheikh Zayed Road, this low-key business-oriented hotel nevertheless has a suave and understated style of its own, from the chic minimalist foyer to the attractively designed rooms with cool cream and pine decor. Its direct connections to the World Trade Centre guarantee a steady flow of business visitors, but there's also a decent-sized pool, gym, spa and massage facilities, plus kids' activities and babysitting, and the hotel complex is also the (slightly unlikely) home of the excellent *Blue Bar* and *Lotus One* see p.104). Around 1100dh.

Shangri-La Sheikh Zayed Rd ☎04-343 8888, ⊛www.shangri-la.com. The most stylish hotel on Sheikh Zayed Road, the *Shangri-La* is pure contemporary class – a beguiling mix of Zen-chic and Scandinavian-cool. Rooms come with smooth pine finishes, beautiful artworks on the wall and mirrors everywhere – even the beds are miniature works of art, with stacked-up pillows and enormous padded headboards. The fourth floor is given over to leisure facilities including a spa, men's salon, an unusually large and well-equipped gym, and one of the biggest pools on Sheikh Zayed Road, and the hotel is also home to several excellent restaurants (see pp.100–102). Not surprisingly, all this doesn't come cheap, but will still make significantly less of a hole in your wallet than the *Fairmont* and *Emirates Towers*, especially in summer, when prices can fall spectacularly. Around 2400dh.

Towers Rotana Sheikh Zayed Road ☎04-312 2320, ⊛www.rotana.com. This no-fuss four-star is one of the cheapest (and plainest) Shekih Zayed Road options. It's distinctly run-of-the-mill compared to other places along the road, but benefits from a good location about halfway down the strip and a decent range of leisure amenities, with a pool, well-equipped gym, sauna, steambath and massage rooms, plus a couple of decent in-house restaurants and the popular *Long's Bar*. But it's still relatively pricey for what you get. Around 1300dh.

Jumeirah and Umm Suqeim

The listings below are shown on the map on p.115m unless, otherwise indicated.

The suburbs of Jumeirah and Umm Suqeim are home to some of Dubai's most memorable beachfront hotels, ranging from the party-atmosphere *Dubai Marine Beach Resort* to the world-famous *Burj Al Arab* – though not surprisingly (apart from the rather uninspiring *Regent Beach Hotel*), none of them comes cheap.

Burj Al Arab ☎04-301 7777, ⓦwww .burj-al-arab.com. A stay in this staggering hotel (for more on which see p.114) is the ultimate Dubaian luxury. The (in)famous "seven-star" facilities include fabulous split-level deluxe suites (the lowest category of accommodation – there are no ordinary rooms here), arrival in a chauffeur-driven Rolls (or charter a helicopter transfer from the airport for an extra 9000dh) and your own butler (while a paltry 40,000dh gets you the royal suite, complete with private elevator and cinema, rotating four-poster bed and your own Arabian *majlis*). As you'd expect, there's pretty much every facility here you could imagine (along with several you hadn't – including a "pillow menu" to ensure the perfect night's sleep), with top-notch business and leisure facilities, amongst them the superlative Assawan Spa and Health Club. There's also the hotel's spectacular collection of hotels and bars to explore and a fabulous stretch of beach to enjoy – or just take one of the hotel's hire cars (choose between a Ferrari, Porsche or Lamborghini) for a spin. Published rates start at 7800dh, but the website sometimes offers discounts of up to fifty percent.

Dar Al Masyaf Madinat Jumeirah ☎04-366 8888, ⓦwww.madinatjumeirah .com. A more intimate (and even more expensive) alternative to the Madinat Jumeirah's big two hotels, *Dar Al Masyaf* consists of a chain of modest, low-rise buildings scattered around the edges of the Madinat complex within extensive, palm-studded gardens; each building contains a small number of rooms, sharing an exclusive pool and decorated in the deluxe Arabian manner of *Al Qasr* and *Mina A'Salam*, whose myriad facilities they share. Around 3800dh.

Dubai Marine Beach Resort Jumeirah Rd, nr Jumeirah Mosque ☎04-346 1111, ⓦwww.dxbmarine.com. See map on pp.108–109. This attractive resort is best known for its superb array of bars and restaurants (see pp.112–113) – a major draw for most visitors, although things can get quite lively after dark, so it's not really the place for a quiet beach holiday and early nights. Its location means that it's the only five-star in Dubai where you can be on the beach but also within easy striking distance of the city centre. Rooms are attractively decorated, set in pleasingly simple modern white "villas" amidst lush gardens stuffed with tropical greenery – a welcome contrast to the interminable concrete of Jumeirah Road outside – and there's a small stretch of white-sand beach, two medium-sized pools and a spa. Around 1700dh.

Jumeirah Beach Hotel ☎04-4068516, ⓦwww.jumeirahbeachhotel.com. The most luxurious and stylish place in town when it opened a decade ago, this iconic hotel (also see p.117) has come down in the world slightly since then, and now caters to a more low-brow crowd of (mainly UK) families and couples. Not that it's necessarily any the worse for it, with a cheery and casual atmosphere and a slightly party atmosphere after dark. The hotel's facilities are among the best in the city, including over twenty restaurants, several top nightspots (see pp.123–125), seven pools, six tennis courts, a golf driving range, PADI diving resort and kids' club, plus a large and lovely stretch of beach with plenty of watersports available and jaw-dropping Burj views; in addition, guests get unlimited access to the Wild Wadi waterpark right next door. The hotel is also home to *Beit Al Bahar*, nineteen freestanding villas, set in lush gardens with beautiful Arabian decor and their own private plunge pools. 3360dh, *Beit Al Bahar* 8000dh.

Mina A'Salam **Madinat Jumeirah** ☎04-366 8888, ⊛www.madinatjumeirah .com. *Mina A'Salam* ("Harbour of Peace") shares the *Madinat Jumeirah's* Arabian theming, with wind tower-topped buildings and quasi-Moroccan decorative touches, although the sheer size (and height) of the place lends it a faint package-resort atmosphere which sits incongruously with its refined traditional Middle Eastern styling. Rooms are beautifully furnished with traditional Arabian wooden furniture and fabrics, and the public areas are full of character. Having said that, the whole place can seem like a slightly watered-down version of the rather more extravagant (and only fractionally more expensive) *Al Qasr* hotel on the opposite side of the Madinat – although you might possibly prefer *Mina A'Salam's* less ostentatious and more homely style. Facilities include a nice-looking stretch of private beach, three pools, the Six Senses Spa and health club, plus the forty-odd restaurants

▼ AL QASR HOTEL

and bars (and myriad shops) of the Madinat Jumeirah complex. 3480dh.

Al Qasr **Madinat Jumeirah** ☎04-366 8888, ⊛www.madinatjumeirah.com. This extravagantly opulent Arabian-themed hotel looks like something out of a film set, from the statues of rearing horses and jaw-dropping views over the Madinat which greet you on arrival, to the many-pillared entrance into the marvellous foyer, with a long tier of cascading fountains and possibly the biggest chandeliers in Dubai. Rooms are similarly dramatic, with show-stopping views over the surrounding attractions and sumptuous oriental decor featuring reproduction antique wooden furniture, plus copious quantities of colourful drapes, cushions and carpets – and of course pretty much every luxury and mod-con you can imagine. There's also a huge pool, the Six Senses Spa and Caritas beauty salon and all the facilities of the Madinat Jumeirah on your doorstep. 3550dh.

Regent Beach Resort **Off Jumeirah Road, 200m south of the** *Dubai Marine Beach Resort* ☎04-344 5777, ⊛www .ramee-group.com. See map on pp.108– 109. If you're absolutely desperate to be in Jumeirah but can't afford a five-star, then this low-key and rather uninspiring little three-star resort is your only option (though it's still no bargain). Rooms are comfortable if characterless, and there's a small pool, and gym. The major drawback is that, although it's on the seafront, it doesn't have its own private beach, so you'll have to mingle with the hoi-polloi on the unattractive stretch of public beach outside. 800dh.

Dubai Marina

The listings below are shown on the map on p.130.

Grosvenor House ☎04-399 8888, ⊛www.grosvenorhouse-dubai.com. Set slightly away from the seafront, this elegantly tapering 45-storey high-rise (spectacular when illuminated by night) is more Sheikh Zayed Road urban chic than bucket-and-spade beach resort. The entire hotel is a model of contemporary cool, from the suave public areas right through to the elegantly furnished rooms, decorated in muted whites, creams and cottons, and with big picture windows affording sweeping views over the Marina and coast. There's also a pool, gym, spa, massage centre and health club, and if you get bored you can take a free shuttle bus to the city centre, the Ibn Battuta Mall and the nearby *Royal Meridien*, whose beach and pools you can use for free. The hotel's very select array of restaurants and bars (see pp.134–137) is a further attraction. Around 1800dh.

Habtoor Grand Resort and Spa ✆04-399 5000, ⊛www.habtoorhotels.com. This rather overblown five-star resort mixes city high-rise and beachside resort styles to rather mishmash effect, with a pair of huge towers overlooking the hotel's busy gardens, pools and beach. It's not the most stylish hotel on the beach, but rooms (either in the two towers or – cheaper – in the grounds) are comfortable and cheery, with bright colours, attractive decor and (from higher levels in the tower rooms) huge views over the Marina, sea and Jumeirah Palm. The extensive facilities include thirteen bars and restaurants, spa, health club, watersports, tennis and squash courts and children's club, plus three pools and a decent stretch of private beach. The sheer size of the hotel, however, means that it's not the most peaceful place on the beach. Tower 2340dh, resort 1800dh.

Hilton Jumeirah Beach ✆04-399 1111, ⊛www.hilton.com/worldwideresorts. This glitzy Hilton boasts lots of shiny metal and an air of cosmopolitan chic – it's more of a city-slicker's beach bolthole than family seaside resort, and the place tends to attract a young and stylish local crowd. Rooms are bright and cheerfully decorated; facilities are relatively limited compared to nearby places, although you do get a health club, a gym and a good range of restaurants and bars, including well-known Italian *BICE* (see p.134). Outside there's a large pool with swim-up bar and lovely terraced gardens running down to the sea, though the hotel beach itself is smaller than at neighbouring establishments, and the sunloungers are rather packed in. There's also a range of gentle watersports available, and a playground and pool for the kids. 750dh.

Le Meridien Mina Seyahi Beach Resort & Marina ✆04-399 3333, ⊛www .lemeridien-minaseyahi.com. The least impressive of the Marina hotels, with patchy service, dull architecture and garish rooms – all in need of an urgent face-lift. Plus points include the extensive grounds and big swathe of beach, the largest of any of the Marina hotels, and parents will welcome the kids' club and babysitting services. However, at this price you can usually get an awful lot more elsewhere. 1800dh.

Oasis Beach Hotel ✆04-399 4444, ⊛www.jebelali-international.com. The only non-five-star in the Marina (though it's still a four-star-deluxe), this cheerful and unpretentious resort hotel offers the area's cheapest rates and plenty of old-fashioned seaside fun. There's a big (though usually very crowded) stretch of beach (complete with colourfully dressed camels for rides), spacious lush gardens, a huge swimming pool and family play area. Activities include watersports, gym, tennis, and there's a wellness centre, plus a good spread of restaurants and bars. Rooms are average, but perfectly comfy. 500dh.

One&Only Royal Mirage ✆04-399 9999, ⊛www.oneandonlyresorts.com. The finest Arabian-themed hotel in town (only *Al Qasr* – see opposite – comes close), this dreamy resort is the perfect 1001 Nights fantasy made flesh, with a superb sequence of quasi-Moroccan-style buildings scattered amidst extensive, palm-filled grounds; the whole place is particularly stunning at night, when the resorts' labyrinthine sequence of beautifully sculpted and tiled courtyards, hallways and corridors – and the thousands of palms – are illuminated to magical effect. The place actually contains three hotels in one: *The Palace*, the *Arabian Court*, and the *Residence & Spa*, each a little bit more sumptuous (and more expensive) than the last. Rooms are attractively appointed, with Arabian decor and reproduction antique wooden furniture and colourful rugs, while facilities include a one-kilometre stretch of private beach, four pools, the delectable Givenchy Spa and Oriental Hammam, and some of the best restaurants and bars in town (see pp.134–137). The *Palace* costs 2630dh, *Arabian Court* 2890dh and *Residence & Spa* 4280dh.

Ritz-Carlton ☎04-399 4000, ⊛www
.ritzcarlton.com. Set in a low-rise,
Tuscan-style ochre building, this very stylish
establishment is one of the classiest (and
most expensive) in the city, and a refreshing
change from the in-your-face high-rises
that surround it, preserving an old-world
European elegance and calming style
amidst the madness of the Marina. Rooms
are spacious, with slightly chintzy European-
style decor, while public areas boast all the
charm of a luxurious old country house,
especially in the sumptuous lobby lounge
and the flagship *La Baie* restaurant (see
p.134). There's also a big and very quiet
swathe of private beach and gardens, while
children are surprisingly well catered for,
with a big kids' club, covered outdoor play
area and their own pool. Other facilities
include tennis and squash courts, a small
golf course, attractive spa and one of the
smartest gyms in town. 1250dh.

Le Royal Meridien ☎04-399 5555,
⊛www.leroyalmeridien-dubai.com. A
large, flashy and slightly pretentious five-
star – comfortable enough, though lacking
the style or charm of some other places
along the beach. There are five hundred
plush but unexciting rooms split between
three different – though all equally uninspiring – parts of the hotel. Facilities are
good, however, with extensive grounds and
beach, two larger-than-average pools, the
ostentatious, Roman-themed Caracalla Spa,
a smart gym, tennis and squash courts, a
kids' club and a decent selection of restaurants. 2000dh.

Sheraton Jumeirah Beach ☎04-399
5533, ⊛www.sheraton.com
/jumeirahbeach. At the southern end of the
Marina, this is the area's most low-key and
flash-free five-star – and usually a bit
cheaper than the competition. Rooms are
passable, if unexciting, but the hotel's real
attraction is its laid-back, family-friendly
atmosphere, and its extensive palm-studded
gardens and beach. The large main pool
has its own swim-up bar and lots of inviting
recliners, while kids get their own pool, shaded playground and the Pirates day-care club.
There's also a range of gentle watersports
available, plus squash courts, gym, wellness
centre and a trio of restaurants. 760dh.

Around Dubai

*The listings below are shown on the
Around Dubai map on the back flap.
If you want to get out of Dubai
completely, you could consider
staying in one of the luxurious resorts out in the emirate's
unspoilt desert hinterlands.*

Bab Al Shams Desert Resort and Spa
☎04-832 6699, ⊛www
.jumeirahbabalshams.com. Hidden out in
the desert a forty-five-minute drive from the
airport, this gorgeous desert resort occupies
a wonderfully atmospheric replica Arabian
fort and offers a complete change of pace
and style from the city five-stars, with
desert camel- and horse-riding or falconry
displays the order of the day, rather than
lounging on the beach. Rooms are decorated in traditional Gulf style, with rustic
ochre walls and Bedouin-style fabrics, and
facilities include a magnificent infinity pool
dotted with huge urns and pavilions, and
an unusual "rain room" where you can take
a dip in a temperature-controlled waterfall.
There's also a good selection of restaurants
including *Al Hadheerah*, Dubai's first traditional Arabian open-air desert restaurant,
complete with the inevitable belly dancers
and live band. 1560dh.

Al Maha Desert Resort and Spa ☎04-
303 4222, ⊛www.al-maha.com. Some
60km from Dubai, en route to Al Ain, in
pristine desert, this very exclusive resort
is styled like a Bedouin encampment
(albeit not the sort that any real Bedouin
are likely to recognize), with grand views
of the surrounding dunes and the Hajar
Mountains. The resort lies within a 225-
square-kilometre conservation area, and
desert wildlife abounds, with gazelles and
rare Arabian oryx sometimes wandering
through the grounds. Accommodation is
in themed tented suites with handcrafted
furnishing and artefacts, and each comes
with its own small private pool. Activities
include falconry, camel treks, horse-riding,
archery, 4WD desert drives and guided
nature walks – or just relax in the resort's
serene spa. From around 3300dh..

Essentials

Arrival

Dubai's massive, ultra-modern international **airport** is very centrally located in Garhoud, on the southern edge of the city centre, and offers a suitably glamorous and glitzy introduction to the emirate, although the whole place can get insanely busy and overcrowded at peak times. The main five-star hotels all have offices at the airport, and there are lots of **car rental** companies here, too, along with a DTCM **tourist information kiosk** (daily 24hr). You can change **money** here, but at poor rates; it's better to pick up some dirhams from the cluster of ATMs by the exit.

All **transport into town** leaves from in front of the terminal building. Many hotels (including even some budget places) offer **free airport transfers** as part of the room rate; check when you book. Although usually busy, transport is all fairly well organized and signed, and there are no touts around. The easiest way to get into town is to take a **taxi**, of which there are always plentiful supplies. Taxis picking up passengers here charge a basic 20dh flag fare, an inexplicable

little rip-off (it's 3dh everywhere else in the city), but fares are still fairly inexpensive: count on around 30–40dh to Deira and Bur Dubai, 40–50dh to Sheikh Zayed Road, 60dh to the Burj Al Arab area, and 70dh to Dubai Marina.

A cheaper but slower alternative is to catch a **bus**, though these are only really useful if you're staying in Deira or Bur Dubai. There are two **airport buses**, which run 24hr. Airport bus #401 travels via Baniyas Road to Al Sabkha Bus Station in central Deira, close to the Gold Souk. Airport bus #402 goes to Al Ghubaiba Bus Station in the middle of Bur Dubai. Other **local bus services** go to the Gold Souk Bus Station in Deira (#4, #11A, #11C, #11M, #48 & #64) and Al Ghubaiba Bus Station (#33 & #44). Fares on all services cost 3dh. Given the number of different local buses running from the airport, you shouldn't have to wait more than about fifteen minutes for a bus between around 6am and 10pm, though after 10pm you'll have to rely on the more intermittent airport bus services.

Information

The Dubai Department of Tourism and Commerce Marketing runs useful little **information kiosks** at various places around the city (all open Sat–Thurs 10am–10pm & Fri 2–10pm, except the airport branch, which is open daily 24hr; for phone enquiries, call ☎04-223 0000). The largest and best-equipped is in the little building in the middle of Baniyas Square in Deira. Others can be found at the airport, in the BurJuman centre, Deira City Centre, Wafi City, Mercato and Ibn Battuta Mall. Staff have a few useful little leaflets to hand out and will do their best to answer any questions you have. The website

ⓦ www.dubaitourism.ae is also a useful source of general information.

The best source of local **listings** is the excellent *Time Out Dubai*, published weekly (5dh) and readily available all over the city, which carries comprehensive information about pretty much everything going on in Dubai. It's particularly good for information about the constantly changing nightlife scene, including new clubs, club nights and one-off promotions, as well as restaurant and bar promotions and new openings. The glossy *What's On* (monthly; 10dh) is also worth a look, though the listings aren't nearly as detailed.

City transport

Pending the opening of the desperately needed Dubai Metro (see box opposite), virtually the only way of getting around Dubai is by **taxi**. These are abundant almost everywhere in the city and at all times of day and night, although you might occasionally have problems finding a free cab in Bur Dubai and Deira around lunchtime and during the evening rush hour. Large malls and big hotels are always good places to pick up a cab; if not, just stand on the street and wave at anything that passes. Taxis are operated by various companies and come in assorted colours – white, sandy-brown and silver are the most common – though all have yellow taxi signs on the roof, illuminated when the vehicle is available for hire. You can also ring for a cab for a very small surcharge. Try ☎04-208 8080 (Dubai Transport Corporation), ☎04-269 3344 (Cars Taxi) or ☎04-339 0002 (National Taxi).

Fares are good value. There's a basic flag fare of 3dh, plus around 1.2dh per kilometre (rising to 3.5dh plus 1.7dh per km between 10pm and 6am), except in airport taxis (20dh flag fare plus 1dh per km). In practice this works out as follows. From Bur Dubai in the city centre count on approximately 15–25dh to Sheikh Zayed Road, 40dh to the Burj Al Arab and 50dh to Dubai Marina, or about an extra 10dh to all these places if travelling from Deira. The good news is that since you only pay for kilometres travelled, if you get stuck in one of Dubai's chronic traffic jams, the journey's not going to cost you any more than it would in light traffic. If you want a taxi to wait for you it will cost around 15dh per 30min, assuming the driver is willing to hang around.

Taxi **drivers** (the vast majority of which are Indian) are reasonably well trained and are familiar with all the main city landmarks, although if you're going anywhere more obscure you might have to help them find the way;

if in doubt, try to have directions or a full address to hand. Rumours of taxi drivers inflating fares by driving newly arrived tourists five times around the block occasionally surface, but appear to have no basis in reality; the whole industry is stringently regulated, and drivers are unlikely to risk their jobs for the sake of a few extra dirhams. Be aware, though, that Dubai's labyrinthine traffic systems often add considerably to the distances between A and B. If you get into a cab and the driver heads off in completely the wrong direction it's likely to be because he has to do so in order to turn around or find the correct exit/entrance to a particular road. If you think you have a genuine grievance and you wish to lodge a complaint, you can phone the number posted in all the cabs. Make sure you take the driver's ID number and explain your problem to him before you leave. **Tips** aren't really necessary, though many taxi drivers have got into the slightly annoying habit of automatically keeping the small change from fares. If, say, you pay for a 13dh taxi ride with 15dh, your driver might well expect to pocket the difference, unless you make it obvious that you want it back.

Note that taxi drivers might occasionally **refuse to take you** if you're travelling only a short distance. This is most frequently the case outside hotels and malls where drivers are obliged to join a long queue to pick up a fare. Strictly speaking, they're obliged to accept your fare, however short the journey, though in practice if they've been waiting for an hour and you only want to go around the block, you can see their point. If this happens, just walk back down the queue of taxis until you find a driver who's happy to take you where you want to go. The only other occasion when a driver is likely to refuse your fare if it's likely to get them stuck in a massive

Dubai Metro

Scheduled to open in 2009, the Dubai Metro will offer a cheap and convenient way of getting around all parts of the city, and hopefully at least slightly ameliorate the city's appalling traffic congestion. The metro will initially consist of two lines, served by almost ninety stations (while plans for a further two lines have also been mooted). The first (the so-called "Red Line") will run from the airport across the city centre and down the coast to Dubai Marina and Jebel Ali. The second (the "Green Line") will run in a loop around the city centre up through Bur Dubai and then back down through Deira to the airport. The metro is being built by a Japanese-led consortium headed up by Mitsubishi and will use state-of-the-art driverless trains running on a mixture of underground and overground lines.

traffic jam (such as when crossing the Creek during the morning or evening rush hours). Again you can see their point of view, though you're perfectly within your rights to take their number and threaten to report them – or alternatively to offer them a decent tip to compensate for their wasted time.

There are a couple of other things to watch out for. Occasional rogue **unmetred taxis** (often from neighbouring emirates) or other unlicenced cars appear on the streets of Dubai touting for custom. If you use one of these you'll have to agree a fare before setting off, and it's unlikely to be to your advantage, unless you bargain very hard – it's best to avoid these cabs unless you're desperate. Even worse are the **hotel limousines** which sometimes try to pass themselves off as conventional taxis (hotel doormen may sometimes try to get you into one of these cars, insisting that they're ordinary taxis, which they're patently not). These vehicles *are* metred, but usually cost around twice the price of a normal cab, and again are best avoided unless you're completely stuck or have a particular need to travel in a car with leather upholstery and an overpowering stink of air freshener. Remember that if it doesn't have the usual yellow taxi sign on the roof, it's not a proper taxi.

Buses

The city has a well-developed and efficient network of bus services, though it's mainly designed for the needs of expatriat Indian and other low-paid workers, rather than tourists, so is only of limited use to visitors. Most services originate or terminate at either the **Gold Souk Bus Station** in Deira or **Al Ghubaiba Bus Station** in central Bur Dubai (and many services call at both). The information offices at either may be able to supply you with a useful free map of the network. The only really obviously useful services are **#8 and #8A** which run from the Gold Souk station to Al Ghubaiba and then head due south, down Jumeirah Road to the Burj Al Arab and on to Dubai Marina, though it takes the best part of an hour to reach the Marina, and buses can also get unbearably hot in summer. Both services run roughly every 20min from early morning till late evening (except on Fri mornings, when services run every 30min and queues can get ridiculously long). Tickets are bought on board from the driver and cost a standard 3dh. In general, though, it makes more sense to cough up the extra cash and take a cab.

Tours, cruises and desert safaris

Tour operators in Dubai are much of a muchness, and all offer a fairly identical set of tours and activities (although prices can vary quite widely depending on how up- or downmarket the company is perceived to be, so you might like to shop around). Popular excursions include Dubai city tours and dhow trips (see p.189), plus day-tours to Sharjah, Al Ain, Abu Dhabi and the east coast. There are also all sorts of more adventurous tours on offer, including half-day, full-day and overnight desert safaris, sand-skiing, dune-buggy riding, dune- and wadi-bashing and camel trekking; some operators also offer various watersports, as well as diving and snorkelling, deep-sea fishing and crab-hunting. It's easiest to book by phone, since most places don't have conveniently located offices (we've only listed addresses for those places that do).

Desert safaris

One thing that virtually every visitor to Dubai does at some point is go on a **desert safari**. Obviously the main attraction of these trips is the chance to see some of the magnificent desert scenery surrounding Dubai, and although virtually all tours put the emphasis firmly on cheap thrills and touristy gimmicks rather than on quiet contemplation of the mighty sands, most people find the experience enjoyable, in a rather tacky sort of way.

Sunset safaris

The vast majority of visitors opt for one of the endlessly popular **half-day safaris** (also known as "sunset safaris"). These are offered by every tour operator in town (see the list opposite), often at surprisingly low prices – currently from as little as 160dh up to around 290dh

– though whoever you decide to go with you'll get more or less exactly the same thing. The only real worry is the often shockingly dangerous driving you'll suffer en route to the dunes, especially with the cheaper tour operators, as tour drivers race one another another along the highway, usually travelling at way over the speed limit, often while steering with one finger and chatting on their mobiles.

Tours are in large 4WDs holding around eight passengers. You'll be picked up from your hotel between 3pm and 4pm and, once you've driven around town collecting the other passengers in your vehicle (usually a rather tedious and time-consuming business, especially if you've had the bad luck to be first on board) you'll be driven out into the desert. The usual destination is the area of desert a forty-five-minute drive out of town on the road to Al Ain, opposite the massive dune popularly known as **Big Red**. This enormous mountain of sand is quite a sight, although it has all the atmosphere of a motorway service station (and rather more noise) thanks to the endless lines of off-road 4WD enthusiasts and quad-bikers cavorting up and down its slopes.

After a brief stop, during which your vehicle's tyres will be partially deflated as a preparation for going off-road, you'll be driven out into the dunes on the opposite side of the highway from Big Red for an hour or so to enjoy the traditional Emirati past-time of **dune-bashing**. This involves driving at high speed up and down increasingly precipitous dunes amidst great sprays of sand while your vehicle slides, skids, bumps and occasionally takes off completely – all good fun, and probably a bit less scary than the average taxi drive down Sheikh Zayed Road (or, indeed, along the main highway to the dunes themselves). Thrills apart, the

Tour operators

As well as the mainstream operators listed below, it's also worth checking out Mountain Extreme (℗07-227 1735, ⓦwww.mountain-extreme.com), an innovative eco-adventure company offering unusual one- and two-day hiking trips in the northern UAE, easily doable from Dubai.

Arabian Adventures Head office at the *Emirates Towers*, plus counters in the *Jumeirah Beach Hotel*, *One&Only Royal Mirage*, *Oasis Beach Hotel*, *Hilton Jumeirah Beach*, *Grand Hyatt*, *Mina A'Salam* and *Al Qasr* hotels ℗04-303 4888, ⓦwww .arabian-adventures.com. An offshoot of Emirates Airlines, this is easily the biggest tour operator in town, with high professional standards and a huge range of interesting trips all over the emirate. More expensive than other operators, but you might consider it money well spent.

Desert Road Tours ℗04-295 9429, ⓦwww.desertroadtours.com. Basic range of tours including all the usual desert activities like sand-skiing, dune-buggy rides and wadi-bashing.

Hormuz Tourism ℗04-228 0668, ⓦwww.hormuztourism.com. One of the cheapest operators in town (though the driving can be appalling), running a large number of tours, among them plenty of desert activities and watery fun, including diving, crab-hunting and deep-sea fishing.

Maly Tours ℗04-223 6881, ⓦwww.malytours.com. Standard selection of desert safaris and other tours at some of the lowest prices in town.

Net Tours *Hyatt Regency*, Deira ℗04-266 6655, ⓦwww.nettoursdubai.com. Standard range of tours at slightly above-average prices.

Orient Tours ℗04-282 8238, ⓦwww.orienttours.co.ae. One of the larger operators, offering a bigger-than-average choice of tours and desert trips, as well as longer UAE and Oman itineraries.

Right Tourism ℗04-397 6625, ⓦwww.righttourism.com. Good for watersports, plus all the usual desert safaris.

Sunflower Tours ℗04-334 4566, ⓦwww.sunflowerdubai.com. Good range of tours, including all the usual desert activites plus more offbeat offerings like deep-sea fishing, crab-hunting and horse-racing tours.

City tours

The Big Bus Company ℗04-324 4187, ⓦwww.bigbustours.com. What better way to see Dubai than from the top of . . . a double-decker London bus. The Big Bus Company's eye-catching vehicles ply two routes, one around the city centre and the other travelling all the way down to Dubai Marina. Buses run roughly every 30min from around 9am to 7.30pm every day. Tickets cost 150dh (children aged 5–15 100dh) and allow you to ride either route, hopping on and off at any of 23 stops, as well as offering various other perks including free entrance to a couple of museums and a free dhow cruise and walking tour.

Wonder Bus Tours BurJuman Centre ℗04-359 5656, ⓦwww.wonderbusdubai .com. The bizarre-looking Wonder Bus – half bus and half boat – offers Dubai city tours with a difference. Departing from the BurJuman centre, you'll be driven down to Garhoud Bridge, where the bus-cum-boat dives into the water and sails you all the way up the Creek to Shindagha. It then emerges once again onto dry land, travelling back to BurJuman by road. Trips last about 1hr 30min (including 1hr on the Creek) and cost 115dh, or 75dh for children aged 3–12. There are four or more trips daily, depending on the tide (book a day ahead to make sure of a place and check latest timings).

dunes are magnificent, and very beautiful at sunset, and although it's difficult to see much while you're being bumped around inside the vehicle, your driver will probably stop near the highest point of the dunes so that you can get out, enjoy the scenery and take some photos (though the throaty roars of dozens of passing vehicles and the clouds of exhaust mean you'll feel more like Michael Schumacher than Lawrence of Arabia). You might also be given the chance to try your hand at a brief bit of sand-skiing. Alternatively, some tour operators take you back to the main road, where you can go for a ride across the dunes on a quad bike – or "dune buggy", as they're usually known here – generally for an additional fee.

As dusk falls, you'll be driven off to the extensive **desert camp**, a further twenty-minute drive back towards Dubai, whose facilities are shared by all the various tour operators. Tucked away in the dunes, the camp boasts a range of activities, all included in the price of your tour. These include (very short) camel rides, henna painting, dressing up in Gulf national costume, and having your photo taken with a fine Emirati falcon perched on your arm – or you could just crash out over the free (albeit rather low-grade) shisha. There's also a reasonably well-stocked and moderately priced bar if you fancy an alcoholic tipple.

After an hour or so, a passable international buffet dinner is served, after which a **belly dancer** performs for another half hour or so, dragging likely-looking members of the audience up on stage with her (choose your seat carefully). It's all good, cheesy fun, although the belly dancer is as likely to be from Moscow as Muscat, and the floor tends to get rapidly swamped with jolly Indian businessmen strutting their stuff, so authentic it most certainly ain't. The whole thing winds up at around 9.30pm, after which you'll be driven (usually at breakneck speed) back to Dubai.

Other safaris

If you want to get more of a feel for the desert, some tour operators will offer you the chance to extend your sunset safari into an **overnight** trip, sleeping out in tents before returning to Dubai after breakfast the following morning. Obviously, this offers you a much better chance of getting some sense of the emptiness and grandeur of the landscape than you're likely to do during the belly-dancing free-for-all.

Some companies also offer **full-day** desert safaris. These usually include a mixture of general sightseeing combined with activities like dune-bashing, camel riding, sand-skiing and dune-buggy riding, probably with a visit to a camel farm for good measure, before returning to Dubai at dusk. These tours are also the best way to experience the popular pastime of **wadi-bashing**, driving through the rocky, dried-up riverbeds that score the easter side of the UAE around the Hajar Mountains – the ultimate off-road UAE adventure. Some operators also offer more specifically **activity-oriented tours** focusing exclusively on things like sand-skiing, camel trekking, dune-buggy riding and traditional falconry.

Boat cruises

A good way of seeing the Creek – and a more comfortable alternative to chartering an abra (see p.51) – is to go on one of the ever-popular **dinner cruises** offered by a string of companies (see below) on both sides of the Creek, most using traditional old wooden dhows. Standard dinner cruises generally cost around 180dh for a two-hour cruise (a bit more if booked through a tour operator), inclusive of a buffet dinner (the food usually being competent rather than outstanding) and on-board entertainment; boats normally leave around 8/8.30pm. Some of the companies listed below also offer cheaper lunch, sundowner and sightseeing cruises.

Bur Dubai side

Bateaux Dubai On the Creek by the UK Embassy, Al Seef Rd, Bur Dubai ☏04-399 4994, ⊛www.bateauxdubai .com. Lunch, sunset and dinner cruises (with four-course à la carte meals and live entertainment) in an unusually long and thin modern vessel – it looks a bit like a floating greenhouse.

Danat Dubai Cruises On the Creek by the UK Embassy, Al Seef Rd, Bur Dubai ☏04-351 1117, ⓦwww .danatdubaicruises.com. Offers a range of cruises in both traditional and modern vessels, including sundowner and dinner cruises, either just on the Creek itself, or heading out into the Gulf.

Deira side

Al Mansour Dhow *Radisson SAS Hotel Dubai Deira Creek Hotel* ☏04-222 2808.

The classiest traditional dhow on the Creek, offering nightly dinner cruises.

Rikks Cruises On the Creek by the Dubai Chamber of Commerce, Deira ☏04-222 2808, ⓦwww.rikks.net. Standard dinner cruises along the Creek with buffet food, belly dancer and live DJ.

Tour Dubai (Creekside Leisure) On the Creek just west of the *Radisson SAS Hotel Dubai Deira Creek* ☏04-336 8407, ⓦwww.tour-dubai.com. Bargain one-hour Creek tours in a smallish wooden dhow (four departures daily 11.30am–5.30pm; 35dh), as well as the usual dinner cruises.

Kids' Dubai

There's plenty to keep the children amused in Dubai, including the beach, Wild Wadi, camel racing, abra rides on the Creek and loads of toy shops, to name just a few possible attractions. In addition, some of the beach hotels have lively programmes of kids' activities and special children's clubs, while all the city's big malls have huge children's entertainment zones, featuring everything from soft-play areas to the latest arcade games. Children's entertainers also lay on free shows in many of the city's shopping malls during the Dubai Shopping Festival and, especially, Dubai Summer Surprises (see p.190).

There are also a couple of dedicated children's attractions worth checking out. At the southern end of Creekside Park in Oud Metha (see p.79) stand the brightly coloured red and blue buildings – modelled after children's play bricks – of **Children's City** (Sat–Thurs 9am–8.30pm, Fri 3–8.30pm; adults 15dh, children aged 3–15 10dh; under 2s free; family ticket – 2 adults and 2

children – 40dh; you also have to pay the 5dh park entry fee as well). The "city" is aimed at kids aged 2–15, with a subtle educational slant. A series of galleries with fun interactive exhibits and lots of touchscreens cover subjects including the human body, physical science, water, international culture, space exploration, computers and nature. There's also a play space, while kids aged 2 to 5 can muck around with sand and water in the toddlers' area.

Less didactic fun can be had at **Wonderland** (daily 10am–10pm; adults 15dh, children aged 4–12 10dh; ☏04-324 1222), immediately south of Creekside Park. This rather old-fashioned theme park has a variety of rides (mostly 5–10dh each) and other attractions including a rollercoaster, powercarts, pirate ship, Western trains, soft-play area, bumper cars, a horror house and the modest Splashland water park. The whole place is usually fairly empty during weekdays – which may or may not be a good thing.

Festivals

Dubai Shopping Festival

ⓦ www.mydsf.com. Only Dubai could dream up a festival devoted to shopping – and only in Dubai, one suspects, would it have proved so popular. Held annually during January and February (see the website for exact dates), the festival sees shops city wide offering all sorts of sales bargains, with discounts of up to 75 percent, while the big malls lay on lots of entertainment and children's events to keep punters' offspring amused during their parents' extended shopping binges. For many people it's a vision of purest hell, but confirmed shopaholics will be in seventh heaven. Bear in mind that the festival's massive popularity means that hotel rates go through the roof and beds get snapped up way in advance.

Dubai Summer Surprises

ⓦ www.mydsf.com. An attempt to draw in the punters during the blisteringly hot summer months from June to August, Dubai Summer Surprises (DSS) is a mainly mall-based event – really more of a marketing promotion than a genuine festival – with a decent selection of shopping bargains on offer and masses of live children's entertainments presided over by the irritating cartoon figure known as Modhesh, whose crinkly yellow features you'll probably quickly learn to loathe. Great if you've got kids in tow, however.

Ramadan

Scheduled to run from approximately Sept 1 to 29, 2008; Aug 21 to Sept 19, 2009; and Aug 11 to Sept 8, 2010, though precise dates vary according to local astronomical sightings of the moon. The Islamic holy month of Ramadan is observed with great attention and ceremony in Dubai, and is the one time of the year when you really get the sense of being in an essentially Muslim city. For Muslims, Ramadan represents a period in which to purify mind and body and to reaffirm one's relationship with God. Muslims are required to fast from dawn to dusk, and as a tourist you will be expected to publicly observe these strictures, although you are free to eat and drink in the privacy of your own hotel room, or in any of the carefully screened-off dining areas which are set up in hotels throughout the city (while alcohol is also served discreetly in some places after dark, but not during the day). Eating, drinking, smoking or chewing gum in public, however, is a definite no-no, and will cause considerable offence to local Muslims; singing, dancing and swearing in public are similarly frowned upon. In addition, live music is also completely forbidden during the holy month (though recorded music is allowed), while the city's nightclubs all close for the duration, and many shops scale back their opening hours.

Fasting ends at dusk, at which point the previously comatose city springs to life in a celebratory round of eating, drinking and socializing known as **Iftar** ("The Breaking of the Fast"). Many of the city's top hotels set up superb "Iftar tents", with lavish Arabian buffets, and the city remains lively until the small hours, when everyone goes off to bed in preparation for another day of abstinence. The atmosphere is particularly exuberant, and the Iftar tents especially lavish, during **Eid Al Fitr**, the day marking the end of Ramadan, when the entire city erupts in an explosion of celebratory festivity.

Major sporting events

Dubai Desert Challenge

ⓦ www.uaedesertchallenge.com. Cars, trucks and bikes race each other across the desert in one of the Middle East's leading motorsports events (and the penultimate round of the FIA Cross Country Rally World Cup). Held at various locations about Dubai and the UAE annually in October/November – see the website for details.

Dubai Desert Classic

Emirates Golf Club ⓦ www.dubaidesert classic.com. Established in 1993, the Dubai Desert Classic has established itself as an important (and very lucrative) event in the PGA European Tour – past winners feature a virtual who's who of the game's leading players, including Ernie Els, Tiger Woods, Colin Montgomerie and Seve Ballesteros. The tournament is held annually in February/March at the Emirates Golf Club near Dubai Marina. Tickets cost a fairly modest 150dh or so per day.

Dubai Duty Free Tennis Open

Dubai Tennis Stadium, Garhoud ⓦ www .dubaitennischampionships.com. Held in late February/early March, this two-week tennis bonanza includes both men's and women's singles tournaments (part of the ATP and WTA tournament calendars respectively). Recent winners include Rafael Nadal, Justine Henin-Hardenne, Lindsey Davenport, Amelie Mauresmo and Roger Federer (who, greedy as ever, has now won the title four times). Tickets can cost as little as 30dh per day.

Dubai World Cup

Nad Al Sheba Horse Racing Stadium
ⓦ www.dubaiworldcup.com. The world's richest horse race, held annually in March, and the climax of the city's annual racing calendar, with a massive $6 million in prize money.

Dubai Rugby Sevens

Dubai Exiles Club ⓦ www.dubairugby7s .com. This annual World Sevens Series tournament is beginning to enjoy an increasingly high international profile, featuring top sevens teams from around the globe, plus lots of enthusiastic local amateur sides; recent winners include the national teams of England, South Africa and New Zealand. Also provides the excuse for some of the city's most strenuous drinking and partying. Held annually in late November/early December.

Directory

Car rental All the major international car-rental companies are represented in Dubai and all have offices at the airport. Alternatively, some of the tour operators listed on p.187 also offer car rental – Arabian Adventures, for example, has a big fleet of vehicles ranging from small Toyotas (135dh per day) to Land Cruisers (650dh per day). Drivers will need to be aged 21 (25 for some larger vehicles) and be in possession of an international drivers' licence; many companies also require a couple of passport photos.

Diving There's some superb diving around the UAE, though it's at its best on the east coast, rather than from Dubai itself; for a list of dive sites and local operators, plus other information about diving in the UAE, visit ⓦ www .emiratesdiving.com or pick up a copy of the detailed *UAE Underwater Explorer* guidebook, available at bookshops throughout the city. One of the city's best diving operators is Al Boom Marine (☎ 04-342 2993, ⓦ www.alboomdiving .com), which runs all types of PADI course from beginner upwards, as well as diving and snorkelling day-trips across the UAE. Diving trips and PADI courses can also be arranged through a number of the beach hotels, including the *Sheraton Jumeirah Beach*, *Le Meridien Mina Seyahi*, *Dubai Marine Beach Resort*, the *One&Only Royal Mirage* and the *Jumeirah Beach Hotel* – the last is the best set-up, with its own dedicated dive school, the Pavilion Dive Centre (ⓦwww .jumeirah.com/diving).

Doctors and pharmacies All Dubai's four- and five-star hotels (and many of the cheaper places too) have English-speaking doctors on call 24hr. There are also reliable pharmacies on virtually every street in the city, who should also be able to refer you to the nearest medical facilities. In an emergency, an ambulance can be summoned on ☎999.

Embassies and consulates Australia, Level 25, Burjuman Business Tower, Bur Dubai ☎04-5087 100; Canada Consulate, Bank Street Building, Suite 701, Bur Dubai ☎04-3145555; New Zealand Consulate General, Suite 1502, 15th Floor, API Tower, Sheikh Zayed Road ☎04-331 7500; South African Consulate General, Khaleed bin al

Golf in Dubai

Golf is big business in Dubai, and the city has an outstanding selection of international-standard courses. All are open to visitors, subject in most places to a handicap limit of 28 for men and 36 or 45 for ladies. Green fees run from around 400dh during weekdays in summer up to 600dh or more during winter weekends.

Al Badia Golf Course Festival City Garhoud ☎04-232 5778, ⓦwww .albadiagolfresort.com. Attractive Creekside course in the southern city centre, though there's only limited access for non-members, so book well in advance.

Desert Course Arabian Ranches, Dubailand ☎04-366 3000, ⓦwww .thedesertcoursedubai.com. Part of the Dubailand development (see p.97), this striking new course (created by Ian Baker-Finch and Nicklaus Design) consists of a links-style grass course set in the middle of natural desert.

Dubai Country Club Ras Al Khor, south of the city near the Nad Al Sheba Horse Racecourse ☎04-333 1155, ⓦwww.dubaicountryclub.com. For something completely different, have a crack at the Dubai Country Club golf course (the oldest in Dubai). The course is made entirely out of sand, with so-called "browns" instead of greens. Players carry a small piece of artificial turf with them to play off on the fairways.

Dubai Creek Golf Club Garhoud ☎04-295 6000, ⓦwww.dubaigolf.com. Famous for its spiky-roofed club house (see p.78), this course (recently redesigned by Thomas Bjorn) enjoys a superb Creekside setting, and there's also a floodlit nine-hole par-3 course for after-dark swingers.

Emirates Golf Club Dubai Marina ☎04-380 2222, ⓦwww.dubaigolf.com. The oldest all-grass championship course in the Gulf, and probably still the most prestigious, centred around a striking Bedouin tent-style clubhouse. Current home of the Dubai Desert Classic (see p.191).

The Montgomerie Dubai Dubai Marina ☎04-390 5600, ⓦwww.themontgomerie .com. Links-style course designed by the eponymous Scotsman, featuring the world's largest green (playable from a 360-degree teeing ground), as well as many other unusual features and top-notch facilities.

Nad Al Sheba Club Nad Al Sheba Horse Racetrack ☎04-336 3666, ⓦwww .nadalshebaclub.com. This fully floodlit 18-hole links-style course (open until midnight) places the emphasis on accuracy rather than length, with double greens and deep bunkers. No handicap requirements for visitors.

The Dubai weekend

The Dubai working week is rather confusing, given that the Islamic "weekend" is traditionally held on Thursday afternoon and Friday. Government departments and some other companies work from Saturday to Wednesday (or noon on Thursday), while most private sector companies work from Sunday to Thursday (although there are rumours that everyone will soon go over to a unified Sun–Thurs working week). This means the city enjoys a kind of indefinitely extended "weekend" running from Thursday lunchtime to Saturday night. Friday is the big day, when the city lets its hair down and eats out, with restaurants all over the city offering extensive Friday brunch menus, the local equivalent of the traditional British Sunday lunch, though a lot more popular. Note, however, that most sights and some shops are closed on Friday mornings, and bus services are also sketchy.

Waleed Street, 3rd Floor, New Sharaf Building, Bur Dubai ☎ 04-397 5222; UK Embassy, Al Seef Street, Bur Dubai PO Box 65 ☎ 04-309 4444, ⓦ www .britishembassy.gov.uk/uae; USA Consulate General, World Trade Center, Sheikh Zayed Rd ☎ 04-311 6000, ⓦ http://dubai.usconsulate.gov.

Internet access is fairly widespread. In the city centre there are places offering very cheap and reliable email access all over Bur Dubai (mainly in the small streets around Al Fahidi St), though, funnily enough, practically nowhere in Deira. Outside the city centre, you'll have to use the Internet facilities at your hotel (usually fairly expensive). Note that the UAE government blocks out large numbers of websites it doesn't like – anything from low-grade smut to massively popular hosting sites like MySpace.com and Youtube.com.

Money, banks and ATMs The UAE currency is the dirham, subdivided in 100 fils. The dirham is pegged against the US dollar at the rate of US$1=3.675dh; other exchange rates at the time of writing were £1=7.2dh, €1=5dh. Notes come in 5dh, 10dh, 20dh, 50dh, 100dh, 200dh, 500dh and 1000dh denominations; there are also 2dh, 1dh, 50fils and 25fils coins. The 5dh, 50dh and 500dh notes are all a confusingly similar shade of brown; take care not to hand over the wrong sort (easily done if, say, you're getting out of a darkened cab at night) – a potentially very expensive mistake.

There are plenty of ATMs all over the city which accept foreign Visa and MasterCards. All the big shopping malls have at least a few ATMs, as do some large hotels. There are banks everywhere, almost all of which have ATMs. The most common are Mashreqbank, Commercial Bank of Dubai, National Bank of Dubai, National Bank of Abu Dhabi and Emirates Bank; opening hours are generally Sat–Wed 8am–1pm, Thurs 8am–noon. All will also change travellers' cheques and foreign cash, and there are also plenty of moneychangers in Bur Dubai (try along and around Al Fahidi St) and Dubai (try Sikkat Al Khail Rd, en route to the Gold Souk).

Opening hours The city's core working hours are Sat–Thurs 8–1am & 4–7pm (or 9am–6pm, with a lunch break); government offices open Sat–Wed 7.30am–2.30pm. Shops generally open roughly daily 10am–10pm, although those in the city's more old-fashioned souks often close between around 1pm and 4pm, while some places don't open on Friday mornings.

Phones The country code for the UAE is ☎ 971. The city code for Dubai is ☎ 04; note that you have to dial the city code even when ringing within Dubai. To call abroad from the UAE, dial ☎ 00, followed by your country code and the number itself (minus its initial zero). To call the UAE from abroad, dial your international access code, then ☎ 9714, followed by the local subscriber number (minus the ☎ 04 city code).

Useful phone numbers

Local directory enquiries ☏181
International enquiries ☏150
Police and ambulance ☏999
Airport enquiries ☏04-224 5555
Department of Tourism ☏04-223 0000

Local Etisalat mobile numbers always begin with ☏050 followed by a seven digit number. Again, you need to dial the code to make the number work. If you've got a number that's not working, try prefixing it with both ☏04 and ☏050 – mobiles are so widely used now that many people don't specify whether a number is a landline or a mobile.

Post The most convenient post offices are the Al Musalla Post Office, Al Fahidi Roundabout, Bur Dubai; and the Deira Post Office, Al Sabkha Road, near the intersection with Baniyas Road. Airmail letters to Europe, the US and Australia cost 3–3.50dh (postcards 2dh); airmail parcels cost 45dh to Europe and 70dh to the US and Australia for parcels weighing 500g to 1kg, or 80dh/130dh for parcels weighing 1kg–2kg. Note that poste restante facilities are not available in Dubai. If you wish to receive mail it's best to have it addressed to your hotel, clearly marked "guest at hotel", and to forewarn the reception desk of their arrival.

Taxes and tipping Room rates at most of the city's more expensive hotels are subject to a ten percent service charge and an additional ten percent government tax; these taxes are sometimes included in quoted prices, and

sometimes not. Check beforehand, otherwise you may have a nasty surprise and find that your bill has suddenly inflated by twenty percent. The prices in most restaurants automatically include a ten percent service charge (though this doesn't necessarily actually go to the waiters themselves); whether you wish to leave an additional tip is, of course, entirely your decision, though it won't necessarily be expected.

Time GMT plus four hours.

Visas Nationals of all Western European countries (bar Cyprus and Malta), the US, Canada, Australia and New Zealand are issued a free sixty-day visa on arrival. You'll need a passport which will be valid for at least six months after the date of entry. Israeli citizens are not permitted to enter the UAE. For futher information, visit ⊛ www.dubaitourism.ae and click on the "Visa Regulations" link.

Watersports Watersports facilities are available at all the beachside hotels. Typical offerings include sailing, windsurfing, kayaking, banana boating, wakeboarding and deep-sea fishing. The Dubai International Marine Club (⊛ www.dimc-uae .com), next to the *Meridien Mina Seyahi* hotel, hosts all sorts of boat races throughout the year, including rowing, sailing and traditional dhow racing.

Chronology

Chronology

c.5000 BC ▶ Earliest human settlement in southern Gulf.

500–600 ▶ Extensive settlement of Jumeirah area in southern Dubai; UAE region is part of an extensive trade network dominated by Sassanian (Iranian) seamen.

c.630 ▶ Arrival of Islam. The Islamic Umayyad dynasty displaces Sassanids as principal power in region. Following the removal of the Islamic caliphate from Damascus to Baghdad in 751, the southern Gulf region experiences a major boom in maritime trade.

1580 ▶ First European reference to Dubai, by the Venetian pearl merchant Gaspero Balbi.

1820 ▶ Dubai ruler Mohammed bin Hazza signs first agreement with British, receiving military protection against powerful neighbouring emirates of Abu Dhabi and the Qawasim (occupying present-day northern UAE and Oman).

1833 ▶ Around eight hundred people of the Al Bu Falasah, a branch of the Bani Yasi tribe from Abu Dhabi, arrive in Dubai and take power under the leadership of Maktoum bin Butti, the ancestor of the current ruling Maktoum family.

1841 ▶ Settlement of Deira begins. Over the next decade the town grows rapidly; by the mid-nineteenth century there are 350 shops in Deira, and a cosmopolitan population of Arabs, Iranians, Indians and Pakistanis.

1892 ▶ The British extend their power in the region through a series of exclusive treaties, or "truces", creating the Trucial States, the forerunner of the modern UAE.

1894 ▶ Foreign traders are offered complete tax exemption in Dubai, which subsequently begins to divert trade from neighbouring Sharjah and Iran. Numerous Iranian merchants begin arriving in the city, settling in Bastakia.

1930 onwards ▶ Gradual collapse of the pearl trade following Japanese discovery of artificial pearl culturing. Trade, the import-export business and smuggling all become increasingly important.

1939 ▶ Sheikh Rashid takes over as de facto ruler of Dubai from his ailing father (although he is only made official ruler on his father's death in 1958). The Creek is dredged and facilities improved to open it up to shipping and trade; Dubai develops into an important regional entrepôt.

1958 ▶ Sheikh Rashid becomes official ruler of Dubai. Huge oil reserves are found in Abu Dhabi.

1960 ▶ Dubai International Airport is opened.

1966 ▶ Oil is discovered in Dubai, though in far smaller quantities than in Abu Dhabi.

1967 ▶ The British announce their intention of quitting the region; discussions are held between the seven Trucial States, Qatar and Bahrain on forming a united country following this withdrawal.

1971 ▶ The British withdraw from the Trucial States, which are reformed as the United Arab Emirates (though without Bahrain and Qatar).

1970s and 1980s ▶ Oil revenues are used to diversify Dubai's industrial base and create massive new infrastructure projects, such as huge new Jebel Ali Port and Free Zone (opened 1983), in southern Dubai and the World Trade Centre (1979). The city's population by the end of the 1980s has risen to over half a million, a fifty-fold increase in less than forty years.

1985 ▶ The creation of the Dubai-based Emirates airline signals a growing emphasis on tourism in the city's economic plans.

1990 ▶ Death of Sheikh Rashid; Sheikh Maktoum becomes ruler of Dubai, though Sheikh Mohammed (appointed crown prince of Dubai in 1995), also exerts increasing influence over the city's aggressive economic development.

1996 ▶ Dubai Shopping Festival held for the first time.

1998 ▶ Opening of *Burj Al Arab*.

2006 ▶ Death of Sheikh Maktoum; Sheikh Mohammed becomes ruler of Dubai.

Language

Language

Language in Dubai is as complicated as the ethnic patchwork of people who inhabit the city. As part of the UAE, the city's official language is Arabic, spoken by nearly a third of the population, including local Emiratis, other Gulf Arabs and various Arabic-speaking expats from countries like Lebanon, Syria, Jordan and further afield. Hindi and Urdu are the mother tongue of many of the city's enormous number of Indian and Pakistani expats, although other Indian languages, most notably Malayalam, the native tongue of Kerala, as well as Tamil and Sinhalese (the majority language of Sri Lanka) are also fairly widely spoken. Other Asian languages are also common, most notably Tagalog (Pilipino), the first language of the city's large Filipino community.

In practice, the city's most widely understood language is actually **English**, even if most people speak it only as a second or third language. English serves as a link between all the city's various ethnic groups, as well as the principal language of the European expat community and the business and tourism sectors. Pretty much everyone in Dubai speaks at least a little English (ironically, even local Emiratis are now forced to revert to this foreign language in many of their everyday dealings in their own city).

Knowing the ethnic origin of the person you're speaking to is the most important thing if you do attempt to strike out into a foreign tongue – speaking Arabic to an Indian taxi driver or a Filipina waitress is obviously a complete waste of time. The bottom line is that few of the people you come into contact with as a tourist in Dubai will be Arabic speakers, except in the city's Middle Eastern restaurants. And unless you're pretty fluent, trying to speak Arabic (or indeed any other language) in Dubai is mainly an exercise in diplomacy rather than a meaningful attempt to communicate, since the person you're addressing will almost certainly speak much better English than you do Arabic (or Hindi, or whatever). Having said that, there's no harm in giving it a go, and the person you're speaking to may be pleasantly entertained by your attempts to address him or her in their own language.

Outside Dubai, the situation is a bit different. English is much less widely spoken outside the city, and a smattering of Arabic can prove genuinely useful in places like Sharjah and Al Ain – although, again, these cities' substantial Indian and Pakistani populations will probably speak English rather than Arabic as a second, link language.

Useful Arabic words and phrases

Hello (formal)	A'salaam alaykum (response: Wa alaykum a'salaam)
Hello (informal)	Marhaba/ahlan wasahalan/Ya hala
Goodbye	Ma'assalama/Fi aman allah
Yes	Na'am/Aiwa
No	La
Please (to a man)	Minfadlack
(to a woman)	Minfadlick
Thank you	Shukran
You're welcome	Afwan
Sorry	Muta'assef/Assef
How much?	Bikaim?
Do you speak English?	Teh ki ingelezi?
I don't speak Arabic	Ma ah'ki arabi

I don't understand	Ma fahemt
My name is . . .	Ismi . . .
What is your name?	Sho ismak?
God willing!	inshallah

Numbers

1	wahid
2	ithnayn
3	theletha
4	arba'a
5	khamsa
6	sitta
7	saba'a
8	themanya
9	tissa
10	ashra

Middle Eastern menu reader

The traditional Middle Eastern meal consists of a wide selection of small dishes known as **mezze** (or **meze**) – akin to Spanish tapas – shared between a number of diners. Most or all of the following dishes, dips and other ingredients are found in the better Middle Eastern (or "Lebanese", as they are usually described) restaurants and cafés around the city, although note that vagaries in the transliteration from Arabic script to English can result in considerable variations in spelling.

baba ghanouj all-purpose dip made from grilled eggplant (aubergine) mixed with ingredients like tomato, onion, lemon juice and garlic

burghul cracked wheat, often used as an ingredient in Middle Eastern dishes such as tabouleh

falafel deep-fried balls of crushed chickpeas mixed with spices; usually served with bread and salad

fatayer miniature triangular pastries, usually filled with either cheese or spinach

fatteh dishes containing pieces of fried or roasted bread

fattoush salad made of tomatoes, cucumber, lettuce and mint mixed up with crispy little squares of deep-fried flatbread

foul madamas smooth dip made from fava beans (*foul*) blended with lemon juice, chillis and olive oil

jebne white cheese

halloumi grilled cheese

hammour common Gulf fish which often crops up on local menus; a bit like cod

humous crushed chickpeas blended with tahini, garlic and lemon; served as a basic side dish and eaten with virtually everything, from bread and vegetables through to meat dishes

kibbeh small ovals of deep-fried minced lamb mixed with cracked wheat and spices

labneh thick, creamy Arabian yoghurt, often flavoured with garlic or mint

loubia salad of green beans with tomatoes and onion

moutabal a slightly creamier version of *baba ghanouj*, thickened using yoghurt or tahini

saj Lebanese style of thin, round flatbread

saj manakish (or *mana'eesh*) pieces of *saj* sprinkled with herbs and oil – a kind of Middle Eastern mini-pizza

shwarma chicken or lamb kebabs, cut in narrow strips off a big hunk of meat roasted on a vertical spit (like the Turkish doner kebab) and served wrapped in flatbread with salad

shisha waterpipe (also known as hubbly-bubbly). Tobacco is filtered through the glass water-container at the base of the pipe, and so is much milder (and less harmful) than normal cigarettes. Tobacco is usually available either plain or in various flavoured varieties; the best shisha cafes may have as many as twenty varieties.

shish taouk basic chicken kebab, with small pieces of meat grilled on a skewer

tabouleh finely chopped mixture of tomato, mint and cracked wheat

tahini paste made from sesame seeds

waraq aynab vine leaves stuffed with a mixture of rice and meat

zaatar a widely used seasoning made from a mixture of of dried thyme (or oregano), salt and sesame seeds

zatoon olives

Glossary

abbeya black, full-length women's traditional robe

abra small boat used to ferry passengers across the Creek

barasti palm thatch used to construct traditional houses

bahar sea

bayt/bait house

burj tower

dar house (or, more figuratively, "world")

dhow generic term loosely used to describe all types of traditional wooden Arabian boat

Eid Al Fitr festival celebrating the end of Ramadan

falaj traditional irrigation technique used to water date plantations, with water drawn from deep underground and carried to its destination along tiny earthen canals

ghutra men's headscarf, usually white or red-and-white check

haj pilgrimage to Mecca

iftar the breaking of the fast after dark during Ramadan

iqal the rope-like black cords used to keep the *ghutra* on the head (traditionally used to tie together the legs of camels to stop them running off)

jebel hill or mountain

kandoura the full-length traditional robe worn by Gulf Arabs (also known as *dishdashas*)

khanjar traditional curved dagger, usually made of silver

Al Khor The Creek

Al Khaleej The Gulf (translated locally as the Arabian Gulf, never as the Persian Gulf)

majlis meeting/reception room in a traditional Arabian house; the place where local or family problems were discussed and decisions taken

mina port

nakheel palm tree

oud Arabian lute

qasr palace or castle

qibla the direction of Mecca, usually indicated by a sign or sticker in most hotel rooms in the city (and in mosques by a recessed niche known as the *mihrab*)

Ramadan see p.190

shayla women's black headscarf, worn with an *abbeya*

wadi dry river bed or valley

small print & Index

A Rough Guide to Rough Guides

Dubai DIRECTIONS is published by Rough Guides. The first *Rough Guide to Greece*, published in 1982, was a student scheme that became a publishing phenomenon. The immediate success of the book – with numerous reprints and a Thomas Cook prize shortlisting – spawned a series that rapidly covered dozens of destinations. Rough Guides had a ready market among low-budget backpackers, but soon also acquired a much broader and older readership that relished Rough Guides' wit and inquisitiveness as much as their enthusiastic, critical approach. Everyone wants value for money, but not at any price. Rough Guides soon began supplementing the "rougher" information about hostels and low-budget listings with the kind of detail on restaurants and quality hotels that independent-minded visitors on any budget might expect, whether on business in New York or trekking in Thailand. These days the guides offer recommendations from shoestring to luxury and cover a large number of destinations around the globe, including almost every country in the Americas and Europe, more than half of Africa and most of Asia and Australasia. Rough Guides now publish:

- Travel guides to more than 200 worldwide destinations
- Dictionary phrasebooks to 22 major languages
- Maps printed on rip-proof and waterproof Polyart™ paper
- Music guides running the gamut from Opera to Elvis
- Reference books on topics as diverse as the Weather and Shakespeare
- World Music CDs in association with World Music Network

Visit **www.roughguides.com** to see our latest publications.

Publishing information

This first edition published October 2007 by

Rough Guides Ltd, 80 Strand, London WC2R 0RL.
345 Hudson St, 4th Floor, New York, NY 10014,
USA.

Distributed by the Penguin Group

Penguin Books Ltd, 80 Strand, London WC2R 0RL
Penguin Group (USA), 375 Hudson Street, NY
10014, USA
Penguin Group (Australia), 250 Camberwell Road,
Camberwell, Victoria 3124, Australia
Penguin Group (Canada), 10 Alcorn Avenue,
Toronto, ON M4V 1E4, Canada
Penguin Group (New Zealand), Cnr Rosedale and
Airborne Roads, Albany, Auckland, New Zealand
Typeset in Bembo and Helvetica to an original
design by Henry Iles.
Printed and bound in China

© Gavin Thomas

No part of this book may be reproduced in any form
without permission from the publisher except for
the quotation of brief passages in reviews.

212pp includes index

A catalogue record for this book is available from
the British Library

ISBN 9-781-84353-742-7

The publishers and authors have done their best
to ensure the accuracy and currency of all the
information in Dubai DIRECTIONS, however, they
can accept no responsibility for any loss, injury, or
inconvenience sustained by any traveller as a result
of information or advice contained in the guide.

1   3   5   7   9   8   6   4   2

Help us update

We've gone to a lot of effort to ensure that the first edition of Dubai DIRECTIONS is accurate and up-to-date. However, things change – places get "discovered", opening hours are notoriously fickle, restaurants and rooms raise prices or lower standards. If you feel we've got it wrong or left something out, we'd like to know, and if you can remember the address, the price, the phone number, so much the better.

We'll credit all contributions, and send a copy of the next edition (or any other DIRECTIONS guide or Rough Guide if you prefer) for the best letters. Everyone who writes to us and isn't already a subscriber will receive a copy of our full-colour thrice-yearly newsletter. Please mark letters: "Dubai DIRECTIONS Update" and send to: Rough Guides, 80 Strand, London WC2R 0RL, or Rough Guides, 4th Floor, 345 Hudson St, New York, NY 10014. Or send an email to mail@roughguides.com

Have your questions answered and tell others about your trip at www.roughguides.atinfopop.com

Rough Guide credits

Text editor: Ruth Blackmore
Layout: Ajay Verma
Photography: Gavin Thomas
Cartography: Ed Wright
Picture editor: Jj Luck

Proofreader: Amanda Jones
Production: Aimee Hamposon
Design: Henry Iles
Cover design: Chloë Roberts

The author

Gavin Thomas has worked for Rough Guides as a writer and editor since 1998; he is also the author of the *Rough Guide to Sri Lanka* and co-author of the *Rough Guide to Rajasthan, Delhi and Agra*. His first experience of Dubai was during an unscheduled six-hour stopover at the airport, which impressed him so much that he decided to go back for more – the only time he has formed a lasting relationship with a major city on the basis of its duty-free facilities. He hopes one day to be able to walk down Al Fahidi Street without being offered a fake watch, and to say something in Arabic which somebody actually understands.

Acknowledgements

Grateful thanks to my editor Ruth Blackmore for making the entire experience smoother than a Burj Al Arab butler; Jj Luck for patiently ploughing through a camel-load of photographs; Ed Wright for maps sharper than a Karama tout; and, as always, to Martin and Kate for putting me on the plane. Thanks also to Matthew Teller; Lucy Blogg; Sofian Hijjawi, Qais Saleh; Hamad bin Mejren; Lejla Charif of Jumeirah (who showed all the other PRs in Dubai how it should be done); and, of course, to Allison, for letting me go in the first place, and then for coming out in person and teaching me how to shop properly.

Photo credits

All images © Rough Guides except the following:

p.36 Dubai Rugby Sevens at the Gulf Emirate's Exiles Rugby Ground © KAMAL MOGHRABI/ AFP/Getty Images.
p.36 Dubai World Cup © 2006 Dubai World Cup.
p.37 Dubai Desert Golf Classic © Ross Kinnaird/ Getty Images.
p.37 Roger Federer returns to his opponent Ivan Ljubicic of Croatia during their ATP Dubai Men's Duty Free © RABIH MOGHRABI/AFP/Getty Images.
p.37 UAE Desert Challenge © UAE Desert Challenge.
p.39 Snorkelling © Al Boom Diving.
p.41 Bab Al Shams. Courtesy of Jumeirah Bab Al Shams Desert Resort & Spa.

p.41 Man with Falcon, Dubai, United Arab Emirates © Hugh Sitton/zefa/Corbis.
p.42 Dubailand, Autodrome © Government of Dubai, Department of Tourism and Commerce Marketing.
p.42 Burj Dubai © Government of Dubai, Department of Tourism and Commerce Marketing.
p.43 The Palm, Jebel Ali and The Palm, Deira © Government of Dubai, Department of Tourism and Commerce Marketing.
p.43 The World © Government of Dubai, Department of Tourism and Commerce Marketing.
p.43 Hydropolis © Government of Dubai, Department of Tourism and Commerce Marketing.

Index

Maps are marked in colour

a

abra cruises 51
abras 38, 51
Abu Dhabi 156–160
  Abu Dhabi 156
  Art Cauldron Café 161
  Beach Rotana Hotel
    restaurants 161
  Corniche 158
  Cultural Foundation 157
  Delma Café 161
  Emirates Palace Hotel 159
  Guggenheim 158
  Hilton Abu Dhabi 161
  Louvre 158
  Marina Mall 160
  Qasr Al Hosn 157
  Saadiyat island 158
  street sculptures, Airport
    Road 157
  transport to and around 155
  UAE Heritage Village 160
accommodation 169–180
adventure activities 188
airport 183
airport buses 183
Al Ahmadiya School 12, 68
Al Ain 147–154
  Al Ain 148
  Al Ain Museum 20, 149
  Al Ain Oasis 20, 151
  Al Ain Souk 21, 151
  Al Kandaq Fort 21, 152
  Buraimi 152
  Buraimi Souk 152
  Camel Souk 153
  highlights of 20
  Hili Gardens and Archeological
    Park 153
  Jahili Fort 153
  Jebel Hafeet 154
  Livestock Market 21, 150
  restaurants and cafés in 154
  Sultan Bin Zayed Fort 21, 150
  transport to and around 147
Al Aqah Beach 164
Al Attar Tower 95
Al-Diyafah Street 83
Al Fahidi Street 55
Al Kandaq Fort, Buraimi
  21, 152
antiques 35
Arabic 201–203
Arabic, useful words and
  phrases 202
Architecture, modern 16
arrival 183
ATMs 193

b

banks 193
bars and pubs (by area)
  Bur Dubai 61
  Deira 76–77
  The inner suburbs 90–91
  Sheikh Zayed Road 103–105
  Jumeirah 112–113
  The Burj Al Arab and around
    122–125
  Dubai Marina 136–137
bars and pubs
  360° 31, 123
  Agency, The 103
  Après 122
  Arabian Courtyard 136
  Aussie Legends 90
  Bahri Bar 124
  Bar 44 30, 137
  Barasti Bar 137
  bars in Dubai, best 30
  Blue Bar 104
  Boudoir 112
  Buddha Bar 31
  Cin Cin 104
  Ginseng 90
  Issimo Cocktail Lounge 76
  Koubba 31, 124
  Ku Bu 76
  Left bank 125
  Long's Bar 104
  Lotus One 104
  Malecon 113
  Pub, The 77
  Rooftop Bar 31, 137
  Sherlock Holmes 61
  Shisha Courtyard 125
  Sho-Cho 113
  Terrace, The 90
  Up on the Tenth 77
  Viceroy Bar 61
  Vintage 91
  Vu's Bar 30, 105
Bastakia 10, 52
beach, Dubai Marina 128
beach, Jumeirah Beach
  Park 108
beaches, Dubai Marina
  hotel 130
belly dancing 188
Bidiya 164
Big Red 186
boat cruises 188
Bur Dubai 7, 47–61
  Bur Dubai 48
Buraimi 20
Buraimi, Oman 152
Buraimi Souk 152

Burj Al Arab 8, 11, 16, 114
Burj Al Arab and around 115
Burj Al Arab, visiting 116
Burj Dubai 42, 96
buses 183, 185
buses, airport 183

c

Cable Car 79
cafés, *see* Restaurants and
  cafés
camel racecourse 95
camel-racing 41, 95
camping, desert 188
car rental 183, 191
carpets 34
changing money 193
Chelsea Tower 95
children's activities 189
Children's City 189
chronology of historical events
  197–198
city tours 187
clubs (by area)
  The inner suburbs 91
  Sheikh Zayed Road 105
  The Burj Al Arab and around
    125, 126
  Dubai Marina 137
clubs
  Apartment 125
  iBO 91
  Kasbar 137
  Mix 91
  Oxygen 91
  Peppermint Lounge 105
  Tangerine 105
  Trilogy 126
  Zinc 105
consulates 192
Covered Souk 67
Creek, The 11, 49, 51
Creek Cruises 38
Creekside Park 79
cruises, dinner 188

d

Deira 7, 62–77
  Deira 64
Deira Fish, Meat and
  Vegetable Market 15, 70
desert activities 41
desert adventure activities 188

desert resorts 41
desert safaris 40, 186
designer fakes 34
dhow-building yards,
    Jaddaf 79
Dhow Wharfage 13, 67
Dhow Wharfage,
    southern 71
Dibba 164
dinner cruises 188
diving 38, 191
Diving Village 56
Diwan 52
doctors 192
drinking, see Bars and pubs
Dubai Cable Car 79
Dubai Chamber of
    Commerce 71
Dubai Creek Golf Club 17, 78
Dubai Creek Yacht Club 78
Dubai Desert Challenge
    37, 191
Dubai Desert Classic 191
Dubai Desert Golf
    Classic 37
Dubai Duty Free Tennis Open
    37, 191
Dubai International Financial
    Centre 94
Dubai Internet City 132
Dubai Marina 8, 127–137
Dubai Marina 130
Dubai Marina Beach 128
Dubai Media City 132
Dubai metro 185
Dubai Museum 54
Dubai Rugby Sevens 36, 191
Dubai Shopping Festival 190
Dubai Summer Surprises 190
Dubai Waterfront 129
Dubai World Cup 36, 97, 191
Dubai World Trade
    Centre 94
Dubai Zoo 107
Dubailand 42, 97
dune-bashing 41, 186
Dusit Dubai 95

e

East Coast, UAE 162–166
East Coast, UAE 163
Eid Al Fitr 190
embassies 192
Emirates Towers 11, 93
English, spoken in
    Dubai 201
Etisalat Tower 71
exchange 193

f

festivals 190
Fish, Meat and Vegetable
    Market, Deira 15, 70
food, Middle Eastern 202
Fujairah 165

g

Garhoud 78
Gate, The 94
glossary 203
gold 34, 63
Gold Souk 14, 62
golf 37, 191
golf courses 192
Grand Mosque 52
Green Art Gallery 107

h

Hajar Mountain 162
Hard Rock Café 132
Heritage House 12, 69
Heritage Village 56
Hindi 201
history 197–198
horse-racing 36, 97, 191
hotels 169–180
hotels (by area)
    Bur Dubai 170–171
    Deira 171–173
    The inner suburbs 174
    Sheikh Zayed Road 175–176
    Jumeirah 177–178
    The Burj Al Arab and
        around 177–178
    Dubai Marina 178–180
    Around Dubai 180
hotels
    Admiral Plaza 170
    Al Hijaz Heritage Motel 172
    Al Karnak Hotel 172
    Al Khayam 173
    Al Maha Desert Resort
        41, 180
    Al Murooj Rotana 176
    Al Qasr 23, 118–119, 178
    Ambassador 170
    Arabian Courtyard 170
    Astoria 170
    Bab Al Shams 41
    Bab Al Shams Desert
        Resort 180
    Burj Al Arab 23, 177
    Carlton Tower 171
    categories 169
    Crowne Plaza 175
    Dallas 170

Dar Al Masyaf 177
Dubai Marine Beach
    Resort 177
Dubai Youth Hostel 172
Dusit Dubai 95, 175
Emirates Towers 175
Fairmont 176
Florida Hotel 172
Four Points Sheraton 171
Gold Plaza Guesthouse 172
Grand Hyatt 174
Grosvenor House 23, 178
Habtoor Grand Resort and
    Spa 179
Hilton Dubai Creek 172
Hilton Jumeirah Beach 179
Hotel Florida International 173
Hyatt Regency 173
Hydropolis 43
Ibis 176
Jumeirah Beach Hotel 177
luxury hotels 22
Meridien Mina Seyahi, Le 179
Mina A'Salam 118–119, 178
New Penninsula 171
Novotel 176
Oasis Beach Hotel 179
One&Only Royal Mirage
    22, 179
Park Hyatt 23, 79, 174
Paz, La 173
Radisson SAS Dubai
    Creek 173
Regent Beach Resort 178
Regent Palace 171
Ritz-Carlton 180
room rates 169
Royal Ascot 171
Royal Meridien, Le 180
Rydges Plaza 174
Shangri-La 176
Sheraton Dubai Creek
    71, 173
Sheraton Jumeirah Beach 180
St George 173
taxes 169
Time Palace 171
Towers Rotana 176
XVA 171
Youth Hostel 172
Hydropolis 43, 130

i

Ibn Battuta Mall 133
Iftar 190
information 183
Inner suburbs, The 80–81
International Exhibition and
    Conference Centre 94
Internet access 193
Iranian Hospital and Mosque,
    Jumeirah 107
Iranian Mosques, Bur
    Dubai 50

INDEX

j

Jaddaf 79
Jambase 125
Jumeirah 8, 106–113
Jumeirah 108–109
Jumeirah Beach Hotel 17, 117
Jumeirah Beach Park 108
Jumeirah Mosque 12, 106

k

Karama 82
Karama Park 82
Khalid Bin Al Waleed Road 55
Khor Fakkan 165
kilims 34

l

language 201–203
limousines 185
listings publications 183

m

Madinat Jumeirah 11, 118
Madinat Theatre 126
Majlis Gallery 53
Majlis Ghorfat Um Al Sheef 13, 110
Mall of the Emirates 119
malls, shopping, see Shopping
Marina Walk 130
Masafi 163
Media City Amphitheatre 132
menu reader 202
Mercato mall 108
metro 185
mezze 202
Middle Eastern menu reader 202
money 193
motorsports 37, 191
Museum of Historical Photographs 56

n

Nad Al Sheba camel racecourse 41, 95
Nad Al Sheba Racecourse 97
National Bank of Dubai 16, 70

nightclubs, see Clubs

o

opening hours 193
opening hours, souks 65
Oud Metha 79

p

Palm, Deira, The 43
Palm, Jebel Ali, The 43, 129
Palm Jumeirah, The 128
Park Hyatt 79
Perfume Souk 66
pharmacies 192
phone codes 193
phone numbers, useful 194
post 194
post offices 194
precious stones 34
pubs, see Bar and pubs

r

Ramadan 190
restaurants and cafés (by area)
Bur Dubai 59–61
Deira 72–76
The inner suburbs 86–90
Sheikh Zayed Road 99–103
Jumeirah 111–113
The Burj Al Arab and around 122–123
Dubai Marina 134–136
restaurants and cafés
Al Dawaar 73
Al Nafoorah 25, 101
Al Qasr 112
Al Tannour 103
Antique Bazaar 60
Après 122
Aquarium 87
Asha's 87
Ashiana 72
Automatic 61
Basta Arts Cafe 59
Bastakiah Nights 25, 61
Bayt Al Wakeel 59
Beirut 29, 86
Benjarong 99
BICE 134
Boardwalk 87
Boudoir 112
Buddha Bar 134
cafés in Dubai, best 28
cheap eats 28
China Club 72
Coconut Grove 88

Creekside 73
Dôme 59
Eauzone 27, 134
Elements 86
Exchange Grill, The 100
Foccacia 74
Glasshouse 74
Hatam 74
Hoi An 100
Il Rustico 89
Indego 135
India House 29, 59
international restaurants in Dubai, best 26
Japengo 111
Kan Zaman 25, 61
La Baie 134
La Moda 74
Latino House 100
Legends 88
Lime Tree Café 28, 112
Malecon 113
Marrakech 101
Medzo 88
Mezzanine 135
Middle Eastern restaurants in Dubai, best 24
Mosaico 101
Nina's 27, 135
Noodle House 28, 101
Ottoman 136
Pierchic 122
QDs 89
Ravi's 87
Sakura 101
Sevilles 89
Shabestan 75
Shahrzad 24, 75
Shakespeare & Co. 102
Shang Palace 102
Sho-Cho 113
Shoo Fee Ma Fee 122
Spectrum on One 102
Tagine 25, 136
Thai Chi 89
Thai Kitchen 26, 90
Trader Vics 103
Verre 26, 75
Vivaldi's 76
Vu's Restaurant 103
XVA Café 29, 60
Yakitori 29, 61
Yum! 76
Zheng He 27, 123
rugby 36, 191

s

Safa Park
Satwa 82
Satwa 82
Sharjah 138–146
Al Hisn Fort 18, 139
Bait Al Naboodah 19, 142
Blue Souk 19, 145
Calligraphy Museum 143

David Roberts 144
Heritage Area 140
highlights 18
Islamic laws in 142
Islamic Museum 19, 141
Koran Roundabout 146
Majlis Ibrahim Mohammed Al
Madfa 143
Museum of Sharjah Herit-
age 144
museums, visiting 139
restaurants and cafés in 145
Sharjah Art Museum 144
Sharjah 140
Souk Al Arsah 18, 35, 143
transport to 138
Sheikh Issa Tower 95
Sheikh Saeed Al Maktoum
House 13, 55
Sheikh Zayed Road 7, 17,
92–105
Sheikh Zayed Road 94–95
Sheraton Dubai Creek 71
Shindagha 47
shopping (by area)
Bur Dubai 57–59
Deira 71–78
The inner suburbs 79–85
Sheikh Zayed Road 98–99
Jumeirah 108–111
The Burj Al Arab and around
118–121
Dubai Marina 133–135
shopping
Al Ghurair City 71
Al Mansoor Video 84
Al Orooba Oriental Carpets 58
antiques 35
Arabian Souk, Mall of the
Emirates 120
Arabian Treasures, Deira City
Centre 83
bargaining 63
Bateel Dates 57
Beach Centre 110
Book Corner 72
BurJuman 33, 57
Camel Company, The 120
carpets 34
Carrefour 57
counterfeits 34, 63
Damas 58
Deira City Centre 78, 83
Deira Tower 72
designer fakes 34, 63
diamonds 121
Emad Carpets 84
Emirates Tower Boulevard 98
Gallery One 121
gold 34, 121

Gold and Diamond Park 121
gold, price of 63
gold, shopping for 63
Harvey Nichols 121
Ibn Battuta Mall 33, 133
International Aladdin Shoes 58
Jewellery Court, Deira City
Centre 84
Jumaira Plaza 111
Karama 35
Karama Centre 82
Karama Souk 84
Khalid Bin Al Waleed Street 58
kilims 34
Magrudy's 111
Mall of the Emirates 32,
119, 121
malls, best 32
Mercato 108, 111
Mercato Mall 33
Persian Carpet House 99
Petals 85
precious stones 34, 121
precious stones, shopping
for 63
Red Sea Exhibitions 111
Souk Madinat Jumeirah
118–119, 121
souvenirs, kitsch 35
tailoring, Bur Dubai 58
Villa Moda 98
Virgin Megastore 59
Wafi City Mall 32, 79, 85
Wafi Gourmet 85
Shri Nathje Jayate Temple 50
Ski Dubai 120
snorkelling 38, 192
Souk Madinat Jumeirah
15, 118
souks
Al Ain Souk 21, 151
Al Qasr 118–119
Buraimi Souk 152
Camel Souk, Al Ain 153
Covered Souk 67
Deira Fish, Meat and
Vegetable Market 15, 70
in Dubai 14
Gold Souk 14
Mina A'Salam 118–119
Perfume Souk 66
Souk Al Arsah, Sharjah 18
Souk Madinat Jumeirah 15,
118–119, 121
souks, Deira 10
Spice Souk 14, 65
Textile Souk 14, 47
souvenirs, kitsch 35
Spice Souk 14, 65
sport in Dubai 36

sporting events 191
sunset safaris 186

Tagalog 201
taxes 194
taxis 184
telephone codes 193
tennis 37, 191
Textile Souk 14, 47
time difference 194
tipping 194
tour operators 187
tourist information 183
Tower, The 95
transport, East Coast, UAE
162
travel agents 187

Umm Suqeim 114
Urdu 201

v

visas 194

w

wadi-bashing 188
Wafi City 79
watersports 129, 194
weekend, definition of Dubai
193
Wild Wadi 38, 117
wind towers 53
Wonderland theme park 189
World, The 43, 128

x

XVA Gallery 53–54

INDEX